Understanding Islamic Law

Contemporary Issues in Islam
Series editor: Aminah Beverly McCloud, DePaul University

Most contemporary books on Muslims tend to see Islam as an exotic, backward, medieval, violent, misogynist tradition that just does not fit with the modern world. Others are simplistic rebuttals of this Islamophobia. The goal of this series is to fill in the gaps of knowledge with accurate information on contemporary issues and comprehensive summaries of the foundations of the Islamic worldview. With this goal in mind, this series explores many aspects of Islam and Muslim life including: both the fundamentals of Islam and Muslim engagement of contemporary issues in Muslim practice, Muslim communities, economics, medicine, law, new configurations of the geography of the Muslim and Islamic worlds, contemporary issues in the Arab world and among Arabs in America, Muslim reform movements in America and in the Muslim world. While this series aims to be comprehensive, it does not claim to be exhaustive. The series seeks to make complex issues comprehensible while still engaging for both students in various disciplines and general readers.

Books in the series
 Understanding Islamic Law, edited by Hisham M. Ramadan

Forthcoming titles include
 Islam, Health, and Medicine, edited by Hamada Hamid
 Islam, Management, and Finance, edited by Rafik Beekun

Understanding Islamic Law

From Classical to Contemporary

Edited By
Hisham M. Ramadan

ALTAMIRA
PRESS

A Division of
ROWMAN & LITTLEFIELD PUBLISHERS, INC.
Lanham • New York • Toronto • Oxford

ALTAMIRA PRESS
A division of Rowman & Littlefield Publishers, Inc.
A wholly owned subsidiary of The Rowman & Littlefield Publishing Group, Inc.
4501 Forbes Boulevard, Suite 200
Lanham, MD 20706
www.altamirapress.com

PO Box 317
Oxford
OX2 9RU, UK

British Library Cataloguing in Publication Information Available

Library of Congress Cataloguing-in-Publication Data

Understanding Islamic law : from classical to contemporary / edited by Hisham
Ramadan.
    p.   cm.— (Contemporary issues in Islam)
    Includes bibliographical references and index.
    ISBN-13: 978-0-7591-0990-2 (cloth : alk. paper)
    ISBN-10: 0-7591-0090-7 (cloth : alk. paper)
    ISBN-13: 978-0-7591-0991-9 (pbk. : alk. paper)
    ISBN-10: 0-7591-0991-5 (pbk. : alk. paper)
    1. Islamic law.   I. Ramadan, Hisham M. II. Series.
KBP144.U53   2006
340.5′9—dc22   2005031797

Printed in the United States of America

♾ ™ The paper used in this publication meets the
minimum requirements of American National Standard
for Information Sciences—Permanence of Paper for
Printed Library Materials, ANSI/NISO Z39.48–1992.

Contents

Series Editor's Introduction: Contemporary Issues in Islam

Aminah Beverly McCloud

Today, texts on Islam and Muslims are generally focused either on rebuttals to Islamophobia, terrorism and analyses of Muslim reform groups, what's wrong with the Islamic religion, Arab Muslim women, the problems in Muslim societies, or the problems Muslim societies have with modernity. Yesterday's texts on Islam and Muslims present Islam as a medieval religion of an extremely exotic nature that oppresses women, whose members are anti-modern, violent, and backward. Readers of either set of texts find that they actually finish reading with opinions on what they read but with little knowledge of Islam as a worldview and even less knowledge of the diverse opinions of over a billion people living all over the globe and their participation in their own modernities. The goal of this series is to fill in the gaps of knowledge with accurate information on contemporary issues and comprehensive summaries of the foundations of the worldview.

With this goal in mind, this series explores many aspects of Islam and Muslim life including: both the fundamentals of Islam and Muslim engagement of contemporary issues in Muslim practice; Muslim communities, economics, medicine, and law; new configurations of the geography of the Muslim and Islamic worlds; contemporary issues in the Arab world and among Arabs in America; and Muslim reform movements in America and in the Muslim world. While this series aims to be comprehensive, it does not claim to be exhaustive. Writing styles and analyses, seek to make complex issues comprehensible while engaging for both students in various disciplines and general readers.

The first text in this series is on the law. The Shari'ah (Islamic law) is a little understood yet critical facet of the Islamic worldview. The operative aspects of Islamic law are contained in fiqh (Islamic jurisprudence). Editor Hisham Ramadan, an accomplished criminal lawyer and Islamic Law professor, provides readers with a variety of texts written by scholars on a number of concerns including an overview of the law, Islamic treatment of punishment, intellectual property, and marriage and divorce issues. This particular volume is a template of other volumes in this series as scholars engage the tradition and its modern, contemporary uses.

Editor's Introduction: Readings on Islamic Law

Hisham M. Ramadan

"Nay, We hurl the Truth against falsehood, and it knocks out its brain, and behold, falsehood doth perish! Ah! woe be to you for the (false) things ye ascribe (to Us)."

—The Holy Qur'an 21:18

"O mankind! We created you from a single (pair) of a male and a female, and made you into nations and tribes, that ye may know each other (not that ye may despise each other). Verily the most honored of you in the sight of Allah is (he who is) the most righteous of you. And Allah has full Knowledge and is well-acquainted (with all things)."

—The Holy Qur'an 49:13

The purpose of this book is to explain several aspects of Islamic jurisprudence fundamentals to the common reader in order to acquaint him with ideologies that are far from his zone of accessible knowledge. The essays presented in this volume were carefully selected to cover several areas of Islamic jurisprudence. Irshad Abdal-Haqq, in chapter 1, lays this volume's foundation by explaining the sources and elements of Islamic law, Islamic major schools of jurisprudence and essential definitions. In chapter 2, I attempt to capture the essence of Islamic criminal law by demonstrating the objectives of Islamic criminal law, its rationales, and the characteristics of the punishment. Ahmed Zaki Yamanai's chapter on international humanitarian law is of utmost importance at the present time, when a number of individuals invoke Islam as a justification for shocking acts of terror, because the essay demonstrates the genuine Islamic ethics of warfare. Professor Noor Mohammed's chapter 4 may assist the reader to understand the essentials of Islamic contract law in a time when a growing number of Muslims are seeking Islamic financial services in the West, and there is a rapid increase in the implementation of the Islamic financial system by many Islamic states.

While Mahmoud Hoballah explains the basics of Islamic family law in chapter 5, Professor Nazeem Goolam clarifies common Islamic family law misunderstandings. The merit of his chapter 6 is not limited to vindication of certain Islamic law positions but also extends to educate numerous Muslims of the true spirit of Islamic law. Professor Ali Khan, in chapter 7, presents a theory on Islam as intellectual property whose significance extends far beyond excellent creativity in academic exercises to raise the question of the validity of the orientalists' analysis of Islamic law. I conclude this volume by including two highly important documents: The Islamic Universal Declaration of Human Rights and The Constitution of Medina supplemented by a commentary. The latter document presents the first constitution made by the Prophet Mohammed in establishing an Islamic state in Medina. The former document, as drafted by the European Islamic Council, a nongovernmental organization, highlights Muslim efforts to codify Islamic human rights apart from oppressive regimes, in a number of states populated by a Muslim majority, and from Western ideologies that might be inconsistent with Islamic law.

This publication is not intended to reconcile Islamic law with positive law or to draw a comparison between Islamic jurisprudence and other laws because any comparison of that sort lacks merit and is erroneous. This is due to the great dissimilarity on many levels between Islamic law and positive law—that is, in origin, in scope, or even in the criterion employed to evaluate the harms and benefits generated by legal and ethical norms.

The crucial timing of this publication occurs during a time when the clouds of misunderstanding Islamic law dominate the skies of academe. Many factors contribute to misstating Islamic law including politically motivated statements against the Islamic world, lack of understanding of Arabic texts necessary to comprehend Islamic law or lack of proper Islamic jurisprudence education. Whether the objective of the academician who misstates Islamic law is entirely virtuous or is driven by unbridled bias, misstating Islamic law produces adverse results. On a local level, it creates a disgraceful environment full of hate and suspicion among citizens of one nation, which in turn, increase hate crimes against Muslims in the non-Islamic state. On an international level, it ignites wars between nations where non-Islamic states, upon erroneous understanding of Islam and Islamic law, claim moral superiority and where these Islamic states are frustrated in their efforts to reach the intellects of non-Islamic states but to no avail.

One might suspect that I exaggerate the importance of understanding Islamic law but a review of history proves the merits of my thesis. Lack of understanding Islam and Islamic law drove the crusaders to free Christians from the alleged Islamic oppression. These wars lasted hundreds of years with atrocities committed by the crusaders against Muslims, Jews, and Middle Eastern Christians alike. Likewise, the hundreds of thousands, if not millions, of European soldiers who died defending what they believed to be just cause should not be forgotten. Perhaps if Europe were armed with correct knowledge of Islamic law and Islam in general, there would be proper unbiased communications between nations such that these wars would have never taken place.

The Muslim world is approximately 1.5 billion people, one-fourth of the world's population, and understanding their laws, which represent their moral identity, is a vital task. It rests on the academician to build bridges of understanding and hope. Accordingly, this publication is not more than a seed in the garden of knowledge. The remainder rests upon the academician crowned by academics' honesty, freedom, and conscientiousness to present Islamic law correctly.

1

Islamic Law: An Overview of Its Origin and Elements

Irshad Abdal-Haqq

I. INTRODUCTION

This chapter surveys the fundamental elements of Islamic law and jurisprudence. It also highlights issues of current concern to American Muslims and examines the prospect for practical application of Islamic law in the United States. Access to information about Islamic law will become increasingly important to American jurists, lawyers, scholars and political leaders as the American Muslim community grows in size and influence. The Muslim population in the United States is estimated to range from five to eight million and Islam is projected to become the nation's second largest religion early in the next century.[1] A distinctive characteristic of Islam is its remarkable synthesis of all aspects of human social interaction and endeavor into a single value system—a system of law. Throughout the entire history of Islam, Islamic law has remained a prime focus of intellectual effort and recognized by Muslims as a religious duty to uphold and protect.[2] Nowhere is this urgency of purpose more pronounced than among American Muslims. On one hand, the Muslim community in the United States, as a minority, must establish institutions that will assure its continuation and development. On the other hand, the Islamic sense of mission readily affirms itself in a society struggling to preserve Judeo-Christian-Muslim values.[3] Added to this dynamic is the fact that the United States is one of only a few places on earth where the global forces of Islamic resurgence are guaranteed the Constitutional freedoms of expression and organization that are required to promulgate their ideals, whether conservative or reformist.

1

Islamic law is likely to become the intellectual focus in the American Muslim community as it synthesizes and matures, for it was a high regard for the law that produced the disciplined and united civilization of Islam's golden era.[4] The all-encompassing law of Islam, emanating from the Qur'an itself, embraces every aspect of human activity, defines Islamic values, and dictates standards of behavior.[5] Therefore, it must command the attention of any Muslim community seeking to preserve and assert itself. The question then is not whether Islamic law will become the intellectual focus of American Muslims, but rather when will it become the focus and how Islamic legal principles will be implemented.

It would appear that in addition to the sense of religious duty to learn and observe Islamic law, both external and internal community pressures are mandating expedited implementation of methods for practicing the law. External pressure stems from the Muslim perception of public prejudice against Islam. Immigrant Muslims are especially sensitive to media reports equating Islam and Arabs to terrorism.[6] The tendency on the part of some media to characterize Islam as an enemy to America and the West is long-standing and well documented.[7] Paradoxically, negative media imagery is serving to galvanize the Muslim community. Islamic political and public relations organizations are enjoying wide appeal because of their role in defending Islamic values and traditions against media and other attacks.[8] As pointed out, Islamic values are delineated through Islamic legal principles. Thus, American Muslim leadership will feel compelled to find ways of implementing the practice and observance of Islamic law in America for the benefit of their growing constituency.

From within the Muslim community, an increasing number of individuals consistently call for the development of stable institutions that will better ensure the preservation and proper application of Islamic values for the benefit of Muslims and the society at large. For example, one leading Muslim imam has suggested formulation of an indigenous school of thought in Islamic law dedicated to addressing the peculiar concerns of American Muslims.[9]

That Islamic law will play an increased role in the affairs of American Muslims appears inevitable. As disputes resulting from Islamic religious obligations and agreements entered under Islamic principles work themselves through arbitration and into the courts, the legal, business and political communities will be asked and sometimes required to address questions of law rooted in Islamic tradition. This tradition will present itself in at least two forms—the first based upon conventional adherence only to those jurisprudential principles and methodology established during Islam's Golden Era, some 900 years ago, and second, those committed to devising new approaches for resolving contemporary concerns where the ancient formulas appear to be inappropriate or inadequate.

Obviously, knowledge of such fundamentals as the origin and elements of Islamic law will be essential in addressing issues emanating from either approach. In the discussion that follows this fundamental material will be discussed along with those areas of law that are likely to be of chief importance to American Muslims. By no means is this article intended to serve as a source of comprehensive information on any Islamic area of law or school of jurisprudence. Rather, it is intended to provide an introductory overview of Islamic law for American readers. Where appropriate, follow-up research and consultation should be conducted.

II. ISLAMIC LAW: DEFINITION AND DESCRIPTION

The term *Islamic law* generally is used in reference to the entire system of law and jurisprudence associated with the religion of Islam,[10] including (1) the primary sources of law (Shari'ah) and (2) the subordinate sources of law and the methodology used to deduce and apply the law (*Islamic jurisprudence* called *fiqh* in Arabic). The Arabic phrase for Islamic law is *qanun ul Islamia*, which has been described as a claque because it is thought not to be a part of original Islamic vocabulary, but rather was devised in reaction to Western influence. Now, however, *qanun ul Islamia* is a part of the vocabulary in every Muslim country.[11]

Some writers use the terms *Islamic law, Shari'ah* and/or *fiqh* interchangeably.[12] This easily could result in confusion for readers seeking to sort out the significance of each concept. In this article, the term *Islamic law* is used in conformity with modern usage and refers to the entire system of law and jurisprudence. The distinction between *Shari'ah* and *fiqh*, however, is an important one and the two terms will not be interchanged. Elaboration on the meaning of each follows in the next two subsections.

At least one writer, Dr. Said Ramadan, has advocated using the term "Muslim jurisprudence" rather than "Islamic jurisprudence" in referring to fiqh because it is his opinion that an incorrect legal conclusion rendered under fiqh, of which there have been many, properly should not be classified as *Islamic*.[13] Adoption of Dr. Ramadan's distinction between "Islam" and "Muslim" would not necessarily result in fiqh being any less identified as Islamic if labeled "Muslim jurisprudence," since Muslims are readily identified as Islamic anyway. Additionally, much of fiqh, in the way of process and findings, comports with sound Islamic standards and principles, and therefore is worthy of being recognized as Islamic.

The more important and substantive distinction is between Shari'ah and fiqh, both of which are considered to be within the scope of the Western description of Islamic law, but with the former of the two being preeminent and ideally forming the basis for all doctrines formulated under fiqh.

A. Shari'ah

There are two primary sources of Islamic law—the *Qur'an* (Koran)[14] and the *Sunnah* (traditions of Muhammad ibn Abdullah, the last prophet of Islam). The Sunnah[15] of Muhammad includes the things he said, i.e. his *hadith*, as well as the things he did or refrained from doing.[16] These two elements, Qur'an and Sunnah, comprise what is known as the Shari'ah—the source from which all principles of Islamic law and life flow.[17]

Shari'ah, or more properly *Al-Shari'ah*, literally means the *pathway*,[18] *path to be followed*,[19] or *clear way to be followed*, and has come to mean *the path upon which the believer has to tread*.[20] In original usage Shari'ah meant the *road to the watering place or path leading to the water*, i.e., the way to the source of life.[21] The technical application of the term as a reference to the law of Islam is traced directly to the Qur'an,[22] wherein the adherents of Islam, *the believers*, are admonished by Allah (God) to follow the clear and right way, the path of Shari'ah: *Then We put thee on the (right) Way of religion; so follow thou that (Way), and follow not the desires of those who know not.*[23]

In this technical sense Shari'ah refers to the canon law of Islam and includes the totality of Allah's commandment.[24] Thus, the principles and injunctions of the Qur'an are regarded as the highest source of guidance under the Shari'ah. From Qur'an flows all authority to make law or to render an opinion on law.[25]

The Sunnah forms the second tier of the Shari'ah. The mandate to establish law and standards of conduct on the basis of the Prophet's behavior flows directly from the language of the Qur'an. The following three ayats represent a sampling of numerous Qur'anic expressions that confirm Muhammad as a guide and model for the believers and mandate obedience to his directives:

> He who obeys the Messenger, obeys Allah, but if any turn away,
> We have not sent thee to watch over them.[26]
> Ye have indeed in the Messenger of Allah an excellent example for him who hopes in Allah and the Final Day, and who remembers Allah much.[27]
> It is not fitting for a believer, man or woman, when a matter has been decided by Allah and His Messenger, to have any option about their decision. If any disobeys Allah and His Messenger,
> he is indeed on a clearly wrong path.[28]

The authentic Sunnah provides insight into the life of Muhammad as the model of conduct all Muslims must strive to emulate as dictated by the Qur'an. This second tier of the primary sources of Islamic law is collected in multi-volume sets (*Hadiths*) that have been translated into English and are discussed more fully in Part III.C.

Where an issue or matter is not specifically addressed in the Shari'ah, it authorizes the use of one's reasoning ability to deduce and apply Shari'ah principles. The following hadith (saying) attributed to Muhammad mandates the use of sound reasoning in reaching legal decisions where the Qur'an and Sunnah are silent on a matter. In this exchange, Muhammad asks his appointed judge to Yemen, Mu'adh Ibn Jabal, the basis upon which he would judge the cases before him.

> *According to what shalt thou judge?* He replied: According to the Book of Allah. *And if thou findest nought therein?* According to the Sunnah of the Prophet of Allah. *And if thou findest nought therein?* Then I will exert myself to form my own judgment. *Praise be to God Who has guided the messenger of His Prophet to that which pleases His Prophet.*[29]

The above hadith embodies the concept of exerting one's judgment within the scope of free thought and individual opinion so long as that opinion does not contravene the plain meaning and spirit of the Shari'ah.[30] This concept of exerting one's reasoning faculty in determining a point of law is called, in Arabic, *ijtihad*. The application of ijtihad was a primary tool used by early Islamic jurists in applying Islamic law, i.e. the process of *fiqh*, in new situations and, as we shall see, the degree of its use has been a major source of contention among Muslim scholars and jurists through the ages.[31] *Ijtihad* literally means "to exert oneself."[32] While its use was encouraged as a tertiary method for deducing Islamic law, Islamic jurists were expected to reason within the scope of the spirit and principles of Shari'ah in all circumstances.

B. Fiqh

The process of *deducing* and *applying* Shari'ah principles and injunctions in real or hypothetical cases or situations is called *fiqh* or *Islamic jurisprudence*.[33] The term *fiqh* also is used to refer to the collective body of laws deduced from Shari'ah through the use of fiqh methodology. While the principles and injunctions of the Shari'ah are infallible and not subject to amendment, fiqh-based standards may change according to the circumstances.[34] The objective of fiqh is to demonstrate the practical application of the Shari'ah. It covers all subject areas of law including religious, political, civil, criminal, constitutional and procedural law; the administration of justice; and the conduct of war.[35] Four methods, often called *sources of law* by Muslim writers, for deducing and establishing fiqh-based law are universally recognized by Islamic jurists. They are: (1) the extraction of Qur'anic injunctions and principles based on interpretations of it; (2) the application of the principles reflected through the Hadith of Prophet Muhammad; (3) the consensus of opinion from among the companions of Muhammad or the learned scholars (*ijma*); and (4) analogical deduction (*qiyas*).³⁶ The third method has been called "collective reasoning," as compared to the "individual reasoning" inherent in the last method.³⁷ In virtually all instances, ijma (consensus) is more highly regarded and given preeminence over qiyas or Ijtihad.³⁸ Both Muslim and non-Muslim scholars regard these four methods of law as the roots of Islamic jurisprudence.³⁹

Fiqh literally means "intelligence" and implies the independent exercise of reasoning power in deciding a point of law, in the absence or ignorance of guidance from the Shari'ah on an issue.⁴⁰ The Arabic verb *faqaha*, means "to comprehend," thus its noun form, *fiqh*, implies comprehension⁴¹ as well as intelligence, and has been more fully translated as *the true understanding of what is intended*.⁴² When accompanied by the definite article *al* (the), as in *Al-Fiqh*, reference usually is being made specifically to the collected works of Muslim jurists rather than the process of analysis and application.⁴³

As noted in our earlier discussion, fiqh-based laws promulgated through fiqh methodology often are referred to as *Islamic law, Islamic jurisprudence*, and even as part of the *Shari'ah* by many scholars, jurists, and theorists. Few would argue with including fiqh under the umbrella of Islamic law,⁴⁴ but designating it as part of the Shari'ah, per se, certainly blurs the line between the infallibility of revealed knowledge (Qur'an) and its demonstration by Muhammad (Sunnah), and fallible attempts by man to infer, deduce and apply the principles of revealed knowledge through ijtihad or otherwise. This blurring of the line between Shari'ah and fiqh has been attributed, in part, to the policy by Muslim leaders shortly after the fall of Baghdad in 1258 C.E. (to the Mongols) to elevate and regard the schools of fiqh as divinely ordained manifestations of Islam.⁴⁵

While there is one Qur'an and Sunnah, no less than nineteen schools of fiqh (*fiqh madhhabs*) developed during the first four centuries of Islam.⁴⁶ By the fall of Baghdad the number of major madhhabs had dwindled to five (four sunni and one shia). These five schools of Islamic jurisprudence continue to exist today and later will be discussed in more detail. Differences between the madhhabs turn on fiqh-related principles of interpretation of the Shari'ah.⁴⁷ Where law in Western culture is secular and separated from religion, in Islam the law touches on every sphere of activity.⁴⁸ While the average citizens of Western society have never even heard of the five Western schools of jurisprudence,⁴⁹ it is not uncommon for an average well-read Muslim to be aware of the existence of and knowledgeable about the five schools of fiqh.

The differences in the fiqh madhhabs during the premodern age eventually deteriorated into fanatical factionalism that has continued to the present time in some parts of the world. For a period of time an individual had to identify with one of the four recognized schools of fiqh to even be considered a Muslim among the Sunni.[50] Anyone refusing to identify and comply with the mandates of one of the four madhhabs was subject to being charged with heresy, as could anyone attempting to change his or her affiliation from one madhhab to another.[51] Factionalism was so acute that in at least one instance a judge prohibited intermarriage between Muslims identifying with different madhhabs.[52] So many Muslims refused even to pray with one another on the basis of differing fiqh madhhabs affiliation that areas of the Grand Masjid (Masjid Al-Haram) in Mecca were reserved for segregated prayer by affiliates of particular madhhabs.[53]

Thus, identification with one or another of the fiqh schools was a very serious matter that became entrenched in the culture of many Muslim societies. As a practical matter, it is likely that American jurists will encounter adherents of a school of fiqh claiming religious customs or obligations that may seem to contradict the claims of Muslims made in another case. It is likely that the differences are legitimate and can be attributed to decisions (fatawa) rendered by Muslim jurists aligned with different fiqh schools or *madhhabs*.

At present, the four major schools of fiqh among the sunni Muslims are: (1) Hanafi, (2) Maliki, (3) Shafi'i, and (4) Hanbali. Among the shia, the Jafari school predominates. A long and continuing line of Muslim scholars advocate new approaches to Islamic law that would encourage renewed, dynamic approaches to fiqh and eliminate rigid allegiances to the traditional madhhabs.[54]

III. ELEMENTS OF SHARI'AH

A. Basic Concepts

Before discussing Qur'an and Sunnah as the primary sources of Islamic law, a descriptive definition of several fundamental terms and concepts are provided in this section. These definitions by no means are intended to be considered comprehensive. Rather, they are meant to provide the minimum information required to better comprehend the more detailed discussion of Shari'ah and fiqh in later sections.

1. Allah

In Islam, Allah is the Supreme Being, creator of all things, the divine reality.[55] The concept of Allah for Muslims is akin to the concept of God for mainstream Jews, Christians, and other monotheistic religions. The unity, oneness, of Allah to Muslims is best expressed by the Qur'an itself in the surah entitled *The Purity of Faith*:

Say: *He is Allah, The One and Only; Allah, the Eternal, the Absolute; He begets not, nor is He begotten, And there is none like unto Him.*[56]

A fundamental tenet of Islam is the principle that Allah is one and that Allah is not a created thing, neither a human being, animal nor other material or spiritual creation.[57] Thus, promulgation of the concept of man as God, or woman as God, or the incarnation of God through a created thing, whether material or spiritual, is anathema in Islam.

2. *Muhammad*

Muhammad ibn Abdullah (PBUH)[58] lived from approximately 570 to 632 C.E. He did not begin to formally teach Islam among his people, the pagan Arabs of Mecca, Arabia, until 610 at the age of forty. From 610 until his death, the foundation of what is called Islam was established. The Qur'an, which was recited by Muhammad (pbuh) to his people, and his reported traditions (*Hadith*), form the foundation of the religion. For more than fourteen hundred years, the Muslim world has painstakingly persevered the sanctity and purity of the Qur'an and have tried to do the same with the Sunnah of Muhammad (PBUH).[59]

Muhammad had a very difficult time establishing Islam among the Arabs of his day. Ultimately he succeeded. Though born an orphan and unable to read or write, he was able to combine the religious with the secular in one of the most backward corners of the earth, to establish a civilization that ushered in the Renaissance in Europe, among other things. For this accomplishment, he has been called *the most influential* person in the history of the world by a non-Muslim historian.[60]

3. *Islam*

Islam is an Arabic word meaning *submission*.[61] In the United States the term is used in reference to the religion or way of life of Muslims. The formal term for the Muslim religion is *Al-Islam*, meaning complete submission to the will of Allah. The definite article *al* in Arabic means *the*, and corresponds with the definite articles *el* in Spanish or French *le*. It is typical to hear Muslims refer to their religion interchangeably in English as Islam or Al-Islam. The use of the term Islam is not considered offensive or wrong in American English, and so is used throughout this article. The term *Muhammadan* now is considered offensive by Muslims, although it was acceptable and widely used by many pre-modern Muslim and non-Muslim scholars.

The words *Islam* and *Muslim* derive from the same Arabic root *s-l-m*, which connotes, among other things, peace, security, soundness, and integrity.[62] It is from this root that the word *salaam* (peace) originates. Consequently, a Muslim is a person who enters into the peace and submits to the will of Allah (God).[63]

There are five fundamental principles of practice in Islam. They are:

(1) Declaration of Belief—That there is no deity besides Allah and that Muhammad Ibn Abdullah of 7th century Arabia is Allah's servant and last messenger;

(2) Prayer—To observe formal prayers five times a day;

(3) Fasting—To observe the Ramadan fast;

(4) Zakat—To give in charity; and

(5) Pilgrimage—To perform pilgrimage (hajj) to Mecca at least once.[64]

The origin of Islam is perceived differently by Muslims and non-Muslims. Where non-Muslims date the beginning of Islam with Muhammad (pbuh) in seventh-century Arabia, Muslims consider all the prophets of the Bible as Muslim and believe that they all delivered portions of the same message that culminated in Muhammad's delivery of the Qur'an.[65] Thus, Muslims do not believe that the message of Islam started with Muhammad—rather they believe that Allah's message to humankind was completed through Muhammad (pbuh). The very last words of the Qur'an as related chronologically by Muhammad[66] read as follows:

This day have I perfected your religion for you, completed My favor upon you, and have chosen for you Islam as your religion.[67]

Approximate 90 percent of all Muslims are identified as *sunni*, with the balance identified as *shia* (also spelled *shiite* or *shiah*).[68] The principle differences are two. First, the shia, found principally in Iran, Iraq, Syria and Lebanon, believe that the leadership of the Muslim community, the caliph, must be a man who is a descendant of Muhammad.[69] They await the emergence of a Muslim leader from the line of the prophet who will embody the wisdom and spiritual power of the Hidden or Twelfth Imam, who went into hiding at the age of four in 873 C.E.[70] In the absence of the Twelfth Imam, his representatives, ayatollahs, provide interim leadership.[71] Sunnis, on the other hand, impose no precondition of physical lineage to be considered for the position of Khalifa.[72] Needless to say, the vast majority of non-Arab Muslims and American converts to Islam readily embrace the latter view, even while taking exception to being labeled or categorized as either *sunni* or *shia*.

The second significant difference is that the shia continue to recognize individual reasoning (ijtihad) as a legitimate source of Islamic law, while the sunni madhhabs forbid the current use of Ijtihad.[73] Relatively speaking, both these distinctions are unremarkable in the lives of ordinary Muslims in the United States. Sunnis and Shias intermarry, pray together, befriend one another, and in all other respects accord full and equal recognition as Muslims to one another.

Numerous organizations through the ages, however, have characterized their religious and social movements as *Islam* or *Islamic*, but were and still are rejected by the greater Islamic community because they promulgated doctrine that contravened the basic five principles of Islam listed above, or other important principles. The most typical doctrinal violations involved claims that someone other than Muhammad ibn Abdullah is the last messenger and/or that Allah is a human being incarnated in a person with whom the group is associated.

Four prominent examples of this phenomenon are:

(1) The *Ahmadiyyah Movement in Islam*, of late nineteenth-century India, which claimed its leader, Ghulam Ahmad of Kadiyan, was the Mahdi and reappearance of Muhammad and Jesus.[74] The Ahmadiyyah continue to exist and have mosques across the world, including the United States.[75] The movement eventually split in two, with the lesser segment, led by Maulana Muhammad Ali, who characterized Ghulam as a *mujaddid* (reviver or renewer of the religion) rather than a prophet.[76] This smaller group consider themselves to be within the framework of mainstream Islam and has published notable scholarly works on Islam;[77]

(2) The *Moorish Science Temple of America*, founded in 1913 in Newark, New Jersey, identified itself with Islam.[78] Its founder, Noble Drew Ali, claimed to be a prophet of Allah and "divinely prepared" a book entitled *The Holy Koran of the Moorish Science Temple of America*;[79]

(3) *The Lost Found Nation of Islam* founded in 1931 by Elijah Muhammad and Wallace Fard claimed to be an Islamic movement.[80] When the Fard mysteriously disappeared in 1931, Elijah Muhammad characterized Fard as *Allah in the person*, while proclaiming himself the *Messenger of Allah*, i.e., Fard's messenger;[81] and

(4) the *Nubian Islamic Hebrews* (aka *Ansaru Allah Community*) which mixes Islam and Christianity into a mystic order that borrows heavily from the Islamic mystic tradition called sufism.[82] Founded in 1967 in New York City[83] the movement's current leader, Isa Muhammad teaches that both Jesus and Muhammad were incarnations of Allah and that he is the current incarnation of Allah.[84]

Thus, there are a number of religious organizations (and their adherents) in America that while identifying themselves as *Islamic* might not embrace the tenets of mainstream Islam and, in turn, might not espouse or identify with the basic principles of Islamic law as set out in this article. This is to say that sunni and shia Muslims share the same Islamic values, in that they seek out the straight path of the Shari'ah precisely as presented in the Qur'an and Sunnah of Muhammad. Other groups, however sincere they might believe in their religious doctrine, embrace values and recognize sources of law that are different from the Shari'ah. As a consequence, the distinction between mainstream Islamic orientation and quasi-Islamic doctrine is an important one of which a jurist must remain sensitive and cognizant.

B. Qur'an

The word *Qur'an* means *that which should be recited, read, or studied* and refers to the book embodying the revelation from Allah to Muhammad (pbuh).[85] It is not unusual to see it referred to as the *Holy Qur'an or Glorious Qur'an*. Islamic law cannot be studied without studying the Qur'an because it is the foundation of the religion. Muslims believe that the Qur'an is the actual word of Allah as it was revealed to Muhammad over a period of twenty-two years, from 610 to 632 C.E.[86] Unlike the Bible with its many books, the Qur'an is but one book comprised of 114 surahs (chapters), 6,666 ayats (verses) and 86,430 words.[87]

Although Muhammad could neither read nor write, prior to his death he made sure that the entire Qur'an was reduced to writing in Arabic.[88] Additionally, some of Muhammad's closest followers committed the Qur'an to memory.[89] Since the time of its recording, the Muslim community has diligently worked to preserve its integrity.[90]

Non-Muslim, Western readers often find the Qur'an difficult to read, in part, because the eloquence and rhythm of the Arabic does not translate into English and other languages.[91] At least one English translation, however, has been highly regarded for its eloquent use of language and scholarly commentary.[92] Muslims consider the Qur'an, itself, a miracle. "There is no end to its miracle," wrote 12th century scholar al-Ghazzali, "it is ever fresh and new to the reciters."[93] The circumstances of its development,[94] the medium of its message,[95] the eloquence and rhythm of its poetry,[96] all are consider a part of the miracle of its being.

The Qur'an is not and does not profess itself to be a code of law or a law book.[97] Instead, it serves as the cornerstone upon which Islamic law is based—the primary source for the principles of law—in addition to selected, specific injunctions.[98] The total number of legal injunctions in the Qur'an has been calculated to be five hundred.[99] The broad Qur'anic categories of legal injunctions that somewhat parallel American subject areas of law include ethics, criminal, business transactions, domestic relations, inheritance, and rules of engagement in war.[100] Additionally, as we shall see, specific Qur'anic ayats (verses) are invoked in support of the devices employed in the science of Islamic jurisprudence, *fiqh*.[101]

C. Traditions of Muhammad: Sunnah and Hadith

The practices and sayings of Muhammad (pbuh) are commonly called *Hadith* or *Sunnah*.[102] The two words often are used interchangeably.[103] In fact, there is a difference in their meanings. Hadith refers to a report of what Muhammad said, that is, an actual verbal expression or opinion on a subject. *Sunnah* implies the mode of life he lived, the example he set through his actions, sayings, judgments, and attitudes[104]—his practices or tradition.[105] In this sense, then, *Hadith* is subsumed under his *Sunnah* because his sayings were one of the things that he did, and reflected his tradition in verbal form. In his own words Muhammad said, *"I have bequeathed to you two things; if you hold fast to them you will never go astray. They are the Qur'an and my Sunnah."*[106] This quotation is an example of a hadith in which the Prophet establishes in Islam the supremacy of the Qur'an and then his Sunnah.[107]

The formal, collected hadiths of Muhammad and reports of his Sunnah came to be called *the Hadith, Al-Hadith*, or *Ahadith*.[108] They are verbalized accounts of what Muhammad said and did as reported by his contemporary followers (companions or *sahaba*) and that have been reduced to writing. Thus, the terms *Hadith* and *Sunnah* are likely to be used interchangeably in much of the current and historical literature on the subject of Muhammad's traditions. This is not problematic because his actions and speech are accorded equal validity in Islamic law and constitute *the exemplification of the message of Islam*.[109]

There are four types of hadith that were reported and recorded: (1) Muhammad's own words; (2) Muhammad's actions (such as descriptions of how he prayed, conducted war, treated the poor, etc.); (3) Muhammad's tacit approval of actions performed in his presence, i.e., his silence on a matter was interpreted as consent; and (4) descriptions of his physical attributes, person-ality, demeanor, and disposition.[110] All four types are referenced as primary sources of Islamic law.

While there is but one Qur'an, scores of scholars compiled Hadiths of the Prophet over a period of three hundred years using varied methodologies.[111] Concern about the accuracy and authenticity of the Hadiths resulted in the advent of the *sahih* movement (meaning authentic, sound or genuine), between 850 C.E. and 915 C.E., during which time dedicated scholars attempted to authenticate each hadith.[112] From this movement came *The Six Books*,[113] six acclaimed *Hadiths* compiled by recognized scholars of high character.[114] These compilers are: (1) Muhammad bin Ismail bin Al-Mughirah Al-Bukhari (called *Al-Bukhari*); (2) Abu al-Hasan Muslim bin al-Hajjaj (called *Muslim*); (3) Abu Dawud Sulayman bin al-Ashath (known as *Abu Dawud*); (4) Abu Isa Muhammad bin Isa (known as *al-Tirmidhi*); (5) Abu Abd al-Rahman Ahmad bin Shuaib (known as *al-Nasai*); and (6) Ibn Majah Muhammad bin Yazid.[115] Of the six, the first two, Al-Bukhari and Muslim, are the most highly regarded and their works are available in English.[116] It took Al Bukhari sixteen years to comb through 600,000 purported hadiths, of which he determined 7,397 to be authentic, and half of those selected are repetitions. Muslim's work contains 12,000 hadiths, with about 8,000 being repetitions.[117]

Most of Muhammad's Sunnah was not recorded in writing until after his death. This was done to prevent mixing up his sayings with the Qur'an.[118] The first generation of transmitters of the Hadith was the Sahabah[119] (contemporary companions), followed by the Successors (*Tabiyun*), who in turn passed along the traditions to the Successors of the Successors.[120] Ultimately the Sahih movement resulted in the analytical treatment of each hadith and its chain of narrators, including their characters and reputations.[121]

Even after assiduous critical study during the sahih period, a small percentage of hadiths now considered to be of questionable authenticity survived scrutiny because they were transmitted by reliable narrators. Consequently, all hadiths are measured against the Qur'an and where there is inconsistency, the latter prevails.[122] The following is an excerpt from a translation of Muslim's collection of hadith from the chapter regarding the meaning of religion:

The Book of Faith
Chapter 24. Religion is Sincerity and Well-Wishing.
    (98) It is narrated on the authority of Tamim ad-Dari that the Apostle of Allah (may peace and blessing be upon him) observed: *Al-Din (religion) is sincerity and well-wishing.* Upon this we said: *For whom?* He replied: *For Allah, His book, His messenger, and for the leaders and the general Muslims.*[123]
    (101) It is narrated on the authority of Jarir[124] that he observed: *I gave [my] pledge of allegiance to the Messenger of Allah (may peace and blessings be upon him) on the observance of prayer, payment of zakat* [obligatory charity] *and sincerity and well-wishing for every Muslim.*

The following excerpt is from a translation of Al-Bukhari's collection of hadith on the same topic:

The Book of Faith
Chapter (43). Religion is to be Sincere and True to Allah.
    On the statement of the Prophet: *Religion is to be sincere and true to Allah; to Allah's Apostle; to the rulers of the Muslims, and to the general Muslims.* And the statement of Allah: *if they are sincere to Allah and His Apostle.*
    54. Narrated Jarir bin Abdullah: *I gave the pledge of allegiance to Allah's Apostle for the following: 1. To offer prayers perfectly; 2. Pay the zakat (obligatory charity); 3. Be sincere and true to every Muslim.*[125]

In this last excerpt, you will note Al-Bukhari's reference to Allah's *statement*, which is found in the Qur'an.[126] His legal notes and other commentary distinguish his work from Muslim's, which was dedicated solely to collecting and organizing the hadith. You can see, however, that the identical principle—that is, that religion is sincerity—is relayed by both Muslim and Al-Bukhari. Many researchers, however, prefer Al-Bukhari over Muslim because he would accept a hadith as authentic only if there was evidence that the transmitter actually met his or her teacher of the hadith. Muslim, who was an admirer and student of Al-Bukhari, is noted for the enhanced arrangement he gave to the Hadith. He would accept a hadith as authentic if the transmitter and teacher were contemporaries, even if he could not find actual evidence of them having met.[127]

IV. THE METHODOLOGIES AND BRANCHES OF FIQH

Fiqh (Islamic jurisprudence) refers to both the science of deducing and applying the principles and injunctions of Shari'ah, as well as the sum total of the deductions by particular jurists.[128] Thus, within the scope of a discussion of Islamic law it is possible to speak of the *fiqh* (the collective body of deductions) or of an individual or tribunal being engaged in *fiqh* (the process of deducing and applying the law). This discussion focuses on the latter.

Fiqh, the process, is divided into two broad divisions—(1) *usul al-fiqh*, called the *roots* of fiqh, refers to the systemized methodology and principles of interpretation used in ascertaining the law;[129] and (2) *faru al-fiqh*, called the *branches* of fiqh, which is akin to the actual "practice of law" and deals with rendering decisions (*fatawa*) that derive from the application of usul al-fiqh.[130]

All five major schools of Islamic jurisprudence are in agreement as to the four primary elements of usul al fiqh,[131] but disagree over the use of subordinate methods and the rules of interpretation and construction, among other things.[132] This section surveys the elements of usul al fiqh, as the base from which fiqh decisions on specific subject areas of law derive, and concludes by discussing the various branches of fiqh.

A. Interpretation of Qur'an (Tafsir)

As we have seen, all of the major schools of Islamic jurisprudence recognize the Qur'an as the primary source of Islamic law.[133] Quite often, the plain meaning (specific directives) and applicability of a principle or injunction of the Qur'an is not clear on its face. In such cases, interpretation is required. Thus, mastery of the science of the interpretation of and commentary on the Qur'an, rank at the very top in Islamic jurisprudence. The science of interpreting and rendering commentary on the Qur'an, i.e., its exegesis, is called *tafsir*.[134] An oft-repeated principle among scholars of Islamic law is that the foremost tafsir of the Qur'an is the Qur'an, itself.[135] This is to say that the Qur'an expounds upon many of its own principles at different places throughout the Qur'an.

While the science of tafsir may be applied to portions of the Qur'an, most works of tafsir are comprehensive, continuous commentaries on each phrase of the Qur'an, in regular order and sometimes word by word.[136] After Muhammad (pbuh), the most highly regarded early exegetes of Qur'an were his Sahaba (companions) and those who succeeded them.[137]

During the period following Muhammad and the Sahaba, the science of exegesis evolved and Islamic scholars established standards for individuals engaged in interpreting the Qur'an. The prerequisites for an exegete of Qur'an were that he/she must:

(1) be an accomplished linguist familiar with Qur'anic (classical) Arabic;
(2) have a thorough understanding of the message of Islam;
(3) have the ability to perceive meanings, abstract relations, and generalizing principles apparent in the various passages of the Qur'an; and
(4) take into consideration the reports of tradition stemming from Muhammad and his companions, i.e., be fully familiar with the Hadith.[138]

While the scholars of Islamic law generally could agree on the prerequisites for engaging in the interpretation of Qur'an, the major madhhabs disagreed as to the actual rules of interpretation.[139] In fact, the rules of interpretation are a fundamental element that separates the madhhabs from one another.[140]

Thus, exegesis of the Qur'an is not an exercise that can be casually performed. Not only should the exegete satisfy the prerequisite qualifications set out above, but he/she also must adhere to a complex set of rules of interpretation, emanating from a particular school of fiqh, or a combination from among the schools, and apply them consistently.[141] Absent the ability to meet these standards, the credible researcher would have to depend upon the tafsir of duly qualified exegetes for definitive interpretations of Qur'anic text and principles, while studying to become qualified in his or her own right.

B. Authenticity and Interpretation of Hadith

The Sunnah of Muhammad (pbuh), as recorded in Hadith, is the second most important source of law. Authenticity is the threshold question regarding the applicability of any hadith.[142] Once a hadith is deemed authentic, the jurist or scholar of hadith would be expected to satisfy the same standards of qualification and employ the same rules of interpretation that are required in the science of tafsir or for the interpretation of any other legal text.[143]

Unlike the Qur'an, which was recorded and organized under Muhammad's direct supervision, most hadiths were recorded and compiled many years after his death.[144] The procedures for determining the integrity of the more than one million hadiths[145] that were in circulation by the end of the second century A.H. developed into highly specialized sciences. They include:

(1) the science of studying and memorizing the text of each and every hadith and its chain of reporters;

(2) the science of establishing and learning the full biography of the hadith reporters;

(3) the science of examining the character of each hadith reporter;

(4) the science of determining whether a hadith has any vitiating cause;

(5) the science of harmonization between hadiths; and, as mentioned earlier; and

(6) the sciences associated with interpreting and explaining the language, hermeneutics.[146]

Differences between the schools of fiqh turn on the conditions of acceptance of hadiths, the use of weak hadiths by some schools, and the unavailability, and therefore nonacceptance, of some sound hadiths by some schools. Of course, differences in the rules of interpretation and construction contributed further in distinguishing the various madhhabs from one another.[147] Despite any differences, the superiority of Muhammad's sunnah over all other law, except the Qur'an, is universally accepted by the schools of fiqh and the Muslim community at-large.

Thus, a jurist, scholar, or researcher would first look to the Qur'an for clearly articulated injunctions and principles of law. Such an exercise could involve extensive study and the application of highly refined interpretive skill. The subordinate primary source of guidance would be the Sunnah of Muhammad as compiled in the Hadith. Where neither source provides express or implied guidance on a particular issue or concern, the Muslim community is directed to exert human reasoning to reach a determination. In so doing, the early leaders of the Muslim community and scholars of law came to recognize several classes of reasoning that are acceptable for deducing and applying the principles of Shari'ah.

C. Other Fiqh Methodologies

The five fiqh methods described in this section would require a jurist or legislator to exercise a degree of individual reasoning (*ijtihad*) in formulating determinations. Limited ijtihad was permitted by all four fiqh schools until the thirteenth century C.E., when the practice was universally discontinued. Currently, only the leader (imam) of the shia school is mandated to use ijtihad in reaching fiqh determinations. Following the descriptions of these ijtihad-based methods, the background and controversy surrounding ijtihad is discussed because its use, especially in the West, is likely to play an important part in the future development of Islamic law.

1. Ijma (Consensus)

Where the Qur'an and Sunnah do not provide specific guidance on an issue, the Muslim community is directed to exert reasoning to deduce the law. Under Islamic law there are two broad classes of reasoning—collective reasoning by consensus, *ijma*, whereby the learned scholars of Islam and/or community of Muslims of a particular era come to agreement on an issue, and individual reasoning via several methodologies, whereby a jurist renders a determination.[148] Of the two, the schools of fiqh give priority to the first. The practice of reaching a legal decision by consensus after mutual consultation (shura) was established by the Sahaba (Muhammad's contemporary followers).[149] Of course to participate in consultation, each participant would have to resort to individual reasoning (ijtihad) in his or her own right.[150] The leading Qur'anic authority for ijma stems from the following ayat:

> O ye who believe! Obey Allah, and obey the Messenger, and *those charged with authority among you*. If ye differ in anything among yourselves, refer it to Allah and His Messenger, if ye do believe in Allah and the Last Day; that is best and most suitable for final determination.[151] (emphasis added)

A point of contention surrounds the question of who may participate in ijma decision making. The general view is that only qualified Islamic scholars who are Muslim and who are qualified for ijtihad are permitted to participate when the purpose is to settle an issue dependent upon the exercise of analogical deduction.[152] Being qualified means a jurist should be knowledgeable of the Qur'an and Sunnah, being able to read, understands and interprets them. He or she would be expected to be able to distinguish between authentic and unauthentic hadiths, and be conversant in the rules of analogical deduction.[153] In other matters, such as elections, practicing the fundamentals of the religion, and perhaps other community affairs, every adult Muslim of sound mind, with exceptions for certain criminals, would be included in the ijma process.[154]

Iqbal considers ijma *the most important legal notion in Islam*.[155] Through it, he believes, Islamic societies should be able to establish permanent legislative institutions. In practical terms, however, ijma has not been used successfully since the time of the Sahaba (immediately following the death of

Muhammad) because of political divisions in the Muslim world and the great distances and circumstances separating the Muslim population.[156] Thus, the recorded ijma of the Sahaba constitute the only ijma-based source of law that is universally recognized.

With new age computer and communications technology and an ever-growing interest among Muslims to work in unity, it is conceivable that ijma will play an important role in Islamic law and relations in the U.S. and elsewhere.

2. Qiyas (Analogy)

Where ijma represents a form of collective ijtihad (reasoning), *qiyas* is an individual form based on analogical deduction.[157] As mentioned earlier, ijma ranks higher than qiyas in fiqh methodology. To participate in ijma involving a matter for which an in-depth knowledge of Qur'anic and Hadith sciences are required, however, an individual first would be expected to be qualified to exercise independent analogical reasoning, or qiyas. By necessity then, the acquisition of the skills required to exercise qiyas precedes an individual's opportunity to participate in ijma determinations, though the latter, reflecting the common concern, is given a higher consideration in fiqh methodology.

At least one Qur'anic reference and two hadiths have been invoked to support the use of qiyas. Abdur Rahim quotes from surah 59, ayat 2, wherein the Muslims are asked by Allah to infer analogically from the example Allah made of treacherous members of the tribe of Banu Nadir. From this, he argues, Muslims are encouraged directly by Allah, to draw analogies from the Qur'an and Sunnah for which there is a similar cause or purpose.[158]

The formal exercise of qiyas as a fiqh method was introduced by Abu Hanifa, for which the Hanafi Madhhab of fiqh is named.[159] Eventually, qiyas was recognized by all four sunni schools of fiqh as a legitimate device for extracting law from the Qur'an and Sunnah, but only where there was no preexisting precedent by ijma.

3. Istihsan (The Public Interest)

Istihsan is the process of selecting one acceptable alternative solution over another because the former appears more suitable for the situation at hand, even though the selected solution may be technically weaker than the rejected one.[160] This process of selecting the best solution for the general (public) interest in a form of ijtihad.[161] The jurists of the various schools gave this concept different names and higher or lesser degrees of importance. *Istihsan* is the label the Hanafi schools adopted. The Hanbali school of thought calls it *Istislah* (equity or public interest), while the Malikis call it

Masalih Al-Mursalah (departure from strict adherence to the texts for the public welfare).[162]

This alternative provided relief where analogy was deficient, opposition to it from other schools prevented it from being fully developed and recognized.[163] Several examples of the application of this device include: (1) the prohibited practice of destroying good food, in this case by Khalif Umar, whereby he ordered the pouring out of milk that had been adulterated with water to punish the dishonest milk salesman and protect the public from being cheated; (2) the practice, under extraordinary circumstances, of allowing physicians to treat patients of the opposite sex even though persons not married to one another normally are prohibited from such intimate contact; and (3) the practice by Khalif Uthman to require a second call to prayer (adhan) for the Friday (Jumah) prayer as a reminder to the general public.[164]

4. Istihab (Presumption of Continuity)

This device is more a rule of evidence than a method of process and is well-known in Western law. Briefly stated, it stands for the proposition that a situation or thing known to exist continues to exist until the contrary is proven. Examples are: (1) the presumption that a missing person is still alive until his or her death is confirmed; (2) that a marriage continues unless dissolution is proved; and (3) the fundamental Islamic law principle that a person is innocent until proven guilty.[165]

5. Urf (Local Custom)

Under fiqh methodology, prevailing customs may be given recognition only where they do not contravene Islamic principles.[166] By necessity, of course, deliberate consideration of the purposes and consequences of a custom must be measured against the Qur'an and Sunnah. It is through this concept that many practices gained recognition under fiqh methodology, and subsequently came to be identified as "Islamic," when in fact a fiqh determination could mean only that the custom did not violate the clear text of the Qur'an or Sunnah. For a custom to be recognized it need not have existed at the time of Muhammad (pbuh) or the Sahaba, but it should be prevalent in the particular country for which it is being considered.[167]

The various fiqh madhhabs give custom differing degrees of importance but they all recognize it as a legitimate method for formulating law.[168] The justification for employing urf as fiqh methodology is traced to Muhammad (pbuh), whose silence on the many customs of the Arab people was interpreted to mean he assented to their continued practice.[169] *Custom* has been defined as that which is practiced by the people more often than not, and would not be invoked on the basis of practice by a few individuals or in a very limited geographic area.[170]

D. Ijtihad (Individual Reasoning)

All of the five fiqh methodologies described in the previous section involve the exercise of a degree of individual reasoning. The exercise of said ability in seeking to formulate a legal determination based on the principles of the Shari'ah is called *ijtihad*.[171] The following hadith was cited earlier in Section IIA and is repeated here for convenience. You will recall the exchange between Muhammad and his newly appointed judge to Yemen, Mu'adh Ibn Jabal, regarding the basis upon which he would judge the cases before him:

> *According to what shalt thou judge?* He replied: According to the Book of God. *And if thou findest nought therein?* According to the Sunnah of the Prophet of God. *And if thou findest nought therein?* Then I will exert myself to form my own judgment. *Praise be to God Who has guided the messenger of His Prophet to that which pleases His Prophet.*[172]

The other hadith involving Muhammad's recognition of the exercise of individual reasoning was reported by both Al-Bukhari and Muslim:

> Amr bin al-As reported that he heard Allah's Messenger (may peace be upon him) as saying: *When a judge gives a decision, having tried his best to decide correctly and is right, there are two rewards for him; and if he gave a judgment after having tried his best (to arrive at a correct decision) but erred, there is one reward for him.*[173]

This hadith again highlights the importance of sincerity in conduct and the reward that flows from it, even when in error. In addition to these examples, there are other reports of the Prophet not only supporting the use of reasoning, but also demonstrating its use to his followers.[174]

The legitimacy of using ijtihad as a fiqh methodology has remained at the center of heated dispute and controversy for more than seven hundred years. During the tenth century C.E., the ulema (jurist class) of Muslim society informally adopted the passive attitude that ijtihad and tafsir should no longer be exercised because any principles of Shari'ah that could be deduced or extracted through ijtihad already had been deduced or extracted. In other words, no jurist or student of law would be permitted to render any determinations on the basis of his own ijtihad—every new decision (fatwa) would be based on previously recorded determinations rendered by the predominate fiqh madhhabs. This restrictive concept is called *taqlid* which means *rigid conformity or blind following*.[175]

The rough equivalent of this phenomenon in American law would be the promulgation of a statute that restricted all judges to render decisions solely via *stare decisis*, that is, adherence to decided cases, under a system of government where the legislative body is defunct and therefore incapable of issuing new law in response to current needs.[176] Needless to say, this policy has had a devastating impact on Islamic law and culture.

On the heels of the Tartar invasion and capture of Baghdad in 1258 C.E., the Iraqi ulema declared the door to ijtihad formally *closed*. This closing of the door to individual reasoning, and thus ijma, was never proven to be legitimate, yet the leaders of the major schools of fiqh, except for the Jafari (shias),[177] readily adopted it as policy and since that time has fought to maintain their influence over the scholarship and application of Islamic law by invoking the closed door principle.[178]

The closing of the door was neither arbitrary nor automatic. It took several centuries to implement. Between the ninth and thirteenth centuries the Muslim community struggled with itself as the conservative *door closers* fought rationalists, corrupt political leaders, and disqualified individuals, all of whom sought to effect changes that the scholars considered threatening to Islam. By closing the door to individual reasoning, they surmised, the guiding principles of Islam would remain intact for posterity.[179]

A long line of scholars and intellectuals has fought against the concept of taqlid and appears to have sparked an entire generation of late twentieth century Islamic scholars into conceiving approaches to fiqh methodology that employ ijtihad in the tradition of Muhammad, the Sahaba and the scholars of the Golden Era of Islam. Many modern writers on Islamic law, including Maududi,[180] Alwani,[181] Doi,[182] Ramadan,[183] Philips,[184] and others, advocate the exercise of individual reasoning consistent with Qur'anic and Sunnah principles. None so eloquently as Mohammad Iqbal expressed the sentiment of this movement:

> The closing of the door of Ijtihad is pure fiction suggested partly by the crystallization of legal thought in Islam, and partly by that intellectual laziness which, especially in the period of spiritual decay, turns great thinkers into idols. If some of the later doctors have upheld this fiction, modern Islam is not bound by this voluntary surrender of intellectual independence.[185]

Maududi affirms Iqbal's view and further maintains that Islamic community development depends upon the exercise of ijtihad and that a key attribute of the leaders of Islamic thought must be the ability (through ijtihad) "to comprehend fundamental principles of the religion, judge contemporary culture and its trends from the Islamic viewpoint, and determine changes to be effected in existing patterns of social life under the Shariah."[186]

That attempts to suppress the exercise of individual human reasoning met and continues to meet staunch opposition is, of course, not surprising. A long line of Muslim philosophers and writers challenged the notion that ijtihad could not be used. Among them was al-Ghazzali, regarded as one of the great philosophers of all time, who revitalized the spirit of ijtihad and urged overall reform in thirteenth century Iraq.[187] Others urging similar reform include Ibn Taymiyah and Muhammad Abduh.[188] Yet despite persuasive arguments supporting it use, change has been slow in coming and virtually nonexistent within the traditional schools of fiqh. Among many American Muslims, the exercise of ijtihad is a given because of the general perception that traditional fiqh is not adequate to address the concerns of Islamic life in the United States.[189]

E. Branches of Fiqh

The *branches of fiqh* refers to the various categories and subject areas of Islamic law and include the following:[190]

(1) Rituals and Liturgy: Prayer, Fasting, Charity, Pilgrimage;
(2) Domestic Relations;
(3) Wills, Trusts, Estates, and Inheritance;
(4) Contracts, Trade and Commerce;
(5) Property;
(6) Torts;
(7) Criminal;
(8) Evidence;
(9) Administrative Procedure;
(10) Taxation and Public Finance;
(11) Constitutional;
(12) International Relations;
(13) Relations with Non-Muslims;
(14) War; and
(15) Ethics.

Not even the largest books on fiqh cover the full range of Islamic law with all its permeations because of the expansive scope of the law.[191] Most fiqh books address the following subject areas in the standardized format and order set out below:[192]

(1) Faith;
(2) Hygiene;
(3) Prayer;
(4) Fasting;
(5) Obligatory charity;
(6) Pilgrimage;
(7) Marriage;
(8) Divorce;

(9) Business Transactions; and
(10) Etiquette.

Islam regulates or provides guidance through its law for all areas of human activity, if the law is ascertained. Thus, regulations range from such personal behavior as bathing and grooming to universal concerns such as the treatment of prisoners of war. The idea that all activities are capable of benefiting from the guidance of the Shari'ah is based on two premises:[193]

1. Commandments (or laws) are issued by Allah for man and creation to follow. Knowledge of the commands as something that should be followed is the essence of all ethical and legal knowledge.
2. Allah's commandments are rational and therefore supported by purposes or values, as found in nature or pertaining to man's ethical and spiritual existence, which correspond to the commandments on ontological grounds.

In a comparative study of the substantive areas of law as between the schools of fiqh, including the shia school, there is a remarkable consistency in the fundamental methodologies employed in applying the law, yet the conclusions held by them on many matters are different, albeit only slightly.[194]

Another characteristic of Islamic law, as a canon law, that distinguishes it from American law are the ways in which actions are assessed. Not all acts are legal or illegal; rather there are intermediate values also made of a person's action. The customary five categories of assessment are: (1) *Obligatory*: there is a reward from Allah for performance of such acts but punishment for neglect; (2) *Recommended*: performance of such acts is rewarded, but neglect is not punished; (3) *Permitted*: such acts garner neither reward nor punishment, (4) *Discouraged*: acts for which there is a reward for avoidance, but no punishment for performance; and (5) *Forbidden*: for which there is a reward for avoidance and punishment for performance.[195]

Perhaps one of the earliest and most significant set of guidelines in assessing and applying the Shari'ah, i.e., engaging in fiqh, was prescribed by the second caliph Umar bin al Khattab, who is credited with instituting the consensus opinions of the sahaba as a tertiary source of law after the Qur'an and Sunnah. Upon the appointment of Shurayh as judge, Umar mandated that he use the following set of principles that has served since that time as a beacon of guiding light in fiqh tradition:[196]

(1) Rendering justice to those who seek it is both an Islamic duty and inevitable;
(2) In the court of law all are equal;

(3) The burden of proof falls on the complainant (plaintiff);
(4) Any party's request for reasonable time to produce relevant evidence must be granted;
(5) A judgment proven false by evidence should be vacated;
(6) All adult Muslims are legal persons except for those convicted of perjury or a crime;
(7) No one may be charged for his intentions—only for his actions when supported by evidence;
(8) Where you find the Qur'an and Sunnah silent on any matter, find a comparable case or principle and deduce or extrapolate the law from it; and
(9) That which the Muslims collectively have found good and desirable is so from the standpoint of Allah.

It is upon this tradition that the schools of jurisprudence were established and flowered. The founders of the lines of reasoning for which the schools are named were men of extraordinary intellect and integrity. At no time did any of them promulgate the policy of restricted fiqh methodology imposed upon the Islamic community that eventually resulted in a sort of resolute stagnation for seven hundred years.

V. SCHOOLS OF JURISPRUDENCE
(FIQH MADHHABS)

The Qur'an embodies all of the principles of Islamic law but few injunctions. Muhammad (pbuh) clarified and exemplified the principles and thereby demonstrated general guidelines for implementing law. After Muhammad's death, Muslims confronted many challenging questions and problems as Islam spread into new lands and confronted new cultures that were not addressed directly by the Qur'an and Sunnah. Within a century of the Prophet's death, all the Sahaba also had died. Principles for validating the derivation of law from revelation were needed because there were too many different reports, opinions, and judgments circulating as new problems and questions constantly arose.

This need and situation gave rise to development of comprehensive fiqh methodology and led to the process of extrapolating new legal directives as they were needed. It was neither a controlled nor instant occurrence. Over a period of three hundred years there developed at least nineteen schools of jurisprudential thought,[197] or in Arabic, *madhhabs*, which literally means *ways of going*.[198] The leading formulators of fiqh methodologies advocated by the madhhabs addressed questions relating to the sources of law, statements of fact versus a judgment or command, the particular and the universal. There emerged from this *Golden Era* of Islam a series of distinguished legal and theological scholars. The five surviving major schools of fiqh are named for some of them. The five schools are the Hanafi, Maliki, Shafii, Hanbal, and Jafari Madhhabs. Each of which was organized long after the death of the person for which it is named. It was not until the fourth century that first school of fiqh, the Shafii school, was organized.[199] It was during this period that the scholars of law set out to expose the methodological principles implicit in lawmaking and to justify them against the critique of other schools, which had reached same or different conclusions using different methodological assumptions.[200]

These schools survive not because of official government support. Rather they continue in spite of government because they are rooted in the tradition of the societies in which their philosophy is prevalent.

Very few traditionally Islamic societies have governments that are founded upon or uphold Islamic law. The combination of taqlid, corrupt leadership during and following the Mongol invasions, and the impact of European colonialism effectively ended government sanctioned Islamic legal systems. Under Western imperialism and colonialism, the practice of Islamic law in Muslim countries diminished considerably. The Shari'ah and fiqh were considered by dominating governments as impracticable in the modern age.[201]

By the end of the nineteenth and first quarter of the twentieth centuries, virtually every Muslim country in the world, except Saudi Arabia, had adopted "Anglo-Mohammedan" and "Franco-Mohammedan" legal codes in place of the Shari'ah and fiqh.[202] New court systems accompanied by legal education programs that focused on European principles of individual rights and constitutional government were established.[203] Currently, Saudi Arabia, Sudan, and Iran stand alone as those countries that fully recognize the Shari'ah as the official law of the land. Qatar, the two Yemens, Kuwait and Bahrain also acknowledge Shari'ah principles but to a lesser degree. All other legal systems in the Muslim world are hybrids of Islamic and European law.

For the most part in every other country, Shari'ah courts administering even just personal and family law have been abolished and fiqh principles have been amalgamated with European concepts in unified court systems.[204] The fusion of the two systems has diluted Shari'ah and created confusion and fostered limited knowledge of Islamic law in Muslim lawmakers, jurists and lawyers in affected countries.[205]

But while official government recognition of the Shari'ah is limited or nonexistent in much of the Muslim world, Islamic resurgence and increasing advocacy for the freedom to practice and implement Islamic law probably will result in a renewed interest in those aspects of traditional madhhab methodology that were established and universally accepted during earlier times.[206]

A. The Hanafi Madhhab.[207]

The Hanafi school was established upon the rules of interpretation developed by Abu Hanifa. Followers of the Hanafi School are found principally in Afghanistan, Guyana, India, Iraq, Pakistan, Surianam, Syria, Trinidad, Turkey and, to a more limited extent, Egypt.

Abu Hanifa was born in the city of Kufa (Iraq) and lived from 702 C.E. to 767 C.E. Until the age of forty he studied under Hammad ibn Zayd, a renown scholar of Hadith. After Hammad's death, Imam Hanifa began teaching and became one of the most highly acclaimed scholars of his day. The strongest element of the methodology he taught was the concept of consultation, *shura*. He would present an issue or problem for his students to solve through consultation, discussion and analysis. Once they reached a consensus on an issue, which could take weeks, the decision was recorded.[208] The order of priority for deducing law by Abu Hanifa and subsequently the Hanafi school was as follows:

1. Qur'an: Abu Hanifa recognized it as the preeminent source of law and guidance.
2. Sunnah: with the stipulation that a hadith not only be accurate, but also that it be widely known, if it is to be used as legal proof.
3. Ijma of the sahaba (unanimous opinion of the Sahaba on any point not specified in Qur'an or Sunnah).
4. The appropriate opinion of an individual sahaba where ijma is not apparent. In this regard, Abu Hanifa gave greater regard to a Sahaba's opinion than his own. Of course in the process of selecting the *appropriate* opinion, he had to exercise his own reasoning and opinion.
5. Qiyas (analogical deduction). Next Abu Hanifa would make his own ijtihad based on the principles of qiyas which he and his students developed and established.
6. Istihsaan: Preference of one proof over another proof when it would be more suitable for a situation.
7. Urf: Local customs given legal weight where no Islamic prohibition existed. This is how customs of a multiplicity of cultures attained legal precedence in the legal system and became classified as Islamic.[209]

B. The Maliki Madhhab

This madhhab is named for Malik Ibn Anas Ibn Amir, who lived from 717 to 801. He was born in Medina (Arabia) where his father was a major Sahaba. Imam Maliki studied hadith under the leading hadith scholars of his time. He is well known for his own compilation of hadith and his forty years of service as a teacher of hadith. A key characteristic of Maliki methodology that distinguishes it from the other schools is the great weight it gives to the customary practices of the people of Medina as a source of evidence of how the Shariah should be applied. Adherents of Maliki fiqh methodology are found in Algeria, Bahrein, Chad, (Upper) Egypt, Kuwait, Mali, Morocco, Nigeria, Qatar, and Tunisia. The priority and weight given to the methods of fiqh are as follows:

1. Qur'an.
2. Sunnah. A hadith was rejected, however, if it was contradicted by the customary practice of the Madinans. A hadith did not have to be well-known as required by Imam Hanifa, but no hadith was acceptable if it had been transmitted by a known liar or someone who was a weak memorizer.
3. Amal. The customs and practices of the people of Medina at-large, who were the direct descendants of the Sahaba of Medina was given special recognition by Imam Malik, based on a presumption that these people naturally followed the Sunnah of Muhammad since he lived his last ten years among them.
4. Ijma of the Sahaba.
5. An individual opinion of a Sahaba also was given a higher regard by Imam Malik than his own opinion.
6. Qiyas.
7. Isolated customs and practices of pockets of Medinans also were given some weight on the same rationale as item 3, above.
8. Istislah. The concerns and welfare of the general community.
9. Urf. The local custom of people throughout the Muslim world could be recognized as law so long as it doesn't contradict the Shari'ah.

C. Shafii Madhhab

The Shafii school is based on the methodology developed by Muhammad Idris ash-Shafi (769–820 C.E.), who was born in Gaza. He studied fiqh and hadith in Medina (Arabia) under Malik ibn Anas ibn Amir, for whom the Maliki school is named. Imam Shafii had a remarkable intellect and memory and is credited with being the first to systematize the fundamental principles of fiqh. Shafii authored the classic *Ar-Risalah* (*The Message*), in which he defined the principles of qiyas from the texts, and established the criteria for their application.[210] Shafii fiqh methodology predominates in Egypt, Indonesia, Kenya, Malaysia, Philippines, Sri Lanka, Surinam, Tanzania, and Yemen. The priority of the application of its methodology is:

1. Qur'an.
2. Sunnah based on authentic hadith. Imam Shafii is credited with having greatly refined the science of hadith criticism.

3. Ijma, where clearly confirmed, also was considered the third most important source of law by this madhhab.
4. Individual opinions of the Sahaba, and where there was disagreement or variances among them, Shafii would choose the opinion closest to the issue being considered.
5. Qiyas. Imam Shafii considered qiyas to the farthest legitimate extent of ijtihad, i.e., no decision could be made on any basis beyond an analogy. He rejected the methods of Istihsaan and Istislah used by Hanifa and Malik as improper innovations (*bida*). As a result, qiyas constitutes the common denominator in fiqh methodology between the four sunni schools.

D. Hanbali Madhhab

The Hanbali school is based on Ahmad Ibn Hanbal's methodology (778–855 C.E). It is the system of methodology upon which Saudi Arabian law is based.[211] Imam Hanbal studied is renown as one of the greatest memorizers and narrators of hadith of his time. He is credited with collecting and preserving over 30,000 hadiths, as found in his collective *al-Musnad*. Hanbal directly under Imam Shafii as well as Imam Abu Yusef, is one of Hanifa's leading students. Hanbal staunchly opposed the concept of taqlid (blind imitation), which had begun to take root and, therefore, forbade his own students from even recording his determinations. Imam Hanbal was brutally persecuted by the khalifs of his country, Iraq, for disagreeing with their Mutazilite philosophy of Islam[212] and was forced into hiding for many years until the leadership changed. The priority of fiqh methodology developed by him is:

1. Qur'an.
2. Sunnah of Prophet Muhammad.
3. Ijma of the Sahaba but no ijma beyond their era because he considered it impossible to reach a consensus among the widely diffused scholars of the Muslim world following the period of the Sahaba.
4. Individual opinions of all of the Sahaba were given consideration, thereby resulting in inconsistent ruling by Hanbali jurists when Sahaba opinions differed.
5. Weak hadiths were preferred over qiyas, but only if its weakness was not attributable to transmission by degenerates or liars.
6. Qiyas was reluctantly employed as a last resort by Imam Hanbal.

All four sunni schools agreed on the primacy of four fundamental fiqh methodologies, namely, the Qur'an, Sunnah, ijma, and qiyas. Differences arose in applying the law because of the rules of process peculiar to each school. These differences may be attributed to three things: (1) the rules of interpretation of word meanings and grammatical construction; (2) the availability, authenticity, conditions of acceptance, and interpretation of hadith, and the treatment of conflicting hadiths; (3) methods of using and even the very decision to use certain principles of reasoning and the emphasis placed on each, including ijma, qiyas, the customs of Madina people, use of individual and collective opinions of the sahaba, istihsaan, istislah and urf.

E. Jafari Madhhab

The Jafari Madhhab is the recognized shia school of jurisprudence.[213] The shia are found principally in Iran, Iraq, and Lebanon.[214] In 1963, Mahmud Shaltut, the rector of Al-Azhar University in Egypt, ruled that the shia were authentically Muslim, but of a different madhhab (school of fiqh) rather than a "sect." His ruling included a directive that Al-Azhar would teach one kind of shia law, that of the Jafari Madhhab (also called Twelver or Imami), alongside the four sunni schools.[215]

The school is named for Abu Jafar Muhammad Al-Baqir and Jafar Sadiq, the fifth and sixth shia imams.[216] Under Jafari fiqh, the following represents the priority given to the methodology of application:

1. Qur'an.
2. Sunnah of Muhammad. The range of acceptable hadith, called akhbar by the shia, is restricted to those traditions that were related or narrated by a shia imam descended from Prophet Muhammad's bloodline.[217]
3. Ijtihad of the Imam (Majamina la'imma) or that which comes from the imams is the third method of ascertaining and applying law by the shia.[218]

Despite the shia doctrine of imamate and its emphasis on lineage as a prerequisite to human worthiness to lead the ummah, the fundamental principles of fiqh and fiqh methodology between the Jafari and sunni schools are comparable.[219] In actual application of the law, however, the same types and qualities of differences that result among the sunni schools are apparent as between the shia and sunni schools.[220]

NOTES

This chapter is an excerpt from an article published in the *Journal of Islamic Law and Culture*. Reprinted with the journal permission. It was originally cited as *7 J. Islamic L. & Culture 27* (2002).

1. FAREED H. NU'MAN, THE MUSLIM POPULATION IN THE

UNITED STATES 11 (1992); *see also* Carole Stone, *Estimate of Muslims Living in America, in* THE MUSLIMS OF AMERICA 25–36 (Yvonne Y. Haddad ed., 1991); John R. Weeks and Saad Gadalla, *The Demography of Islamic Nations*, POPULA-TION BULLETIN, Dec. 1988, at 52; and Yvonne Y. Haddad, *A Century of Islam in America*, THE MUSLIM WORLD TODAY, 1986 at 1 [hereinafter Haddad, *A Century of Islam in America*], predicting 2015 as the date at which Islam will become America's second largest religion. It is not uncommon to encounter publications and articles citing other data that already places Islam as America's second largest religion or that predicts a sooner date than 2015. *See, e.g.*, IRA G. ZEPP, JR., A MUSLIM PRIMER xxi (1992) [hereinafter ZEPP], citing the year 2000 as the year during which Islam will surpass Judaism and become America's second largest religion.

    2. Normal Calder, *Legal Thought and Jurisprudence, in* 2 THE OXFORD ENCYCLOPEDIA OF THE MODERN ISLAMIC WORLD 450, 456 (John L. Esposito ed., 1995) [hereinafter Calder].

    3. John O. Voll, *Islamic Issues for Muslims in the United States, in* THE MUS-LIMS IN AMERICA 205, 213–214 (Yvonne Y. Haddad ed., 1991).

    4. ISMAIL R. al-FARUQI & LOIS L. al-FARUQI, THE CULTURAL ATLAS OF ISLAM 279 (1986) [hereinafter al-FARUQI].

    5. FRANCIS ROBINSON, ATLAS OF THE ISLAMIC WORLD SINCE 1500, 30 (1982) [hereinafter ROBINSON].

    6. Haddad, *A Century of Islam in America, supra* note 1, at 1.

    7. *See generally* EDWARD W. SAID, COVERING ISLAM—HOW THE MEDIA AND THE EXPERTS DETERMINE HOW WE SEE THE REST OF THE WORLD (1981) (highlights the deleterious impact of negative media coverage on Islam, Muslims and Arabs, which he attributes, in part, to the loss of well-rounded Western scholars of Islamic civilization such as Joseph Schacht, Philip Hitti, and H. A. R. Gibb, among others).

    8. Two notable examples are the AMERICAN MUSLIM COUNCIL and COUNCIL ON AMERICAN-ISLAMIC RELATIONS, both based in Washing-ton, D.C.

    9. W. D. MUHAMMAD, IMAM W. DEEN MUHAMMAD SPEAKS FROM HARLEM, N.Y. 33 (1985).

    10. al-FARUQI, *supra* note 4, at 265.

    11. Calder, *supra* note 2, at 450.

    12. *See, e.g.*, YVONNE Y. HADDAD & ADAIR T. LUMMIS, ISLAMIC VAL-UES IN THE UNITED STATES 18–20, 98 (1987) [hereinafter HADDAD & LUM-MIS]; AL-HAJ M. AHMED, THE URGENCY OF IJTIHAD 20–21 (1992) [hereinafter AHMED]; ABDUR RAHMAN I. DOI, SHARI'AH: THE ISLAMIC LAW 6 (1984) [hereinafter DOI]; and MOHAMMAD H. KHAN, THE SCHOOLS OF ISLAMIC JURISPRUDENCE 5 (1991) [hereinafter KHAN]. *See also*, JOHN L. ESPOSITO, ISLAM—THE STRAIGHT PATH 79, 147, 203 (1991), wherein he attributes this phenomenon, at least in part, to the great deference some Muslims give to fiqh as compared to those calling for reform.

    13. SAID RAMADAN, ISLAMIC LAW, ITS SCOPE AND EQUITY 62 (1970) [hereinafter RAMADAN].

    14. The word *Qur'an* corresponds to the Westernized spelling for the same word as Koran. Throughout this article the former spelling will be used.

15. RAMADAN, *supra* note 13, at 43. Ramadan effectively refutes research conclusions on Muhammad's Sunnah reached by a series of non-Muslim orientalists including H. A. R. Gibb, John Schacht, Majid Khadduri and Alfred Guillaume. He argues that these scholars confused *Sunnah* as a legal, Islamic term with its literal Arabic meaning which relates to the customs of pre-Islamic Arabia. The result, concludes Ramadan, has been the undermining of the authenticity of the traditions of Muhammad by orientalists on the basis of their misconception of how Muhammad's Sunnah was established.

16. DOI, *supra* note 12, at 49.

17. RAMADAN, *supra* note 13, at 52.

18. ABDUR RAHIM, THE PRINCIPLES OF ISLAMIC JURISPRUDENCE 389 (Kitab Bhavan 1994) (1911) [hereinafter ABDUR RAHIM].

19. DOI, *supra* note 12, at 2.

20. VII E. J. BRILL'S FIRST ENCYCLOPEDIA OF ISLAM 1913–1936, 320 (M.Th. Houtsma et al. eds., 1987) [hereinafter BRILL].

21. ROBINSON, *supra* note 5, at 29; VII BRILL, *supra* note 20, at 320.

22. VII BRILL, *supra* note 20, at 320.

23. Holy Qur'an, Surah 45, Ayat 18 (A. YUSEF ALI, THE HOLY QUR'AN, TEXT, TRANSLATION AND COMMENTARY 1359) (Amana Corp. 1983) (1934). [hereinafter Holy Qur'an]. *Surah* is the technical Qur'anic term for *chapter*, while ayat is the term for *verse*. Each surah of the Qur'an is composed of a varying number of ayats. In future citations the number of the surah will precede the number of the ayat, with the two being separated by a colon.

24. VII BRILL, *supra* note 20, at 320. *See also* THE HANS WEHR DICTIONARY OF MODERN WRITTEN ARABIC 465 (J. Milton Cowan ed., 1976) [hereinafter HANS WEHR]; HARITH SULEIMAN FARUQI, FARUQI'S LAW DICTIONARY 149 (1972); and IBRAHIM I. AL-WAHAB, LAW DICTIONARY ENGLISH-ARABIC 131 (1972).

25. RAMADAN, *supra* note 13, at 42. *See also* al-FARUQI, *supra* note 4, at 240; Calder, *supra* note 2, at 451; DOI, *supra* note 12, at 21; and ROBINSON, *supra* note 5, at 29.

26. HOLY QUR'AN, *supra* note 23, at 4:80.

27. *Id.* at 33:21.

28. *Id.* at 33:36.

29. RAMADAN, *supra* note 13, at 75, citing original Arabic sources. *See also* DOI, supra note 12, at 71; TAHA JABIR al ALWANI, SOURCE METHODOLOGY IN ISLAMIC JURISPRUDENCE 12 (Yusuf T. DeLorenzo & Anas S. Al Shaikh-Ali trans., 1994) [hereinafter ALWANI]; A. D. AJIJOLA, INTRODUCTION TO ISLAMIC LAW 92 (2d ed. 1983) [hereinafter AJIJOLA]; ABDUR RAHIM, *supra* note 18, at 135; and MUHAMMAD HAMIDULLAH, INTRODUCTION TO ISLAM 106–107 (1959) [hereinafter HAMIDULLAH], all citing the same hadith.

30. RAMADAN, *supra* note 13, at 75.

31. A. BILAL PHILIPS, THE EVOLUTION OF FIQH 100 (3d ed. 1992) (1988) [hereinafter PHILIPS].

32. RAMADAN, *supra* note 13, at 75.

33. II BRILL, *supra* note 20, at 101; RAMADAN, *supra* note 13, at 62.

34. PHILIPS, *supra* note 31, at 2.

35. *Id.*

36. KHAN, *supra* note 12, at 5.

37. RAMADAN, *supra* note 13, at 84–85.

38. MUHAMMAD IQBAL, RECONSTRUCTION OF RELIGIOUS THOUGHT IN ISLAM 137 (2d ed. 1989) (1929) [hereinafter IQBAL]. But see PHILIPS, *supra* note 31, at 39, where he discusses the right of the early caliphs of Islam to overrule a decision by consensus.

39. *See* II BRILLS, *supra* note 20, at 887 (for Professor John Schacht's description of fiqh); PHILIPS, *supra* note 31, at 60 and 91 (description of the four basic sources of Islamic law); and IQBAL, *supra* note 38, at 131.

40. RAMADAN, *supra* note 13, at 84.

41. *Id.*

42. PHILIPS, *supra* note 31, at 1.

43. RAMADAN, *supra* note 13, at 84.

44. But *see* RAMADAN, *supra* note 13, at 61–63, where he argues that though juristic thought by Muslims is meant to be Islamic, it must be measured against the Qur'an and Sunnah before being deemed Islamic. Therefore, he argues, the process of juristic reasoning and application should not be called Islamic law before being qualified as such by the Muslim community, at-large.

45. PHILIPS, *supra* note 31, at 107. C.E. means *Christian Era* and corresponds with A.D. typically used by non-Muslims. A.H. means *After the Hijra* (Muhammad's flight from Mecca to Medina) in 622 C.E., which marks year one in the Islamic calendar.

46. IQBAL, *supra* note 38, at 131.

47. PHILIPS, *supra* note 31, at 91–100.

48. al-FARUQI, *supra* note 4, at 265. Here the authors eloquently explain how the values of the Shari'ah became everyday facts of knowledge for the common people, who, whether literate or illiterate, understood and pursued the ideal values of the religious law.

49. Those being: (1) the natural law school, (2) analytical school, (3) historical school, (4) comparative school, and (5) sociological school.

50. PHILIPS, *supra* note 31, at 107–108.

51. *Id.*

52. *Id.*

53. *Id.*

54. *Id.* at 142; IQBAL, *supra* note 38, at 131; RAMADAN, *supra* note 13, at 61–63; S. A. MAUDUDI, A SHORT HISTORY OF THE REVIVALIST MOVEMENT IN ISLAM 97 (3d ed., 1976) (1963) [hereinafter MAUDUDI].

55. WARITHUDDIN MUHAMMAD, PRAYER AND AL-ISLAM 2 (1982) [hereinafter W. D. MUHAMMAD]; ZEPP, *supra* note 1, at xxxix.

56. Holy Qur'an, *supra* note 23, at 112:1–4.

57. W. D. MUHAMMAD, *supra* note 55, at 2.

58. Whenever Muhammad or another prophet is mentioned verbally or in writing, it is traditional for Muslims to invoke Allah's peace and blessing. Thus, in many

writings and speeches Muhammad's name often will be followed by the parenthetical (*PBUH*) or its Arabic equivalent, meaning "May the peace and blessing of Allah be upon him." Throughout the balance of this article it will appear from time to time. A common alternative parenthetical apparent in the writings of others will contain the transliterated Arabic abbreviation of the same words—(*SAAW*).

59. *Id.* at 6–15. *See, generally*, ABDUL HAMEED SIDDIQUI, THE LIFE OF MUHAMMAD (PBUH) (1975), for a comprehensive account of Muhammad's life.

60. MICHAEL H. HART, THE 100: A RANKING OF THE MOST INFLU-ENTIAL PERSONS IN HISTORY 3 (1992).

61. W. D. MUHAMMAD, *supra* note 55, at 16; *Islam at a Glance* (The Muslim Students' Association of the U.S. & Canada, 1996); ZEPP, *supra* note 1, at 1–3; and HANS WEHR *supra* note 22, at 424.

62. HANS WEHR, *supra* note 24, at 424.

63. W. D. MUHAMMAD, *supra* note 55, at 16.

64. *Id.* at 37.

65. *Id.* at 23. *See also* Holy Qur'an, *supra* note 23, at 2:131–132, wherein it is revealed that Abraham submitted to Islam and left his example as a legacy to his sons.

66. W. D. MUHAMMAD, *supra* note 55, at 15.

67. Holy Qur'an, *supra* note 23, at 5:3.

68. Thomas J. Abercrombie, *The Sweep of Islam, in* GREAT RELIGIONS OF THE WORLD 238, 255 (NATIONAL GEOGRAPHIC SOCIETY, ed. 1971).

69. *Id.*

70. ZEPP, *supra* note 1, at 153–155.

71. *Id. See, infra* note 215, for an explanation of Shiism.

72. *Id.* at 158.

73. *Id.*

74. I BRILLS, *supra* note 20, at 301.

75. *Id.*

76. *Id.*

77. *Id. See also,e.g.*, Maulana Muhammad Ali's *The Religion of Islam* (1951) and his *Translation of the Holy Quran* (1928).

78. C. ERIC LINCOLN, RACE RELIGION AND THE CONTINUING AMERICAN DILEMMA 159 (1984) [hereinafter LINCOLN].

79. This work now is out of print. It was self-published and has no copyright date. More of a pamphlet than a book, it was 62 pages long and comprised of 47 chapters.

80. LINCOLN, *supra* note 66, at 160. *See also, generally*, C. ERIC LINCOLN, THE BLACK MUSLIMS IN AMERICA (1961); ADIB RASHAD, THE HIS-TORY OF ISLAM AND BLACK NATIONALISM IN THE AMERICAS (1991); and MUSTAFA EL-AMIN, THE RELIGION OF ISLAM AND THE NATION OF ISLAM: WHAT IS THE DIFFERENCE? (1991).

81. *See, generally*, ELIJAH MUHAMMAD, MESSAGE TO THE BLACK-MAN IN AMERICA (1965), beginning with the preface. When Elijah Muhammad died in 1975, the Nation of Islam changed its orientation by entering into mainstream Islam under the leadership of Elijah's son, W. D. Muhammad. Several years later, Louis Farrakhan broke with the younger Muhammad and reconstituted, for the most

part, the old Nation of Islam. It continues to represent Elijah Muhammad as the *Messenger of Allah* and Wallace Fard (aka *Master W. Fard Muhammad*) as *Allah*. See, THE FINAL CALL newspaper of the Nation of Islam (FCN Publishing, Chicago & Washington) for a listing of Nation of Islam beliefs. *See also* Steven Barboza, *A Divided Legacy*, EMERGE, April 1992, at 26, in which he summarizes the history of the Nation of Islam. In the latter piece, Barboza mistakenly characterizes W. D. Muhammad's embrace and teaching of mainstream Islam as a fervent preaching of *love for whites*. In fact, the literature reveals that W. D. Muhammad has been teaching mainstream Islam in the purest sense, which condemns all racism, but which also celebrates the value of all races of humankind. Researchers on Islam in America should contrast this article with Barboza's, *My Islam*, AMERICAN VISIONS, December 1988, at 26, that does not acknowledge at all the Nation of Islam's transition following Elijah Muhammad's death.

82. ABU AMEENAH BILAL PHILIPS, THE ANSAR CULT IN AMERICA 17 (1988).

83. *Id.* at 9.

84. *Id.* at 17–18.

85. HAMIDULLAH, *supra* note 29, at 16.

86. DOI, *supra* note 12, at 21.

87. *Id.* at 23.

88. HAMIDULLAH, *supra* note 29, at 16. But see, ROBINSON, supra note 5, at 28, who maintains that it cannot be confirmed whether the entire Qur'an was written down during the life of Muhammad.

89. AJIJOLA, *supra* note 29, at 57–58.

90. *Id.*; HAMIDULLAH, *supra* note 29, at 16.

91. ROBINSON, *supra* note 5, at 28.

92. A. YUSEF ALI's, HOLY QUR'AN, TEXT, TRANSLATION AND COMMENTARY, *supra* note 23, is noted for its eloquent use of English. *See for example*, A. R. Kidwai, *Translating the Untranslatable—A Survey of English Translations of the Qur'an*, THE MUSLIM WORLD BOOK REVIEW, Summer 1987, in which he recommends A. Yusef Ali's translation despite the fact that he was a mere civil servant and not a scholar, and whose commentary Kidwai sometimes disagreed with. In addition to A. Yusef Ali, Kidwai also highly recommends the English translations of Muhammad Marmaduke William Pickthall, Muhammad Asad and T. B. Irving, though he expresses dissatisfaction with all current English translations of Qur'an.

93. ROBINSON, *supra* note 5, at 28.

94. DOI, *supra* note 12, at 21.

95. MICHAEL H. HART, THE 100: A RANKING OF THE MOST INFLUENTIAL PERSONS IN HISTORY 3 (1992).

96. ROBINSON, *supra* note 5, at 28.

97. AJIJOLA, *supra* note 29, at 57–58.

98. *Id.*

99. DOI, *supra* note 12, at 36.

100. *Id.* at 40–42. Professor Doi provides an excellent and comprehensive listing of each subject area of law and cites the exact surah and ayat in the Qur'an for each type of injunction.

101. *Id.*

102. W. D. MUHAMMAD, *supra* note 55, at 13.

103. *Id.*

104. al-FARUQI, *supra* note 4, 252.

105. W. D. MUHAMMAD, *supra* note 55, at 13.

106. MUHAMMAD ABDUL RAUF, AL-HADITH 11 (1974) [hereinafter AL-HADITH].

107. *Id.*

108. *Id.*

109. al-FARUQI, *supra* note 4, 252.

110. AL-HADITH, *supra* note 106, at 11.

111. *Id.* at 19.

112. *Id.* at 20.

113. *But see*, al-FARUQI, *supra* note 4, at 261, how some scholars recognize the Hadith of Imams Malik and Ibn Hanbal as two additional collections, while discounting Ibn Majah's, thereby bringing the total number of "books" to seven.

114. AL-HADITH, *supra* note 106, at 23.

115. *Id.* at 20–23.

116. IMAM MUSLIM, SAHIH MUSLIM (Abdul Hamid Siddiqui trans., 1976) [hereinafter SAHIH MUSLIM]; IMAM AL-BUKHARI, SAHIH AL-BUKHARI (Muhammad Muhsin Khan trans., undated) [hereinafter AL-BUKHARI].

117. AL-HADITH, *supra* note 106, at 20.

118. *Id.* at 17.

119. See RAFI A. FIDAI & N. M. SHAIKH, THE COMPANIONS OF THE HOLY PROPHET (1988), for biographical accounts of fifty-three close companions of Muhammad.

120. AL-HADITH, *supra* note 106, at 15.

121. *Id.* at 16.

122. *Id.* at 25.

123. I SAHIH MUSLIM, *supra* note 116, at 39. Muslim supports the authenticity of this hadith by citing the names of several other narrators who attribute this transmission to Tamim ad-Dari, a well known Sahaba (companion of Muhammad), who was a monk prior to his conversion to Islam in year 9 of the Islamic calendar (631 C.E.).

124. *Id.* Jarir embraced Islam forty days before the death of Muhammad and has had a large number of hadith transmissions attributed to him. Muslim couples the hadiths transmitted by ad-Dari and Jarir and others on the same theme to support the principle that religion is sincerity.

125. I AL-BUKHARI, *supra* note 116, at 48–49.

126. HOLY QUR'AN, *supra* note 23, at 9:91.

127. AL-HADITH, *supra* note 106, at 21.

128. RAMADAN, *supra* note 13, at 84. *See also* II BRILL, *supra* note 20, at 887, providing numerous examples of this word being used in both ways.

129. al-FARUQI, *supra* note 4, at 267.

130. KHAN, *supra* note 12, at 5.

131. al-FARUQI, *supra* note 4, at 267.

132. PHILIPS, *supra* note 31, at 91.

133. *See* references at note 27.

134. VII BRILL, *supra* note 20, at 603.

135. al-FARUQI, *supra* note 4, at 244, stating: "Exegesis of the Qur'an by the Qur'an, wherever it is possible, must take precedence over tradition. This is the first criterion." *See also,* KHAN, *supra* note 12, at 19; AJIJOLA, *supra* note 29, at 57; and, DOI, *supra* note 12, at 23.

136. VII BRILL, *supra* note 20, at 603.

137. *See* al-FARUQI, *supra* note 4, at 244, for the names and renowned works of highly regarded exegetes.

138. *Id.* at 244–246. Qur'anic Arabic is not the idiom of discourse in modern Arabic speaking societies, just as Elizabethan English is not the standard of communication in English-speaking societies. Obviously, a bona fide exegete of Qur'an would have to be familiar with the Arabic language, vocabulary, idioms, etc., existent during the time of Muhammad. Additionally, a thorough knowledge of the historical context in which the Muslim community was established also would be essential. Finally, al-Faruqi also would expect that the sincere exegete's only loyalty be to truth rather than dogmatic allegiance to a particular school of fiqh or other philosophy. *See also,* DOI, *supra* note 12, at 34–36.

139. PHILIPS, *supra* note 31, at 91.

140. *Id.; See* ABDUR RAHIM, *supra* note 18, at 73–110, for a comprehensive exposition of the rules for interpreting Qur'an, including those addressing the treatment of homonyms, apparent conflicting texts or prepositions, construction, dependent clauses, and a host of other complex linguistic occurrences. *See also,* KHAN, *supra* note 12, at 19, wherein he delineates four basic principles of interpretation of the Qur'an. These same four principles are prescribed by Maulana Muhammad Ali in virtually identical format and language in his THE RELIGION OF ISLAM at 46 (1950).

141. Like individual reasoning (ijtihad) discussed in Section IV D, supra, the practice of tafsir (which also involves the exercise of individual reasoning) was limited and eventually barred by the four sunni Islam schools of fiqh after the thirteenth century. Of course this restriction placed on jurists identified with those schools has not prevented scholars who disagree with them from exercising the freedom to engage in the discipline of tafsir. *See,* DOI, *supra* note 12, at 68.

142. ABDUR RAHIM, *supra* note 18, at 67.

143. *Id.* at 73.

144. The general assumption is that Muhammad's hadiths were not recorded during his lifetime. In fact many hadiths were recorded in his presence. *See,* RAMADAN, *supra* note 13, at 48–50, citing numerous examples of hadiths that were recorded contemporaneously.

145. al-FARUQI, *supra* note 4, at 260.

146. *Id.*

147. PHILIPS, *supra* note 31, at 95–97.

148. DOI, *supra* note 12, at 64.

149. *Id.* at 66.

150. *Id.*

151. HOLY QUR'AN, *supra* note 23, at 4:59.
152. ABDUR RAHIM, *supra* note 18, at 113.
153. *Id.* at 114.
154. *Id. See also* KHAN, *supra* note 12, at 40.
155. IQBAL, *supra* note 38, at 137.
156. *Id. But see*, KHAN, *supra* note 12, at 35, listing a dozen ways in which ijma was used in early Islam to settle issues relating to the collection, organization, classification, division and pronunciation of the Qur'an. In recent years, the Muslim Ummah (community) has come together to consult on issues of mutual interest and importance.
157. ABDUR RAHIM, *supra* note 18, at 132–157. *See also*, DOI, *supra* note 12, at 70–81.
158. ABDUR RAHIM, *supra* note 18, at 135.
159. DOI, *supra* note 12, at 70. Abu Hanifa desired on the one hand to sanction a method of reasoning that would provide for flexibility and growth in Islamic jurisprudential activities, but that would also curb digressive thinking from an Islamic point of reference or framework. Qiyas apparently was adequate, to the view of Muslim jurists, to meet both needs.
160. DOI, *supra* note 12, at 81.
161. AHMED, *supra* note 12, at 38.
162. DOI, *supra* note 12, at 81.
163. AHMED, *supra* note 12, at 38. You will recall that during the time these concepts were being formulated there were as many as nineteen schools of fiqh. The Shafii school is the only major sunni one that rejects this form of ijtihad. The Hanafi jurist, Abu Bakr al Razi al Jassas is credited with refuting Shafii's arguments against istihsan. Absent its availability and use, al-Faruqi concludes that Islamic law stood "condemned to fossilization." al-FARUQI, *supra* note 4, at 277.
164. DOI, *supra* note 12, at 81.
165. *Id.* at 83.
166. *Id.* at 84; and AHMED, *supra* note 12, at 39.
167. ABDUR RAHIM, *supra* note 18, at 131–132.
168. *Id.*
169. *Id.*
170. *Id.*
171. *See, generally*, DOI, *supra* note 12, at 78–80.
172. *See* note 31 and accompanying text.
173. III SAHIH MUSLIM, *supra* note 116, at 930; *See also* PHILIPS, *supra* note 31, at 136.
174. ABDUR RAHIM, *supra* note 18, at 136, and DOI, *supra* note 11, at 70. Both authors discuss several examples of how Muhammad and, subsequently, the sahaba employed qiyas for the advancement of the Islamic community. Perhaps the most notable example has been the extension of the prohibition of using intoxicants, which meant wine during the Prophet's time, to include a wide variety of other alcoholic and nonalcoholic intoxicants. As a matter of Islamic law, this application of qiyas has been universally accepted. Without the device of qiyas, this would have been difficult to achieve.

175. *Id.*, at 69.

176. In point of fact, Western jurists are required to apply the principles ascertained in previous decisions but not when they are discovered to be wrong, such as the *separate but equal doctrine* of *Plessy v. Ferguson* that was rejected in *Brown v. Board of Education of Topeka*, or when the facts are sufficiently different that application of the previously articulated principle would be inadequate, unjust, or unfair.

177. The shias (shiites) believe that ijtihad is available but that it only may be used by their imams, who are presumed to be infallible. *See*, DOI, *supra* note 12, at 80.

178. DOI, *supra* note 12, at 69.

179. PHILIPS, *supra* note 31, at 128.

180. *See, generally*, S. A. MAUDUDI, A SHORT HISTORY OF THE REVIVALIST MOVEMENT IN ISLAM (1963) [hereinafter MAUDUDI] and THE ISLAMIC LAW AND CONSTITUTION (1955), addressing the qualifications of individuals engaged in ijtihad as well as techniques for employing and applying ijtihad in modern government, e.g., legislative assembly.

181. ALWANI, *supra* note 29, at 12–15.

182. DOI, *supra* note 12, at 69.

183. RAMADAN, *supra* note 13, at 83.

184. PHILIPS, *supra* note 31, at 142. In fact, Philips proves that taqlid, which he defines as *blind rigid imitation*, is against everything taught by the early scholars of Islamic law and that it must be avoided. This author, among others, attributes the advent of sectarian-type division of the Muslim community to taqlid and its required allegiance to one particular school of thought. During the period following the fall of Baghdad, the four sunni schools of fiqh came to be considered divinely ordained manifestations of Islam and there are reported cases of the prohibition of marriage between persons identified with different schools, the prohibition of mixed prayer by persons from different schools (even at the Kaba in Mecca), and the sanction of punishment for persons attempting to transfer allegiance to another school. Anyone refusing to declare affiliation with a particular school was declared non-Muslim and subject to punishment. Such is the nature and legacy of taqlid. That taqlid still is endorsed is remarkable. *Id.* at 106–109.

185. IQBAL, *supra* note 38, at 141.

186. MAUDUDI, *supra* note 180, at 38–39. Later, at 52, Maudedi emphasizes the fact that the four famous schools of fiqh founded by highly acclaimed imams used ijtihad as a basic principle, and that no Muslim leader of the future can afford to discard the principles they developed, as they were *men of deep insight and extraordinary intellectual powers*, who evolved profound principles of universal application.

187. Many of Islam's most gifted intellects turned to what is loosely called by Western observers as *Islamic mysticism*, sufism, as a method for exercising and achieving the freedom of thought suppressed in the institutions of learning because of taqlid. Abu Hamid al-Ghazzali was one of many such young men. In its distorted extreme, sufism garnered what Iqbal called an obscure "other-worldliness" mentality as sufis struggled for total egolessness and become one with God. Tenth century sufi, Al-Hallaj, was executed for his proclamation that he was the "ultimate reality" as a result of his mystical experiences. Abu Yazid, a ninth century sufi, proclaimed after his mystical experience "Praise be to me." Of course these extreme examples in no

way depict the balanced outlook of the typical sufi who balances the mystical and the mundane as he seeks an expanded consciousness of sufi reality. The word *sufi* comes from *suf*, the coarse woolen cloth worn by early sufis to keep them warm during their solitary desert vigils. See, IQBAL, *supra* note 38, at 119–120 and ZEPP, *supra* note 1, at 159.

188. *Id., generally,* Throughout this work, Maududi summarizes the backgrounds, accomplishments and arguments for change and revitalization of a stream of Islamic scholars, imams, and leaders, all of whom he believes are worthy of being recognized as mujaddids, or renewers ("revivalists") of Islam, and who exercised ijtihad in their efforts to bring about change. *But also see*, PHILIPS, *supra* note 31, at 114, in which he discusses Abduh's tafsir of the Qur'an and the extremist views espoused by Abduh.

189. n189 W. D. MUHAMMAD, IMAM W. DEEN MUHAMMAD SPEAKS FROM HARLEM, N.Y. 33 (1985), in which Imam Muhammad opines the need for an American fiqh, which by definition implies the exercise of ijtihad. *Also see*, the statement of the Fiqh Council of North America in *Muslim Legal Directory & Guide to Your Legal Rights 1995–96*, AMERICAN MUSLIM FOUNDATION LEGAL FUND of WASHINGTON, DC, at 60–62, wherein Yusef Talal DeLorenzo explains that the Council uses methods of employing fiqh that departs from traditional usage. Also note that the Council is presided by Taha J. al Alwani a proponent of modern day ijtihad; and PHILIPS, *supra* note 31, at 141–143, calling for a dynamic new approach to fiqh that would include the exercise of ijtihad. It is important to emphasize that all the referenced authors express the importance of exercising ijtihad within prescribed limits consistent with and subordinate to Qur'an, Sunnah, and ijma.

190. *See, generally,* LALAH BAKHTIAR, ENCYCLOPEDIA OF ISLAMIC LAW: A COMPENDIUM OF THE MAJOR SCHOOLS (1995), as a convenient and well-organized source for examining commonalities and differences between the Hanafi, Hanbali, Shafii, Maliki, and Jafari schools on most points of what might be described in Western discourse as civil law, i.e., this work does not address issues of crime, war, or government [hereafter BAKHTIAR]. Also see, al-FARUQI, *supra* note 4, at 274 for a succinct listing of the "departments" of law. Other authorities cited throughout this article, including DOI, ABDUR RAHIM, and AJIJOLA, discuss and compare the positions of the various sunni schools on most of the branches of fiqh listed above including criminal law, international relations, and war. The following two other works provide a comprehensive treatment of crime and punishment in Islamic law: MOHAMED S. EL-ALWA, PUNISHMENT IN ISLAMIC LAW (1982), and YUSUF al-QARADAWI, THE LAWFUL AND THE PROHIBITED IN ISLAM (1984).

191. A. Kevin Reinhart, *Introduction* to BAKHTIAR, *supra* note 190, at xxxiii.

192. PHILIPS, *supra* note 31, at 104.

193. al-FARUQI, *supra* note 4, at 279.

194. BAKHTIAR, *supra* note 190, at xxix.

195. A. Kevin Reinhart, *Introduction* to BAKHTIAR, *supra* note 190, at xxxvii.

196. al-FARUQI, *supra* note 4 at 275. al Faruqi provides an eloquent, lucid and sublime treatment of Islamic law and jurisprudence from a philosophical, abstract, and even mystical perspective. The principles for applying law, their origins, and the

meaning and purpose of law as it relates to man's relationship with Allah (God) are stunning and thorough. Mrs. al-Faruqi's photographs contribute a dimension of Islamic cultural achievement and diversity rarely encountered in other works on the religion. DOI, *supra* note 12, at 14, provide the full text of the letter from which these nine guiding principles are extracted. However, Doi, attributes them to a letter written by Umar but addressed to Abu Musa Ashari rather than Shurayh. Umar, in fact, appointed them both as judges and in all likelihood counseled them to use the same principles in rendering justice.

197. al-FARUQI, *supra* note 4, at 274–275.

198. RAMADAN, *supra* note 13, at 88.

199. RAMADAN, *supra* note 13, at 91–92. By this fact, Ramadan asserts that the so-called founders never intended to establish schools; instead it was their purpose to exert all their means of knowledge as a contribution to healthy relation between Muslims and the Shari'ah.

200. al-FARUQI, *supra* note 4, at 276.

201. DOI, *supra* note 12, at 450.

202. *Id.*

203. *Id.* at 452.

204. AJIJOLA, *supra* note 29, at 361, explaining that those Shari'ah courts still functioning in the Middle East are restricted to reviewing family law issues.

205. DOI *supra* note 12, at 255.

206. *See, e.g.*, THE SHARIA: A GLOBAL MUSLIM DEMAND, INQUIRY MAGAZINE OF EVENTS AND IDEAS (Jan. 1987), wherein numerous Muslim writers proffer methods for reasserting the exercise of ijtihad and reestablishment of Shariah law in Muslim countries.

207. The listing of fiqh methodologies for the four sunni schools presented in this section are commonly acknowledged and are repeated in the works of the following authorities: PHILIPS, *supra* note 31, at 63–90; DOI, *supra* note 12; KHAN, *supra* note 12; and AJIJOLA, *supra* note 27.

208. PHILIPS, *supra* note 31, at 64.

209. *Id.* at 67.

210. al-FARUQI, *supra* note 4, at 276.

211. During the mid-eighteenth century, Muhammad Abd al-Wahhab led the Islamic movement of purification and renewal in the Arabia peninsula. This period of renewal was not confined to Arabia but was apparent throughout the Muslim world in reaction to the deleterious effects of European expansionism and the contaminating influences that were seeping into Islam by virtue of the compromising laxity of Muslim rulers. The Wahhabi movement reflected the culmination of dissatisfaction that began more than a century earlier as expressed by such scholars as Maulana Abd al-Haqq and Sheikh Ahmad Sirhindi in the Indian subcontinent. While the numerous scholars wrote about the dilution of Islamic practices, Abd al-Wahhab was the first "to steer the movement out of the studies of the learned and onto the field of action." A scholar and follower of the Hanbali school of jurisprudence, Abd al-Wahhab aligned his forces with Muhammad ibn Saud in 1744. Although Wahhab and Saud suffered numerous setbacks subsequent to a period of successful expansion in the areas north of Arabia, ultimately the Wahhabi purification movement based, in

part, on Hanbali fiqh philosophy firmly established itself under the House of Saud, the present-day rulers of Saudi Arabia. *See* ROBINSON, *supra* note 5, at 118–121, for a more detailed discussion of the Wahhabi movement. *See also*, PHILIPS, *supra* note 31, at 130, for a description of twentieth century Wahhabi purification efforts at Saudi Arabian cemeteries (by removing monuments and shrines, which contravene Islamic principles) and the present day usage of *Wahhabi* as a euphemism for extremism by those who opposed the changes.

212. The mutazilites represented the minority theological view of Islam as a religion. They stressed reasoning power over revelation as the final authority, and employed more innovative approaches to interpreting Qur'an, placing special emphasis on individual freedom. *See*, ZEPP, *supra* note 1, at 149.

213. Shia, also spelled *shiah* or *shiite*, which means *partisans* (of Ali, the fourth Khalif) is that significant segment of the Muslim community, who believes that the leader of the community must be elected from among the descendants of Muhammad, i.e., the leader must be from Muhammad's bloodline. The overwhelming majority of the Muslim world, typically called *sunni*, believe that the leader may be any man who manifests appropriate qualities of leadership and character as demonstrated by Muhammad, and thus reject this shia view. Subsequent to Muhammad's death (632 C.E.), the majority of the Muslim community elected Abu Bakr as khalif, while a minority believed Ali, the Prophet's cousin and son-in-law, should have been deemed the new leader. Despite Abu Bakr, Umar, and Uthman's tenure as khalifs, the shia recognize Ali, the fourth khalif, as the first legitimate imam after Muhammad and declared the other three disbelievers (kafirs). Like Uthman, Ali was assassinated (in 661 C.E.). Upon Ali's death the governor of Syria, Muawiyah, who had served in that capacity since the time of Abu Bakr, declared himself khalif and his son, Yazid, successor, to the consternation of the shias. In 680 C.E. at the battle of Kabala, Ali's youngest son, Husain, was defeated and killed by Yazid's forces in a civil war over the leadership of the ummah. The shias attribute Husain's defeat in part to shia betrayal and desertion. Each year in commemoration of the defeat at Karbala, the shias flagellate themselves in atonement. Although there are subgroups among the shia (and sunnis for that matter), the most recognized and leading component of them is the *Twelvers*, those who ascribe to the theory of the twelve imams. The twelfth descendant of Ali was named Muhammad. In 873 C.E., at the age of four, he went into hiding and has not to this day revealed himself. He is therefore known as the *Hidden Imam, The Twelfth Imam or Mahdi*, and the faithful among the shias await his return. During his absence, ayatollahs (literally *the reflection of Allah on earth*) serve in his stead. [Prior to his death, some followers of Ayatollah Khomeini believed he was the Twelfth Imam.] In the sixteenth century, the Safawi dynasty established the Twelvers as the authority on Islamic religious matters in Iran and nearby Iraq, where they have dominated ever since. Besides the issue regarding succession to the leadership of the Muslim community (the *imamate doctrine*), another significant difference between shias and sunnis involves the application of the fiqh methodology of ijtihad—individual reasoning. Originally among the sunni, it was a viable method for use by appropriately qualified individuals. Later, its use was officially discontinued. Among the shia, its use is considered legitimate but only may be exercised by an imam, not just any educated scholar of Islam. Under shia fiqh, only

a descendant of Muhammad could be entrusted to exercise the human capacity to reason in matters involving Islam. For more detailed introductory description of the shia and their subgroups: *See,* PHILIPS, *supra* note 31, at 150 and ZEPP, *supra* note 1, at 151–158.

214. BAKHTIAR, *supra* note 190, at xxix.

215. A. Kevin Reinhart, *Introduction* to BAKHTIAR, *supra* note 190, at xxxii. It is worth noting here that although Jafari fiqh is the most widely recognized, there are dozens of shia subgroups (or subsects) that may be at variance with the Jafari view on fiqh application. *See,* AJIJOLA, *supra* note 29, at 42, for a reference to the number of shia subgroups. *See also,* Abdulaziz Sachedina, *Shi'i Schools of Law,* in 2 THE OXFORD ENCYCLOPEDIA OF THE MODERN ISLAMIC WORLD 463 (John L. Esposito ed., 1995) [hereinafter Sachedina].

216. Sachedina, *supra* note 215, at 463.

217. KHAN, *supra* note 12, at 126. This methodology is based upon shia allegorical interpretations of the Qur'an called *tawil.*

218. *Id.* at 128. Under shia philosophy the imam is the law-giver, the walking, talking Qur'an, who by virtue of the privilege to render interpretations resorts to a method of analogical reasoning that is comparable to qiyas, called *aql. See* DOI, *supra* note 12, at 77–78.

219. *See, generally,* RAMADAN, *supra* note 13, at 90–91, in which he discusses the rather minimal differences between sunni and shia Islam, apart from the concept of imamate, citing, among other, Asaf Fyzee, the esteemed shia scholar, and I. Goldziher.

220. BAKHTIAR, *supra* note 190, at xxx, reports that in fiqh application the Jafari school more often agrees with the Hanafi and Maliki schools, while the Shafii and Hanbali schools more often disagree.

2

On Islamic Punishment

Hisham M. Ramadan

INTRODUCTION

The purpose of this chapter is not only to educate the reader on the fundamentals of the Islamic punishment scheme but also to permit the reader to enter a law sphere that might be atypical and indeed at odds with the legal concepts already rooted in the reader's mind. The reason for the peculiarity is that most readers living in the west are most familiar with positive law,[1] applying its norms, as a criterion, to the examination of Islamic law doctrines and philosophy. This criterion is—to a certain extent—dysfunctional because its source significantly differs from Islamic law in principle and in application. That is because Islamic law—according to Islamic beliefs—is of divine origin while the vast majority of laws in the modern world are based upon a group of principles developed gradually over the past ten centuries. The divine basis of Islamic law is reflected in many aspects of the law including its constructions of rationales, punishments, rules and limits of interpretation, and so forth. For instance, one of the rationales of the punishment in Islamic law is to cleanse the Muslim offender by imposing the appropriate punishment. In essence, it is a spiritual salvation method that influences the individual's behavior in an Islamic legal system.[2] A Muslim who has committed a crime—one that is virtually impossible to be proven because he is beyond the reach of law enforcement or otherwise—may surrender to the authorities and confess of the crime only because he is driven by a desire to be cleansed from the crime committed.[3] It was reported that a man went to the Prophet Mohammed (the Prophet of Islam) asking him to inflict the punishment of *Zina* (fornication or adultery) although the crime was neither reported nor was seen by eyewitnesses and thus, would go unpunished.[4] In another incident, an individual brought his son to the Prophet Mohammed to adjudicate and enforce the punishment of *Zina* offense thus breaking with family loyalty.[5] In these cases the offenders, knowing that they will answer for their deeds before God, not only renounced the criminal act but also sought retribution from the prohibitory norm violation by submitting themselves to the punishment. Since there is no parallel consideration in positive laws to the divinity aspect of the law, the reader may not fully comprehend the functionality of Islamic law if the concept of divinity of Islamic law is overlooked.

The divinity feature of Islamic law is an example of many atypical concepts that might be a challenge for some readers. Accordingly, I will endeavor, in this chapter, to shed light upon punishment fundamentals, a topic that has neither been explored adequately nor been examined objectively in the non-Muslim world or for that matter in the contemporary Muslim world in the face of new challenges.

A. Islamic Law Objectives

The interests and the values that Islamic law aims to protect differ significantly from its counterpart in positive laws, which in turn reflect on the rules of law. Generally Islamic law's objectives are: the protection of religion, life, intellect, procreation and property.[6] The principle is that the Islamic legislature ought to protect these objectives by all means necessary to ensure the social welfare. Accordingly, Islamic law prohibits *Zina* (fornication or adultery) because it constitutes aggression against procreation. It prohibits consumption of intoxicants because it constitutes an aggression against the intellect. It prohibits homicide because it constitutes aggression against life and wealth. In each of these crimes one or more social interest/Islamic law objectives is shattered. Consequently, the role of Islamic society is to eliminate the threat to its interests by imposing the appropriate sanction.

In cases of conflict of interest, Islamic law strikes a fine balance between competing interests by: (a) averting the greater of two harms by assumption of the lesser, (b) preferring averting harm over procuring benefits, or (c) averting public harm by the private assumption of loss.

The typical example of the competing interests appears in *Zina* offense. *Zina* offense impinges upon a number of interests including the protected interests of procreation. Therefore it is subjected to severe punishment. Because the punishment is severe and in order to safeguard individuals from false accusation of unchastity, Islamic law imposes a very difficult rule of evidence to fulfill. To prove the crime, either four just and credible witnesses testify that they actually saw the actual act of penetration or the alleged perpetrator offers an uncoerced confession. The preparatory acts of sexual copulation and other forms of sexual acts that do not involve penetration do not suffice as *Zina*. Moreover, Islamic law assures the right to privacy, an indispensable doctrine, which enhances the difficulty of proving the offense. The strict evidential requirements in *Zina* offense is the solution for balancing the social interest, manifested in preventing the innocent's wrongful conviction with the alleged perpetrator's interests, manifested in the false accusation of unchastity and wrongful conviction and the severity of the punishment. Such a balance between the severity of the punishment and the rules of evidence hardly exists in modern positive laws.

The renowned Islamic scholar, Abu Zahra, has made valuable remarks regarding the interests that are worth consideration:

(1) The interests that deserve consideration are the *real* interests which are based upon one or more of the five objectives listed above.[7]

(2) The interests that the legislature considers might cause harm to a number of individuals and it may sacrifice present interest to gain future interest. In this case, the legislature must advance the most general, enduring major interests.[8]

(3) An interest is not synonymous with desire. Desires might be temporary or based on whim. Whim on many occasions might cause lawlessness and disorder because it might be based upon deviation from rationale thinking. Consequently, it may, in effect, cause more crimes.[9]

(4) A group of individuals' desires does not necessarily correspond to the general interests/goals protected in Islamic law. Rather Islamic law protects only the interest that corresponds to the general public interest.[10]

Essentially, the keystone of the Islamic justice system is in procuring a *real* social benefit. In this context, the punishment is not beneficial in itself nor is it favorable; rather what is important is to protect the considerable legitimate interests, to be precise, to avoid harm and/or to gain a benefit. Indeed, several actions might produce benefits (i.e., consuming alcohol) but the harm generated may greatly outweigh the benefits.[11] Subsequently, the prohibition of such actions was required to avoid the harm. Perhaps the actions that are purely beneficial are limited; and that numerous actions produce great social benefit and a certain amount of harm to a number of individuals. In that case, the Islamic legislature has favored the interest of society as a whole. A contrast between permitting consuming milk and consuming alcohol is highly beneficial to illustrate this policy. While alcohol produces some benefits, its harm affects the individual consumer and the entire society. The harm outweighs the benefit; therefore it is prohibited. In contrast milk produces benefits to the individual consumer and to the society. However, in some cases consuming milk causes harm to lactose intolerant individuals.[12] In weighing the benefits and harms, one must realize that the vast majority of individuals benefit from milk without incurring harm, though in a very few cases harm can occur in a limited number of individuals. Accordingly, because the benefits greatly outweigh harm, consuming milk is permissible. However consumption of alcohol, in which the harm to the general population outweighs the benefits, ought to be prohibited. It should be noted that, according to Muslims beliefs, affirming a prohibition in either Quran or Sunna suffices for its implementation. However, the harm/benefit rationale analysis is useful only for conducts that were not adjudicated specifically in the basic sources of Islamic law.

Remarkably, the objectives of Islamic law are very important in construing the Islamic penal policy because it stands as a barrier from individual(s) desires and whims especially if those individuals are in places of power which influence the penal policy.

B. Characteristics of the Punishment

1. Stability, Consistency and the Flexibility of the Law

The chief characteristics of Islamic criminal law are the stability and consistency while remaining able to offer the flexibility necessary to meet social changes. The stability and the flexibility stems from the fact that the basic jurisprudential doctrines never change while the secondary applications of the doctrines tolerate various interpretation and methodological analysis. The basic sources of Islamic criminal law, Quran and Sunna lay the foundational jurisprudence that generate doctrinal consistency while Islamic law scholars' analysis and methodologies of interpretation of the basic sources offers the flexible secondary jurisprudence needed to meet the ever-changing social demands.[13]

The structure of the Islamic penal system evinces the harmony between the characteristics of consistency, stability and flexibility. Very basic foundations necessary to maintain social order were laid down in the detailed list of *Hudud* and *Qusas* crimes while the elastic category of *Tazeer* crimes offers the flexibility required to meet the changes in the prohibitory norm.[14] It should be noted that *Tazeer* crimes are not left to the whim of the Islamic legislature but rather is always guided by the five Islamic law objectives discussed earlier and by the prohibitory norm general directions explained in *Qusas* and *Hudud* crimes.

2. Merciful Law but Firm

The Holy Quran suggests that justice is the ultimate goal of Islamic jurisprudence.[15] In conjunction with justice, two basic rules are maintained: a power to protect and enforce it and the mercy to deal with extraordinary circumstances.[16] Mercy, in this context, is not limited to a particular set of circumstances, rather it is a universal doctrine that covers an unlimited range of circumstances.

Although the concept of mercy is a universal doctrine, it certainly does not follow that every wrongdoer is routinely excused.[17] The blanket pardon of the offenses encourages the offenders and the potential offenders to offend or re-offend. Such action would constitute an ultimate act of cruelty toward the society in general.[18] In this context, typically the highest degree of mercy materializes in strict adherence to the rule of law deterring potential harmful conducts.[19] However, the offender's circumstances or the extraordinary social circumstances may trigger mercy. On an individual level, extraordinary circumstances may reduce, delay or even preclude the punishment. It was reported that the Prophet Mohammed ordered a stay of exaction of the punishment of adultery until the woman offender delivers the baby and completes the nursing period. The Muslims Caliph (ruler) Omar Ibn Al-Khatab excused a slave from the punishment of theft of a food upon knowing that the slave master failed to provide sufficient food to the slave.[20] On a social level, circumstances may also affect the application of a punishment. Omar Ibn Al-Khatab had suspended the punishment for theft in the famine year. However, under no circumstances could the severity of the punishment alone be the basis for punishment mitigation.[21]

The application of the concept of mercy covers the entire sphere of judicial proceedings including the execution of a punishment. The famous Islamic law scholar Ibn Taymia suggests that executing the capital punishment must be by a sword or the like because it is the fastest and least painful method of execution.[22] The implication from this proposal is that if a modern method of execution (e.g., lethal injection) is less painful and faster than the sword it should be allowed.[23]

3. Equality Before the Law

Numerous verses in the Holy Quran and Hadith affirm absolute equality before the law.[24] Chief among these is the fact of the unity of the origin of mankind which is stated as follows:

> O mankind! reverence your Guardian-Lord, who created you from a single Person, created, of like nature, his mate, and from them twain scattered (like seeds) countless men and women; fear Allah, through Whom ye demand your mutual (rights), and (reverence) the wombs (that bore you): for Allah ever watches over you.[25]

A careful examination of this verse suggests that reminding humanity that all mankind is of one origin renders the very basic premise of inequality inconceivable because it is unimaginable to discriminate between identical individuals. In fact, the concept of origin unity destroys any basis to discriminatory practices based upon race, color, and so forth, because the underpinning of this concept assumes identicalness, as a general rule, among mankind.

A decisive test to the equality doctrine occurred in the very early stages of establishing the Islamic state. It was reported that when a noble lady, a member of the dominant tribe, committed larceny the members of her tribe sent a close acquaintance to the Prophet Mohammed to exempt her from the punishment. The Prophet refused maintaining "the people before you (past nations) were destroyed because they used to inflict the punishments on the poor and forgive the noble. By him in whose hand my soul is (God)! If Fatima (the daughter of the Prophet) did that (that is, stole), I would cut off her hand."[26]

4. Proportionality Doctrine

The proportionality doctrine is explicitly stated in a number of verses of the Holy Quran.[27] The scope of the proportionality doctrine is not limited to the harm caused by an offender(s) but also extends to the benefit(s) lost.[28] Perhaps proportionality is one of the most controversial doctrines in Islamic law. The controversy emerges from the application of corporeal punishments in Islamic law. In one view, punishment in Islam, particularly corporeal penalties, are disproportionate, harsh, cruel and inhuman. Cutting the hand of a thief, flogging the fornicator and slanderer cannot be said proportionate to the harm caused. Before discussing the merit of this criticism, one ought to know that the corporeal punishment is not an Islamic law innovation rather it is virtually a form of punishment known before Islam, predominantly in the Bible.[29]

Labeling Islamic law as inhuman and cruel exclusive of proper understanding of the Islamic justice system reflects the common state of ignorance among a large number of commentators. Initially one should realize that the Islamic justice system is entirely different from other justice systems. The Islamic justice system, as Muslims believe, is of divine origin while almost all contemporary legal systems are positive laws. The divinity of the law and the basic Islamic belief that a Muslim ought to surrender his will to God alone would create an atmosphere of acceptance of God's commands and obligations as well as resentment of external interference from non-Islamic ideologies.

On the other hand, Islamic law utilizes its normative dogmas, which hardly exist in other legal systems, to characterize the relationship between the punishment and the crime. Cutting the hand of the thief is subject to the fulfillment of strict elements of the offense and absence of the defenses. While a number of criminal law defenses in Islamic law might coincide with that of other legal systems, the elements of the offenses, in particular larceny differs noticeably. To cut off the hand of the thief, the value of the stolen property should not be less than certain value *Nessab* otherwise the punishment will be commuted to a less severe one.[30] Comparably when the crime of *Zina* (fornication or adultery) prescribes severe punishment, flogging for the fornicator and stoning to death for the adulterer, it is balanced with a very heavy burden of proof requirement. No less than uncoerced confession or the testimony of four credible witnesses, who witnessed the actual act of penetration, is adequate to inflict the punishment. Ultimately the punishment scheme in Islamic law is applicable only in a proper Islamic state where the individual necessities of life are obtainable to disperse the possibility of excusable larceny and where the moral norms prohibit extra-matrimonial sexual intercourse.[31]

The common state of ignorance among a large number of commentators is due to lack of knowledge of the comprehensive Islamic justice scheme that covers the entire sphere of the Muslims lives from the basic ethical questions to the method of enforcement of capital punishment. It is also stems from utilizing different criterion in assessing the degree, source and effect of the harm caused by violating the prohibitory norm. Islamic jurisprudence broadens the scope of the harm to include any harm encroaching upon the five protected interests, namely, life, property, procreation, religion and intellect. In contrast, other legal systems typically utilize a narrow view of the possible harm caused by violating the prohibitory norm. For instance, extramatrimonial sexual intercourse in a non-Islamic legal system is not a crime unless it contains the lack of the consent element as in rape or involves the encroachment of a right of another person as in adultery. Islamic law adopts a broader view that considers the socioeconomic impact of extra-matrimonial sexual intercourse. Prohibited intercourse risks the welfare of the offspring and the innocent partner by increasing their chances of infection by sexually transmitted diseases. Furthermore, the socially destructive effect of adultery manifested in destabilizing and destroying the family unit should not be ignored.[32] In these cases, the protected Islamic law objectives of procreation, life and property are undermined greatly.

Similarly, in larceny, the thief, who steals a few dollars, without necessity, causes damage that is not limited to the property stolen. He creates a general mode of untruthfulness in society. Larceny actually infuses guardedness, mistrust and unrest in the community. In contrast, the damaged incurred by embezzlement is less severe because the harm is limited to the property stolen and to the relationship between the offender and the victim. For this reason the punishment for theft is higher than the punishment for embezzlement, "*Al Ghaseb*."

In sum, because Islamic law recognizes the proportionality doctrine, the punishment must always match the harm caused. However, defining the zone of harm in Islamic law does not necessarily reflect the assumed harm zone in positive laws.

5. *Fostering Crime Denunciation*

The condemnatory symbolic significance of Islamic punishment is manifest in the public engagement in the criminal proceedings. The trial is public, the execution of the punishment is public and yet, the community, in some cases, executes the punishment under the supervision of the proper authority. In other words, when individuals, in a given Islamic society, stone the convicted adulterer they are, in fact, unequivocally expressing their condemnation of the violation of the prohibitory norm, i.e., adultery. This sort of social condemnation embodies the denunciation, enmity and hatred of the offender's acts as distinguished from the offender himself.[33]

Conversely, Islamic law encourages the offender's "private" condemnation of his harmful acts.[34] Encouraging the denouncement of the offender's crime has a number of benefits including raising the offender's feeling of guilt leading to the expressive determination not to re-offend. Also it eases the authorities' task in restoring justice and equity. Typically, it occurs by the offender's surrender and pledge to authorities to desist from further crimes.

However, Islamic law scholars presented various views with respect to the denunciation and repentance timing and limits. In general, the schools of thoughts are divided into three categories:

• Some scholars of Al-Hanblee and Al-Shafee schools of thoughts concluded that repentance will avail the offender from the punishment even after the arrest and conviction. The supporting evidences are:

A. A number of Quranic verses preclude the punishment in case of sincere repentance. Most significantly, the preclusion of the punishment in armed robbery (*Hiraba*), if the offender repents before arrest, bearing in mind that armed robbery is a heinous offense.[35] Accordingly, lesser offenses should be included under this rule.

B. Repentance cleanses the offender from the wrongdoing, therefore the punishment is not justified.

However, a stay of execution is limited to crimes involving social rights exclusively (e.g., Zina, voluntary intoxication). If the crime committed involves the victim's rights solely or a combination of the victim's rights and the social right, repentance makes no effect on the execution of the punishment. Some of the scholars who adopt this approach conditioned the stay of execution of the punishment upon showing the intention not to re-offend in the future. This condition requires the elapsing of a period of time sufficient to show continuous desire not to re-offend. Noticeably this approach adopts the individual's point of view and disregards the deterrence effect of the punishment

• Imam Malek and Imam Abu Hanifa suggested that repentance does not preclude the punishment after the crime commission with exception of armed robbery offense. They advanced the following argument:

A. *Hudud* crimes cleanse the offenders only by executing the prescribed punishment. The Quranic verses prescribe the punishment for an offense, unmistakably demanding the enforcement of the punishment.[36] Hence, precluding the punishment upon repentance opposes the clear direction stated in these verses.

B. As a general rule, the deterrent effect of the punishment should be maintained. Opening the door for pardonable repentance after committing the crime promotes wrongdoing.

• The renowned scholars Ibn Al-Kyam and Ibn Taymia suggested that repentance does not preclude the punishment if the crime committed affects only an individual's rights, such as theft. In contrast, repentance does preclude the punishment if the crime committed affects the social right, for example, voluntary intoxicant consumption.

Plausibly Imam Malek's and Imam Abu Hanifa's opinion is worthy of endorsement, otherwise the entire justice system may collapse because offenders will claim repentance once they are caught.

6. *The Principle of Legality*

According to the principle of legality the punishment is not justified unless the prohibited conduct and its punishment thereof is defined by statute. Under Islamic law there are three categories of crimes: *Hudud*, *Qusas* and *Tazeer*. Crimes of *Hudud* and *Qusas* are well defined and their punishments are prefixed. However, *Tazeer* crimes are not defined exclusively in Islamic law. It was left to the Islamic legislature, in a given era, to define according to the social needs. To be sure, it ought not to be exclusively defined to enable the legislature to confront new legislative challenges with solutions guided by clear jurisprudential doctrines. A nonexclusive list of these doctrines includes:

1. Knowledge of the prohibition is an indispensable punishment requirement.[37]
2. An act or omission is not an offense under *Tazeer* crimes category unless it is a prohibited conduct under Islamic law or is legislatively designated prohibited conduct for the purpose of serving public interest.[38] Again, the legitimacy of a legislatively designated prohibited conduct is established only if it serves public interest.

3. The law of *Qusas* and *Hudud* crimes draws clear guidelines for *Tazeer* crimes. These guidelines give the legislature indication as to the nature of *Tazeer* prohibitions and its applicable punishments. For instance, when the Islamic legislature stated clearly the crime of intentional homicide and its punishment, it is indicative that conducts that cause comparable harm but to a lesser degree are also prohibited. Accordingly, attempted murder is prohibited. Furthermore, the majority of scholars suggest that the punishment for lesser harmful conducts should not exceed the original crime's punishment.[39]

4. The sentencing discretionary power is vested in the judiciary according to various factors including the defendant's character, his criminal history, the impact of the particular crime on the victim, the impact of the crime on the community, recidivism . . . etc. In this context, the sentence is not subject to the judge's unbridled discretion rather it is always controlled by the necessary means to rehabilitate the offender and to remedy social problems.[40]

7. The Impact of the victim's forgiveness on the punishment

Crime victims are strongly encouraged to forgive the offender resulting in punishment preclusion.[41] Yet, forgiveness is feasible only if the crime committed violates the victim's right solely or violates the victim's right and a social right but the victim's right is prevailing. Accordingly, the impact of the victim's forgiveness is totally dependant on the nature of the crime committed. Because *Hudud* crimes violate social rights, forgiveness is unattainable.[42] However, in a number of *Hudud* offenses such as theft offenses, the victim owns the exclusive right of pressing charges. Once the charge is made to the proper authority it is not possible to preclude the punishment.[43] Logically this supposition is unrealistic with respect to the intentional consumption of intoxicant offense because in that case the entire society, not a solitary individual, is the victim.

In *Qusas* crimes (homicide and bodily injury offenses) it is the victim's (or his heirs in case of death) exclusive right to press charges or enforce the punishment. The victim may intervene in the judicial process at any moment to withdraw the charges or to preclude the punishment if the offender is convicted.

It should be noted that victim forgiveness, if effective, does not erase the prohibitory norm violation; rather it precludes only the original punishment. Consequently, authorities may impose supplementary *Tazeer* punishment if it serves social needs.[44]

8. The impact of common violation of the prohibitory norm

When a large number of individuals, in a given society, have challenged the prohibitory norm by defying one of its rules, the value of that rule decreases dramatically. Consequently, it promotes noncompliance among the population and nonenforcement of the sanction prescribed for the rule disobedience. For instance, long before legalizing prostitution in a number of states, it was widely practiced and its sanction was not enforced. In contrast, Islamic law has severe punishment for general disobedience. The original punishment for intoxication offense varies according to the circumstances but ordinarily is never elevated to the capital punishment level. If intoxication becomes commonly practiced in an Islamic state, the legislature ought to enhance the punishment, up to capital punishment, to face the widespread defiance.[45] The underlying ideology of this position is that when an offense is commonly practiced the magnitude of the social harm radically increases. It threatens public order and peace in the society in addition to promoting de facto law nullification. Hence, it is necessary to enhance punishment for those who collectively challenge the prohibitory norm.

9. Punishment gradations scheme in Islamic law

Islamic law noticeably adopted a punishment gradations scheme based upon the nature of the harm caused and the crime victim. In *Qusas* offenses (homicide and bodily injury) the harm is more personal than social, thus only the victim owns the right of proportionate retribution. When the threat to the society is moderate, i.e., petty theft, and the stolen property is valued at less than the specified amount, *Nessab*, the original punishment for theft is substituted by a lesser punishment. When the society faces utmost threat to its institution, the punishment is enhanced to the highest degree. Thus, in the crime of armed robbery when a number of individuals threaten the indispensable social right of safety and security, society must respond to such a threat by imposing the ultimate penalties for such offenses.

C. Punishment Rationales

A number of punishment rationales are explicitly stated in the Quran and Sunna. Nevertheless, there are also a number of possible rationales implicitly instituted in Islamic law. The following rationales are the explicit and the *possible* rationales.

1. Retribution

Although committing a crime, homicide in particular, harms the victim(s), his heir(s) and the entire society, the permissible right of retribution is conferred to the victim(s) or his heirs exclusively.[46] Using this right, the victim (or his heirs in case of death of the victim) may seek either retributive capital punishment for the death of the victim or seek to inflict identical bodily injury to that caused by the offender. This right might be invoked by the victim or his heirs (in case of death of the victim) upon the commission of intentional or quasi-intentional homicide or bodily harm.[47] The victim (or his heirs in the case of victim's death) does not have to exercise his right of retribution; he may forgive or demand fair compensation.[48] However, forgiveness is strongly encouraged in Islamic law.[49]

The retribution doctrine is always subject to the limitation of proportionality. The victim or his heirs cannot, under any circumstances, demand retribution or compensation disproportionate to the harm that occurred.

2. Education

Law, in general, influences and is influenced by the social morals and norms. By enhancing the social morality standards to reflect the law, individuals respect, support and uphold the legal norms. In this context, the law will be the mirror which individuals look at to measure their actions. From this perspective, Islamic law instrumented the law and the penal policy in particular, to establish the ideal society. Initially the Quran directed individuals to enjoin the right conduct and suppress the wrong.[50] This sort of direction elevates the general sense of accountability among individuals. It shapes their characteristics by making them active members in their community enforcing the rule of law. This active participation in enforcing the law creates an educational environment in which the individuals educate themselves and each other of the law. In sum, these Quranic directions generate a reciprocal beneficial relationship between the law and individuals. Individuals support and enforce the law, and the law facilitates and contributes to educating them of the rights and wrongs.

Several Islamic guidelines educate individuals of not only the prohibitory norm but also of the expected demeanors from them. Chief among them is the severe prohibition of impudent crimes that causes dual harmful effects: the harm caused by committing the crime and boldness while committing the crime.[51] Impudent violations of the prohibitory norms encourage potential offenders to offend especially if such violations occur among a class of individuals sharing geographical location, age group, race or culture, and so forth. The psychological premise for severing the prohibition for impudent crimes might be that humans are social creatures who constantly strive to blend into the surrounding environment. If committing a particular crime becomes common and impudent, a number of individuals may commit this crime in an attempt to simulate the surrounding environment, which in turn, undermines the prohibitory norm.

The Islamic law's criminal procedure also supports the policy of severe prohibition for impudent violations of the prohibitory norm but to a lesser degree. Under the Islamic criminal procedural system, in a number of crimes, such as theft, the victim has the exclusive option of forgiving the offender or of reporting the offense to the authorities. Once it is reported, the charge becomes a social right and therefore the victim cannot withdraw the charge.[52] This procedural policy encourages forgiveness, however, when the offense become public, it becomes a matter of public order that requires inescapable prosecution to maintain the integrity of the prohibitory norm.

3. Deterrence

Perhaps the prime punishment rationale in Islamic law is deterrence. Long before western jurists recognized the deterrent effect of the punishment, the Holy Quran explicitly affirmed that applying and enforcing the law of *Qusas* saves lives.[53] From one point of view, one may realize that individuals, by nature, tend to act upon their interests even if such interests conflict with the greater social interests.[54] The threat of the punishment improves individuals by changing the individuals' balance of good and evil since the prohibited conduct, which triggers the punishment, outweighs its benefits.[55] On this basis individuals can be deterred from performing a prohibited conduct.

Uniquely, Islamic law realizes that methods of inflicting punishment maximize the impact of deterrence. It orders execution of the punishment publicly to promote long-term survival in the memory of the witnesses.[56] The merit of this stance is that visualizing an incident is unlike hearing or knowing about it. The more senses that an individual uses to memorize an incident the more likely he will remember it. For that reason, the impact of witnessing an execution on potential murderers is thought to be much greater than on those who are only aware of the law that prescribes capital punishment for murder.

The eminent jurist Ibn Taymia suggested that the limb amputation punishments prescribed for specific offenses generate a great deterrent impact on the society in general and on the potential offenders in particular.[57] It may exceed the deterrent impact of capital punishment in a sense that execution of an offender could be forgotten.[58] Yet the offender who received the limb amputation punishment becomes a symbol of the threat of the punishment wherever he goes.[59]

Remarkably the deterrent effect of the punishment is not universally successful. A number of offenders may choose to re-offend endlessly. In this context, the Islamic jurist Al-Kassani suggested that the rationale of the punishment is to prevent the offenders from re-offending. When an offender chooses to re-offend continuously after inflicting the *Hadd* punishment on him following every offense, further punishment may not be warranted.[60]

4. Rehabilitation

According to Islamic theology, inflicting the punishment cleanses the offender from the moral stigma of the crime which gives the offender the opportunity to proceed with his life thereafter normally and without the shame of the crime. Accordingly, it has been reported that the Prophet Mohammed forbade an individual from calling a woman convicted and punished for adultery, "the adulterer."

Yet, the Islamic rehabilitation scheme is not limited to cleansing the stigma of the crime but it also extends to aiding the offender in every possible way to re-integrate successfully into the community.[61] In this context, a number of Islamic law scholars have emphasized that the punishment purpose of the *Tazeer* category of crimes is to deter future crimes as well as rehabilitate the offender.[62]

5. Incapacitation

Incapacitation is a possible punishment rationale in the Islamic justice system. The basic premise of the incapacitation rationale is that the offenders who challenge the prohibitory norm and possess future threat must be prevented from re-offending by incapacitation. One may infer that Islamic law's adoption of the corporeal punishment scheme, which includes capital punishment and limb amputation, utilizes the incapacitation rationale to a great extent which may undermine the importance of other punishment rationales. In fact, there might be some supporting evidence for incapacitation rationale with regards to *Hudud* and *Qusas* crimes but in *Tazeer* crimes, where the vast majority of crimes are found, the prime rationales are deterrence and rehabilitation.[63]

6. Instituting the perfect society

This rationale combines several earlier rationales such as rehabilitation and crime prevention as well as promotion of large numbers of ethical values embodied in Islamic law. In the following paragraphs, I will shed light on a number of features of the institution of the perfect society that was not explained in the previous rationales.

In the crime of *Qazaf* "slander or false accusation of unchastity" the victim exclusively has the right of pressing charges. The majority of scholars concede that the victim may intervene in the judicial process either by withdrawing the charges at any stage or even by requesting a stay of execution if the offense has been proven.[64] The minority opinion suggests that once the issue has been raised it has become a social right, therefore the authorities have the exclusive control over the judicial proceedings.[65] Whatever the case may be, the victim is strongly encouraged to forgive. Upon careful analysis of the Islamic law position in *Qazaf* offense, one may realize that Islamic law promotes justice, commendable social morality and mercy. The victim is encouraged to forgive (mercy). But his right not to be labeled falsely is guaranteed (justice). To maintain the social relationships between individuals, the victim has the exclusive right to prove his innocence by pressing charges or even by halting the punishment once his innocence is proven upon a judgment (social welfare). Yet the threat of the punishment of *Qazaf* remains unaffected by this judicial proceeding scheme to deter future crimes. Nevertheless, the treatment of *Qazaf* offense is merely an example of the Islamic legislative methodology that artfully drafted a unique solution to the social problems with considerations of social rights, social integrity, victims' rights, mercy and justice.

The Islamic religious beliefs have a dual effect: preventing crimes by elevating the social moral sense and positively influencing the criminal proceedings. With respect to the crime prevention effect, one may realize that in an Islamic state, negative feelings of hate and jealousy are to be eradicated by enforcing compassion and mercy between individuals. The rich pay charity hence that the poor would not feel overlooked with no social protection while the rich enjoy wealth. Charitable deeds are strongly encouraged even when it exceeds the moral and the legal obligation of *Zakah* charity.[66]

That Islamic religious beliefs have an influential effect on criminal proceedings is clearly noticeable. Offenders may voluntarily confess crimes that are virtually impossible to discover. It has been reported that during the reign of Imam Ali, an offender went to him confessing of murder to prevent inflicting the punishment on the convicted innocent individual. However, when the undisclosed crime has limited social harm such as the consumption of intoxicants the offender need not reveal it and may privately repent such action.[67] If the offender disclosed it the authorities should inflict the punishment prescribed.[68] Ultimately, every individual in the Islamic state is under obligation to enjoin the right conduct, including crime prevention, and forbid the wrong conduct.[69] These are a few examples of the Islamic legislature's employment of faith as instrument to attain ideal society.

NOTES

1. Law established or recognized by governmental authority, *Merriam-Webster's Dictionary of Law.*

2. According to Islamic belief, if the offender does not suffer the pain of the punishment for the crime he committed, in the hereafter, God, the all-knowing, will question the offender for the crime committed and may subject him to a greater punishment.

3. O ye who believe! stand out firmly for justice, as witnesses to Allah, even as against yourselves, or your parents, or your kin, and whether it be (against) rich or poor: for Allah can best protect both. Follow not the lusts (of your hearts), lest ye swerve, and if ye distort (justice) or decline to do justice, verily Allah is well acquainted with all that ye do. *See* THE HOLY QURAN 4:135.

4. A person from among the Muslims came to Allah's Messenger (may peace be

upon him) while he was in the mosque. He called him saying: Allah's Messenger, I have committed adultery. He (the Holy Prophet) turned away from him, He (again) came round facing him and said to him: Allah's Messenger, I have committed adultery. He (the Holy Prophet) turned away until he did that four times, and as he testified four times against his own self, Allah's Messenger (may peace be upon him) called him and said: Are you mad? He said: No. He said: Are you married? He said: Yes. Thereupon Allah's Messenger (May peace be upon him) said: Take him and stone him. SAHIH MUSLIM (BOOK OF AL-HUDUD) Hadith # 3202.

5. One of the desert dwellers came to Allah's Messenger (may peace be upon him) and said: Messenger of Allah, I beg you in the name of Allah that you pronounce judgment about me according to the Book of Allah. The second claimant who was wiser than him said: Well, decide among us according to the Book of Allah, but permit me (to say something). Thereupon Allah's Messenger (may peace be upon him) said: Say. He said: My son was a servant in the house of this person and he committed adultery with his wife. I was informed that my son deserved stoning to death (as punishment for this offense). I gave one hundred goats and a female-slave as ransom for this. I asked the scholars (if this could serve as expiation for this offense). They informed me that my son deserved one hundred lashes and exile for one year, and this woman deserved stoning (as she was married). Thereupon Allah's Messenger (may peace be upon him) said: By Him in Whose Hand is my life, I will decide between you according to the Book of Allah. The female-slave and the goats should be given back, and your son is to be punished with one hundred lashes and exile for one year. And, O Unais, go to this woman in the morning; and if she makes a confession, then stone her. He (the narrator) said: He went to her in the morning and she made a confession. And Allah's Messenger (may peace be upon him) ordered that she be stoned to death. SAHIH MUSLIM (BOOK OF AL-HUDUD) Hadith # 3210.

6. MOHAMMED ABU ZAHRA, AL-GARIMA [THE CRIME] 30–31[hereinafter ABU ZAHRA].

7. *Id.* 32.

8. *Id.* 32.

9. *Id.* 32–34.

10. *Id.* 33–34.

11. They ask thee concerning wine and gambling. Say: "In them is great sin, and some profit, for men; but the sin is greater than the profit." They ask thee how much they are to spend; say: "What is beyond your needs." Thus doth Allah make clear to you His Signs: in order that ye may consider. THE HOLY QURAN 2:219.

12. Lactose intolerance is the inability to digest significant amounts of lactose, which is the predominant sugar of milk.

13. Sunna is the Standard practice of the Prophet Mohammed, including his sayings, deeds, tacit approvals or disapprovals. The authentic Sunna is as binding as THE HOLY QURAN as stated in THE HOLY QURAN. (Obey Allah, and obey the Messenger, and beware (of evil): if ye do turn back, know ye that it is Our Messenger's duty to proclaim (the Message) in the clearest manner.) THE HOLY QURAN 5:92, *See also* 136 MAJID KHADDURI, ISLAMIC CONCEPTION OF JUSTICE 136. Interestingly enough, some commentators argue that Islamic law is inflexible

because, as the jurist concedes, God offers a solution to every problem, *See* MATHEW LIPPMAN ET AL., ISLAMIC CRIMINAL LAW AND PROCE-DURE 25 (1988). The diversity present in the opinions of the Muslim schools of thought and the flexible rules of legislation including Ijtihad (exerting oneself to find the correct judgment of God) that these authors acknowledge refutes the foundation for their claim.

14. *Hudud* crimes consist of adultery or fornication, slander or false accusation, theft, intoxication, brigandage or armed robbery, apostasy, rebellion or treason. *Qusas* Crimes are intentional or quasi-intentional homicide and bodily injury crimes. All other crimes are *Tazeer* crimes.

15. We sent aforetime Our Messengers with Clear Signs and sent down with them the Book and the Balance (of Right and Wrong), that men may stand forth in justice; and We sent down Iron, in which is (material for) mighty war, as well as many bene-fits for mankind, that Allah may test who it is that will help, unseen, Him and His Messengers: for Allah is Full of Strength, Exalted in Might (and able to enforce His Will). THE HOLY QURAN 57:25.

16. According to Abu Zahra, verse 57:25 in the HOLY QURAN draws an analogy between justice and iron in an attempt to explain that as iron is tough and strong, justice need an iron fist to endorse and protect it. ABU ZAHRA, *Supra* note 6, at 8.

17. (We sent thee not, but as a mercy for all creatures). THE HOLY QURAN 21:107.

18. ABU ZAHRA, *Supra* note 6, at 7.

19. Allah's Messenger (The prophet Mohammad, May peace be upon him) said: He who shows no mercy to the people, Allah, the Exalted and Glorious, does not show mercy to him. SAHIH MUSLIM Hadith # 4283.

20. It should be noted that although Islam has tolerated slavery, all its teachings and prescriptions lead to its abolition. During the short period in which slavery was practiced, Muslims were instructed to treat slaves well and with dignity. The Prophet said: Your slaves are your brethren; therefore whoever has a brother who depends upon him must feed and clothe him in the way he feeds and clothes himself; and should not impose upon him tasks which exceed his capacity; should you ask them to do such things, then you are obliged to help them. In the long term, manumitting a slave has always been regarded as one of the most meritorious of all acts. The HOLY QURAN even requires it as a means of expiation for serious faults.

21. (The woman and the man guilty of adultery or fornication flog each of them with a hundred stripes: let not compassion move you in their case, in a matter pre-scribed by Allah, if ye believe in Allah and the Last Day: and let a party of the Believ-ers witness their punishment.) THE HOLY QURAN 24:2. As a general rule, once the offense is reported to the authorities neither the severity of the punishment nor the offender's social status preclude the punishment, *See* TAFSEER IBN KATHEER [Ibn Katheer interpretation of the Holy Quran] associated with the previous verse.

22. TAKEE AL-DEEN IBN TAYMIA, AL-SAYSAH AL-SHARIA FE ESLAH AL-RAEE WA-AL-RAYA 86 [hereinafter IBN TAYMIA].

23. This is especially true bearing in mind that the Prophet Mohammed ordered the Muslims to be kind to all creatures even when slaughtering an animal for food. He said "Verily Allah has enjoined goodness to everything; so when you kill, kill in

a good way and when you slaughter, slaughter in a good way. So every one of you should sharpen his knife, and let the slaughtered animal die comfortably." SAHIH MUSLIM (BOOK OF *US-SAID WAL—DHAB'IH WA MA YUKALU MIN AL-HAYAWAN*).

24. For example, See the Hadith "The lives of all Muslims are equal" SUNAN ABU-DAWUD (*KITAB AL-DIYAT*) [BOOK OF FAIR COMPENSATION].

25. THE HOLY QURAN 4:1, *See also* the same meaning in this verse "O mankind! We created you from a single (pair) of a male and a female, and made you into nations and tribes, that ye may know each other (not that ye may despise each other). Verily the most honored of you in the sight of Allah is (he who is) the most righteous of you. And Allah has full Knowledge and is well-acquainted (with all things)." 49:13.

26. SAHIH AL-BUKHARI (THE BOOK OF AL-*HUDUD*) Hadith # 11.

27. (The prohibited month, for the prohibited month, and so for all things prohibited, there is the law of equality. If then any one transgresses the prohibition against you, transgress ye likewise against him. But fear Allah, and know that Allah is with those who restrain themselves.) THE HOLY QURAN 2:194, (We ordained therein for them: "Life for life, eye for eye, nose for nose, ear for ear, tooth for tooth, and wounds equal for equal." But if anyone remits the retaliation by way of charity, it is an act of atonement for himself. And if any fail to judge by (the light of) what Allah hath revealed, they are (no better than) wrong-doers.) THE HOLY QURAN 5:45.

28. ABU ZAHRA, *Supra* note 6, at 9 & 34.

29. For example: Kill Homosexuals (If a man lies with a male as with a woman, both of them shall be put to death for their abominable deed; they have forfeited their lives.) (Leviticus 20:13 NAB). Kill fortunetellers (A man or a woman who acts as a medium or fortuneteller shall be put to death by stoning; they have no one but themselves to blame for their death.) (Leviticus 20:27 NAB). Death for adultery (If a man commits adultery with another man's wife, both the man and the woman must be put to death.) (Leviticus 20:10 NLT) Death for fornication; (A priest's daughter who loses her honor by committing fornication and thereby dishonors her father also, shall be burned to death.) (Leviticus 21:9 NAB); Death to followers of other religions (Whoever sacrifices to any God, except the Lord alone, shall be doomed. (Exodus 22:19 NAB). Kill nonbelievers; (They entered into a covenant to seek the Lord, the God of their fathers, with all their heart and soul; and everyone who would not seek the Lord, the God of Israel, was to be put to death, whether small or great, whether man or woman. (2 Chronicles 15:12–13 NAB).

30. *See* MOHAMMAD IQBAL SIDDIQI, THE PENAL LAW OF ISLAM 27–28 (1985).

31. *Id.* at 29–30

32. ABU ZAHRA, *Supra* note 6, at 38.

33. It has been reported that the Prophet Mohammed forbade an individual to call a convicted adulterer "the adulterer."

34. (Allah accepts the repentance of those who do evil in ignorance and repent soon afterwards; to them will Allah turn in mercy: for Allah is Full of Knowledge and Wisdom. Of no effect is the repentance of those who continue to do evil, until death faces one of them, and he says, "Now have I repented indeed;" nor of those

who die rejecting faith; for them have we prepared a punishment most grievous.)
THE HOLY QURAN 4: 17–18; *See also* (By the Soul, and the proportion and order
given to it; And its enlightenment as to its wrong and its right; Truly he succeeds that
purifies it, And he fails that corrupts it!) THE HOLY QURAN 91:7–10.

35. (The punishment of those who wage war against Allah and His Messenger, and
strive with might and main for mischief through the land is: execution, or crucifixion,
or the cutting off of hands and feet from opposite sides, or exile from the land: that
is their disgrace in this world, and a heavy punishment is theirs in the Hereafter;
Except for those who repent before they fall into your power: in that case, know that
Allah is Oft-Forgiving, Most Merciful.) THE HOLY QURAN 5:33–34: *See also* (But
if the thief repents after his crime, and amends his conduct, Allah turneth to him in
forgiveness; for Allah is Oft-Forgiving, Most Merciful.) THE HOLY QURAN 5:39,
(If two men among you are guilty of lewdness, punish them both. If they repent and
amend, leave them alone; for Allah is Oft-Returning, Most Merciful.) THE HOLY
QURAN 4:16. Moreover, the authentic Hadith of the prophet Mohammed states
(whoever repent from committing sins as the one who committed no sins).

36. (The woman and the man guilty of adultery or fornication flog each of them
with a hundred stripes: let not compassion move you in their case, in a matter prescribed by Allah, if ye believe in Allah and the Last Day: and let a party of the Believers witness their punishment.) THE HOLY QURAN 24:2, (As to the thief, male or
female, cut off his or her hands: a punishment by way of example, from Allah, for
their crime: and Allah is Exalted in Power. Full of Wisdom.) THE HOLY QURAN
5:38.

37. Quran and Sunna unequivocally state this requirement. *See* (Who receives
guidance, receives it for his own benefit: who goes astray doth so to his own loss: no
bearer of burdens can bear the burden of another: nor would We visit with Our
Wrath until We had sent a Messenger (to give warning).) THE HOLY QURAN
17:15, (Nor was thy Lord the one to destroy a population until He had sent to its
centre a Messenger, rehearsing to them Our Signs: nor are We going to destroy a
population except when its members practice iniquity. THE HOLY QURAN 28:59,
(Messengers who gave good news as well as warning, that mankind, after (the coming)
of the Messengers, should have no plea against Allah: for Allah is Exalted in Power,
Wise.) THE HOLY QURAN 4:165; Furthermore, the prophet Mohammed never
punished for a prohibited conduct until the Quran specified the offense and its penalty. See AHMED FATAHEY BAHNASI, AL-SYASAH AL-GANAAEYAH FE
AL SHARIA AL-ISLAMIAH [THE PENAL POLICY IN ISLAMIC LAW]
357(1988).

38. ABD AL-QADER ODAH, 1 AL TASHRI' AL-GANAI' AL-ISLAMI
[ISLAMIC CRIMINAL LEGISLATION] 149–152(1977) [hereinafter ODAH].

39. ABU ZAHRA, *Supra* note 6, at 142–143.

40. ODAH, *Supra* note 38, at 148–149.

41. (O ye who believe! The law of equality is prescribed to you in cases of murder:
the free for the free, the slave for the slave, the woman for the woman. But if any
remission is made by the brother of the slain, then grant any reasonable demand, and
compensate him with handsome gratitude. This is a concession and a Mercy from
your Lord. After this, whoever exceeds the limits shall be in grave penalty.) THE
HOLY QURAN 2: 178.

42. See footnote 235.

43. The Prophet Mohammed said: Forgive the infliction of prescribed penalties among yourselves, for any prescribed penalty of which I hear must be carried out. SUNAN ABU-DAWUD (*KITAB AL-HUDUD*) [BOOK OF AL HUDUD] HADITH # 4363.

44. ABU ZAHRA, *Supra* note 6, at 73.

45. It has been reported that Daylam Al-Hameri asked the Prophet Mohammed saying: We are in a land doing a very hard job and we consume a drink made from wheat aiding us in the performance of our work and to help us in this cold country. The Prophet Mohammed inquired, "it is an intoxicant?" I said yes. The Prophet Mohammed said do not consume it. I said, "but people will not give it up." He said "if they do not refrain from consuming it, kill them." Narrated in *Musnad* Ahmed.

46. See (On that account: We ordained for the Children of Israel that if anyone slew a person—unless it be for murder or for spreading mischief in the land—it would be as if he slew the whole people: and if any one saved a life, it would be as if he saved the life of the whole people. Then although there came to them Our Messengers with Clear Signs, Yet, even after that, many of them continued to commit excesses in the land.) THE HOLY QURAN 5:32.

47. Regarding intentional homicide, *See* (Nor take life—which Allah has made sacred—except for just cause. And if anyone is slain wrongfully, We have given his heir authority (to demand Qusas or to forgive): but let him not exceed bounds in the matter of taking life; for he is helped (by the law).) THE HOLY QURAN 17:33.

48. There are a number of opinions regarding demanding fair compensation. The jurist Malek and others suggested that, in the case of homicide, the victim's heirs have the choice of retribution or forgiveness unless the offender accepts the payment of fair compensation. The jurists, Shafee, Ahmed, Dawod and Abu Thour suggested that the victim heirs have the right of fair compensation regardless of the offender's acceptance or refusal of the compensation payment. Similar debate arose regarding compensation in the case of bodily harm. *See* IBN ROSHED AL-KORTOBY (THE BOOK OF AL-*QUSAS*), 2 BADAYET AL-MOGTAHED WA NAHAYET AL-MOKTASED 595–607.

49. *See* (We ordained therein for them: "Life for life, eye for eye, nose for nose, ear for ear, tooth for tooth, and wounds equal for equal." But if anyone remits the retaliation by way of charity, it is an act of atonement for himself. And if any fail to judge by (the light of) what Allah hath revealed, they are (no better than) wrongdoers.) THE HOLY QURAN 5:45, *See also* IBN HAZEM, 11 AL-MOHLA-BE AL-ATHAR, inquiry # 2080 at 113.

50. *See* these verses of THE HOLY QURAN: (Ye are the best of Peoples, evolved for mankind, enjoining what is right, forbidding what is wrong, and believing in Allah. If only the People of the Book had Faith, it were best for them: among them are some who have Faith, but most of them are perverted transgressors.) 3:110, (Let there arise out of you a band of people inviting to all that is good, enjoining what is right, and forbidding what is wrong: they are the ones to attain felicity.) 3:104 (Invite (all) to the Way of thy Lord with wisdom and beautiful preaching; and argue with them in ways that are best and most gracious: for thy Lord knoweth best, who have strayed from His Path, and who receive guidance.) 16:125.

51. (Those who love (to see) scandal published broadcast among the Believers, will have a grievous Penalty in this life and in the Hereafter: Allah knows, and ye know not.) THE HOLY QURAN 24:19; the Prophet Mohammed said (all the sins of my followers will be forgiven except those of the *Mujahirin* 'those who commit a sin openly or disclose their sins to the people.' An example of such disclosure is that a person commits a sin at night, and though Allah 'God' screens it from the public, then he becomes in the morning and say, 'O so-and-so, I did such and such (evil) deed yesterday,' though he spent his night screened by his Lord (none Knowing about his sin) and in the morning he removes Allah's Screen from himself) SAHIH AL-BUKHARI (THE BOOK OF AL-ADAB) Hadith # 6069.

52. The Prophet Mohammed said: Forgive the infliction of prescribed penalties among yourselves, for any prescribed penalty of which I hear must be carried out. SUNAN ABU-DAWUD (*KITAB AL-HUDUD*) [BOOK OF AL HUDUD] HADITH # 4363, *See Also* ABU ZAHRA, *Supra* note 6, at 52.

53. (And there is (a saving of) life for you in al Qusas (the law of equality in punishment), O men of understanding, that you may became Al Muttaqun 'the pious'). THE HOLY QURAN 2: 179.

54. ODAH, *Supra* note 38, at 68–69.

55. *Id.*

56. See (The woman and the man guilty of adultery or fornication flog each of them with a hundred stripes: let not compassion move you in their case, in a matter prescribed by Allah, if ye believe in Allah and the Last Day: and let a party of the Believers witness their punishment.) THE HOLY QURAN 24:2.

57. IBN TAYMIA, *Supra* note 22, at 86.

58. *Id.*

59. *Id.*

60. AL-KASSANI, 7 BADAH'A-SANAH FE TERTEEB AL-SHARAH' 172.

61. The following event explains both equality before the law and aiding the offender after inflicting the punishment ('A'isha, the wife of Allah's Apostle (may peace be upon him), reported that the Quraish were concerned about the woman who had committed theft during the lifetime of Allah's Apostle (may peace be upon him), in the expedition of Victory (of Mecca). They said: Who would speak to Allah's Messenger (may peace be upon him) about her? They (again) said: Who can dare do this but Usama Ibn Zaid, the loved one of Allah's Messenger (may peace be upon him)? She was brought to Allah's Messenger (may peace be upon him) and Usama Ibn Zaid spoke about her to him (interceded on her behalf). The color of the face of Allah's Messenger (may peace be upon him) changed, and he said: Do you intercede in one of the prescribed punishments of Allah? He (Usama) said: Messenger of Allah, seek forgiveness for me. When it was dusk Allah's Messenger (may peace be upon him) stood up and gave an address. He (first) glorified Allah as He deserves, and then said: Now to our topic. This (injustice) destroyed those before you that when any one of (high) rank committed theft among them, they spared him, and when any weak one among them committed theft, they inflicted the prescribed punishment upon him. By Him in Whose Hand is my life, even if Fatima daughter of Muhammad were to commit theft, I would have cut off her hand. He (the Holy Prophet) then commanded about that woman who had committed theft, and her hand was cut off.

'A'isha (further) said: Hers was a good repentance, and she later on married and used to come to me after that, and I conveyed her needs (and problems) to Allah's Messenger (may peace be upon him).) SAHIH MUSLIM (BOOK OF AL-HUDUD) Hadith # 4188.

62. See MOHAMMED S. EL-AWA, PUNISHMENT IN ISLAMIC LAW 96–97.

63. *See Id.*

64. *See* ABD AL-QADER ODAH, 2 AL TASHRI' AL-GANAI' AL-ISLAMI [ISLAMIC CRIMINAL LEGISLATION] 487 (1977).

65. *Id.*

66. *See* (The prophet Mohammed said: Giving charity is obligatory upon each Muslim. It was asked: What do you say of him who does not find (the means) to do so? He said: Let him do manual work, thus doing benefit to himself and give charity. It was asked: What about one who does not have (the means) to do so? He said: Then let him assist the needy, the aggrieved. It was asked: What do you say of one who cannot even do this? He said: Then he should enjoin what is reputable or what is good. He asked: What if he cannot do that? He (the Holy Prophet) said: He should then abstain from evil, for verily that is charity on his behalf.) SAHIH MUSLIM EXPLAINED BY NAWAWI Hadith # 1676.

67. It was reported that the Prophet Mohammed said that the hidden sin harms only its committer but if disclosed it will harm the entire society. *See* IBN TAYMIA, *Supra* note 22, at 133; (A person from among the Muslims came to Allah's Messenger (Mohammed may peace be upon him) while he was in the mosque. He called him saying: Allah's Messenger, I have committed adultery. He (the Holy Prophet) turned away from him, He (again) came round facing him and said to him: Allah's Messenger, I have committed adultery. He (the Holy Prophet) turned away until he did that four times, and as he testified four times against his own self, Allah's Messenger (may peace be upon him) called him and said: Are you mad? He said: No. He said: Are you married? He said: Yes. Thereupon Allah's Messenger (may peace be upon him) said: Take him and stone him.) SAHIH MUSLIM Hadith # 3202; the Prophet Mohammed said (All the people of my *Ummah* (nation) would get pardon for their sins except those who publicize them. And (it means) that a slave (of Allah) may do a deed during the night and tell the people in the morning that he has done so and so, whereas Allah has concealed it. And he does a deed during the day and when it is night he tells the people, whereas Allah has concealed it.) SAHIH MUSLIM Hadith # 5306.

68. *See Id.*

69. (Ye are the best of Peoples, evolved for mankind, enjoining what is right, forbidding what is wrong, and believing in Allah. If only the People of the Book had Faith, it were best for them: among them are some who have Faith, but most of them are perverted transgressors.) THE HOLY QURAN 3:110.

3

Humanitarian International Law in Islam: A General Outlook

Ahmed Zaki Yamanai

I. HUMANITARIAN LAW AND
HUMANISTIC LAW

Needless to say, any monograph on humanitarian international law in Islam is perforce lengthy, because divine law is beyond the grasp of the human endeavor. All I can promise is to try to cover as much ground as possible rather than fight shy of exposing my inadequacy—the principle being "If you cannot take it all. Don't leave it all." What then do we mean by humanitarian international law?

Authors of international law books use two different terms, namely, "humanitarian law" and "the rights of man." To me the rights of man refer to humanistic law. *Humanitarian law* is derived from humanity or humanitarianism, while *humanistic law* is a derivative of man or humanism. Authors attribute to these two terms different meanings.

I personally prefer that each term should have a separate meaning: humanitarian law in this review shall mean the law which has as its object the rights of man in time of war and during armed conflict, while humanistic law shall mean the law that regulates the rights of man in time of peace.

Some people may feel uneasy when I speak of humanitarian international law in Islam. For how can we identify a branch of Islamic international law and specifically call it "humanitarian" when we know that all Islamic law is a humanitarian law and that Islam's name itself is derived from the Arabic word "peace." I was beset by that same feeling. But I set it aside as rooted in nonessential considerations. Indeed I intend to study a term used in contemporary language and given a restricted meaning; and the truth is that although peace is the spirit of Islam, yet peace is not the only truth in the human community which also knows competition and internecine fighting in a savage way.

The tolerant religion of Islam was largely responsible for moving humanity from the darkness of Greco-Roman ideas about war to the light in which the enemy was guaranteed certain rights and the fighting man was assured of certain protections. This move was great in relation to the ferocity of war as it was known to the Greeks and the Romans, and is still great in relation to that which we are witnessing today despite the efforts, exerted over four centuries of contemporary international law to curb the horrors of war and alleviate its woes.

A Word of Truth

Islamic *Shari'ah*[1] has established guideposts for the Islamic state to follow in its international relations, and has set the lines of its behavior toward other states. The Holy Qur'an contains numerous verses in this connection from which I quote the following as an example: "Who, if we establish them in the land, will observe the Prayer, and pay the *Zakat,* urge to what is reputable and restrain from what is disreputable—to Allah belongs the issue of affairs." [22(42)][2]

War in Islam has one of two goals: protection of the land of Muslims against invasion; or consolidation of the Islamic religion lest it should be wiped out. This is why war pursues virtue, establishes justice and honors the individual. The *Qur'an* points out the purpose of war when it says, "Fight them until there is no dissension and the religion is entirely Allah's." [12(193)]

Philosophy of Humanitarian International Law: The Islamic Concept

Under the conditions mentioned above, what is the role of humanitarian international law? Humanitarian international law must reconcile two contradictory issues: humanitarian considerations and the requirements of necessity. Humanitarian considerations urge amity and compassion, while necessity pushes for force and competition. The Prophet summed up this role of humanitarian international law in Islam when he said, "I am the Prophet of gentle compassion; I am the Prophet of fierce battle."[3] He combined passion and battle, placing compassion before battle in order to impress upon the Muslim fighter that he is the hand of justice, and not the sword of depravity. As regards the term "fierce battle," although it means a "bloody fight" and a "slaughter," it also connotes the fighting of sedition rather than mere combat. The Arabic word for "fierce battle" also implies "repair," "reform," or "adjustment"; these are the objects of fighting in Islam and are a control on the behavior of Muslim fighters. It is in these sublime meanings that "compassion" and "fierce battle" meet.

Swiss jurist Jean Pictet attempt to summarize the philosophy of humanitarian international law in an encompassing sentence. The best he could come up with was the principle "Do to others what you would have done to yourself."[4] We know that the noble Prophet said, "one will not be a believer unless one wishes for one's brother what one wishes for oneself." This means that adherence to the philosophy of humanitarian international law is, in Islam, a branch of the faith, and, after the five basic elements of Islam, is itself a basic pillar.

It was the culture of Islam that was the first to innovate the rules that constitute humanitarian international law. Returning crusaders carried some of these rules back and some others were studied in Italian land Spanish universities from which the fathers of modem international law emerged. Although modern humanitarian international law, the law that governs the rights of man during times of war, has been recorded in written documents, largely as a result of the efforts of the Swiss humanist Henry Dunant,[5] its principles cannot be divorced from their customary origins. This fact was recorded in the preamble to the Second Protocol supplementing the Geneva Conventions. It expressly states that whatever is not governed by the written rules is indeed governed by the rules of international custom, and protected by the principles of humanity and the dictates of the common conscience.[6] The role of Islamic Shari'ah in establishing those customs is well known; its merits are without limits and its injunction to adhere to the directives of conscience is a principle without limitation.

It is true that the rules of humanitarian international law are insensitive, but in Islam instinct is commanded by God who formulates its requirements in the Qur'an, his Holy Book, and in the traditions of Muhammad, his gentle Prophet, as a duty of mankind and an obligation decreed for enforcement and respect. "He has formed people by nature to follow, there is no alteration of the creation of Allah. That is the right religion, but most of the people do not know." [30(30)]

Assuming that necessity is the human limitation affecting the principle of "wishing good for others," Islamic Shari'ah has taken a stance which is not taken in the West. It urges the Muslim to be altruistic even in case of necessity, and makes altruism a desirable quality of the Faithful: "But preferring (them) over themselves even though there was want amongst them." [59(9)] Even if Muslim wishes to invoke necessity, his right to do so is qualified and limited by the Holy Qur'an which says, "But if anyone is compelled, without oppression or deliberate transgression, no guilt rests upon him." [2(173)]

[6(145)] [16(115)] The Qur'an ensures that a Muslim's action in cases of necessity is not left to his whim, for he is required to act without oppression and without deliberate transgression.

II. GENERAL CONCEPTS OF HUMANITARIAN INTERNATIONAL LAW IN ISLAM: ARMED CONFLICT OF A NONINTERNATIONAL NATURE AND ARMED CONFLICT OF AN INTERNATIONAL NATURE

Moving from this introduction to a direct discourse, I think it is best to follow the method of the Swiss jurist Jean Pictet. Hence, I will first deal with the general principles of humanitarian international law in Islam in the light of presently established international humanitarian principles in positive law. Armed conflict—or fighting—in the established Islamic nation is divided into two general categories: conflicts referred to by Al-Mawardi[7] as "wars of public interest" and "wars against polytheists and apostates."

A. Wars of Public Interest

By way of clarification, I would like to say a few words about the various types of wars of public interest.[8]

1. Fighting Belligerents and Highway Robbers

Belligerents and highway robbers are corrupt individuals grouping themselves to raise arms and commit highway robbery, taking property and life and hindering travel. Obviously, we are dealing here with a kind of fighting which falls within humanistic law, the law that regulates the rights of man in times of peace, rather than humanitarian international law, which regulates the rights of man during times of war. Therefore, the rules pertaining to the former represent a penal legislation to be applied by the state within its territory to the inhabitants of such territory by virtue of state sovereignty. The stern penalty prescribed by the Noble Verse is attributable to the ugliness of the crime and to the fact that it threatens the security of the community.

2. Fighting Rebels and Dissident Kharijites

Rebels and dissident Kharijites[9] are Muslims who rebel against the *Imam* (ruler), differ with the community, and adopt a reprehensible, innovated school of thought—Mazhab. In Islamic history dissident Kharijites differed with 'Ali Ibn Abu Talib and rebelled against him when he agreed to arbitration with Mo'awiyah; they settled in a place called Harura and were therefore known as the Haruriyah. Their leaders were 'Abd Allah Ibn al-Kawwa al-Yashkari and Shabat at-Tamini. A group of these dissidents interrupted 'Ali while he was delivering a sermon from his pulpit with shouts of "The only Arbiter is God." To which Ali answered: "A word of truth intended to cover up a falsehood." We owe you three things: "We shall not bar you from the mosques of God where you will invoke the name of God; We shall not take the initiative of fighting with you; We shall not withhold booty from you as long as your hands are with us."

If these rebels should show their dissent while they are mingled with the loyal Muslims the rule is that the *Imam* should clarify to them the unsoundness of their belief and the invalidity of their innovation so that they return to the true and agree with the community. The *Imam* may impose punishment upon those who show overt corruption in order to discipline them or deter others from following them, but this punishment should not reach execution or the infliction of a *Hadd* (one of the penalties prescribed in the Qur'an for certain capital crimes). The position toward dissidents is similar to that toward opposition parties. Their freedom to express their opinions is guaranteed so long as their opposition is not accompanied by acts of violence or supported by force. If they do either, the *Imam* shall have the right to punish them with *Ta'zir* (discretionary penalty below a *Hadd*). This case has nothing to do with humanitarian international law.

As a matter of fact, disobedience of the *Imam*, whether the disobedient group aggregates under a leader or not, is a kind of civil war which requires fighting the rebels voluntarily. The Holy Qur'an says in this connection; "If two parties of the believers fight, set things right between them, and if one of the two parties oppresses the other, fight the one which is oppressive until it returns to the affairs of Allah, then if it returns, set things right between them justly and act fairly; verily Allah loves those who act fairly," [149(9)] Oppression here may include transgression in combat or turning away from peace.

Fighting against rebels and Kharijites corresponds to the fighting referred to in article 3 of all the Geneva Conventions.

In case of armed conflict not of an international character occurring in the territory of one of the high Contracting Parties, each Party to the conflict shall be bound to apply, as minimum, the following provisions:

1. Person Taking no active part in the hostilities, including members of armed forces who have laid down their arms and those placed hors de combat by sickness, wounds, detention, or any other cause, shall in all cases be treated humanely without any adverse distinction founded on race, color, religion or faith, sex, birth or wealth or any similar criteria.

To this end, the following acts are and shall remain prohibited at any time or in any place whatsoever with respect to the above mentioned persons:

    a. Violence to life and person, in particular murder of all kinds, mutilation, cruel treatment and torture;

    b. Taking of hostages;

    c. Outrages upon personal dignity, in particular, humiliating and degrading treatment;

    d. The passing of sentences and the carrying out of executions without previous judgment pronounced by a regularly constituted court affording all the judicial guarantees which are recognized as indispensable by civilized people

2. The wounded and the sick shall be collected and cared for.[10]

Exclusive attention was given to this category of fighting by the second of the two protocols that came out of the 1976 General Conference for the Development of Humanitarian law.[11] This protocol, however, was beset with so many stumbling blocks that one can safely say that it was almost stillborn. Like the article quoted above, this protocol's basic guarantees are restricted to those who do not play a positive role in the acts of aggression, including the wounded, the sick, and prisoners. To these people it offers guarantees which do not go beyond those granted by the previously quoted article. In connection with the ways and methods of war, the protocol adds provisions which prohibit vengeance and treachery and do not allow that the living be deprived of the right to seek refuge. It also establishes principals for the protection for civilians and children. These protections and these guarantees are but a part of the provisions extended to those involved in armed conflict having an international nature, as I shall explain in part B of this section.

It may behoove us here to compare these provisions with the statement made by Ali Ibn Abu-Talib to his soldiers during his war with Mo'awiyah.

> If you defeat them, do not kill a man in flight, do not finish off a wounded man, do not uncover a pudendum, or mutilate the dead, do not rip open a curtain or enter a house without permission, do not take any of their property, do not torture or harm their women even though they may insult your leaders, and member God, mayhap you will have knowledge.

The regulations of the Geneva Conventions pertaining to armed conflict of a noninternational are less bold and their guarantees are much weaker than those contained in the provisions pertaining to international armed conflict. The philosophy underlying the division of the Convention provisions on humanitarian law into two protocols is, itself, based on the desire to withhold the greater guarantees from combatants in noninternational armed conflict. As for the Islamic system, it takes a diametrically opposed stance. It takes a more sympathetic view of armed conflict with rebels und Kharijites, offering them rules and guarantees that it withholds from polytheists and apostates engaged in international armed conflict.

3. *The Fight Against Apostates*

The fight against apostates is the fight against people who were declared Muslims but who later reneged their Islam. About these, the prophet said, "He who changes his religion, kill him." He also said, "A Muslim's blood shall not be lawfully shed except for three causes; atheism after belief; adultery after marriage; or killing a person otherwise than in retaliation for another person." The relationship between this fighting and international law falls within the sphere of humanistic law, the law that regulates the rights of man in times of peace, rather than humanitarian law.

But if apostates should move to a land separate from the land of Muslims where they cannot be reached, if they become a de facto government exercising sovereignty over part of the Islamic territory, then they should be fought on account of their apostasy. War shall be waged against them, after due notice and warning, in much the same manner that war is waged against foreign enemies. There are, however, four differences between a war against such apostates and a war against foreign enemies:

(1) No truce can be negotiated, nor peace concluded with apostates in their own land, whereas peace can be made with foreign enemies;

(2) It is not permissible to compromise with apostates by acknowledging their apostasy in return for a financial consideration though such compromise can he concluded with a foreign enemy;

(3) Apostates cannot be enslaved, nor can their woman be taken captive though foreign enemies can be enslaved and their women can be taken captive (jurists differ on this point); and

(4) The property of apostates shall not be acquired as booty, whereas the victorious combatants shall own the spoils taken from a foreign enemy.

Those who refrain from paying the *Zakat* (alms) to the *Imam* shall be likened to apostates and accorded the same treatment in the fighting. It is on the basis of the opinion (Fatwah) of Abu Bakr and the Prophet's Companions[12] that the Apostasy War was justified.

B. Wars against Polytheists and Apostates

I now move on to armed conflict having an international nature. As promised, I shall cover briefly the provisions of humanitarian international law dealing with this kind of encounter, by reviewing the most important of the general principles governing it. Without fear of being blamed for generalization, I can say that, in positive law, all these principles stem from an important general concept stated in the preamble of the St. Petersburg Declaration of 1868 to the effect that the only legitimate object of war to be pursued by states is to weaken the enemy's military strength.[13] Consequently, whatever lies within the purview of this object does not conflict with the requirements of humanitarian international law, while anything beyond this purview is not precluded by a customary or contractual rule will constitute a transgression against what was called in the Second Protocol "the principles of humanity and the dictates of the universal conscience." In this sense, the Holy Qur'an says, "Fight in the cause of Allah those who fight you, but do not transgress limits, for God loves not transgressors." [2(190)] God has thus prohibited that fighting should go beyond its goals and regards excess as a transgression which He does not love. The Holy Verse is explicit in setting the goal of the fight as the repelling of aggression.

The Prophet is reported to have said, "A powerful and aggressive people once waged war on a weak and tranquil people and God helped the latter to overcome their enemy, but the victors abused and oppressed the vanquished, thereby incurring the wrath of God to the day of resurrection." This is the general principle or basis for a number of rules limiting the freedom of the Islamic State with regard to its mode of conduct. I will group these rules under three headings: (1) the use of arms; (2) the treatment of the enemy in battle; and (3) the treatment of prisoners of war.

1. The Use of Arms

Humanitarian thought is keen on alleviating the ferocity of military conflict as much as possible. As a means of reducing the cruelty of war, it restricts the combatant's right to choose the arms used and precludes the use of arms that cause unwarranted pain. However, it still shies from laying a definitive rule in this connection and the general rules formulated to achieve this end are weak and fragmentary.

The latest of such rules are laid in article 35 of the first Protocol of the Geneva Convention of 1949.[14] This article contains two rules relevant to this discussion. The first states, "In any armed conflict, the right of the Parties to the conflict to choose methods or means of warfare is not unlimited."[15] This wording is so vague that we can safely say that it reads more like advice or an entreaty than a binding obligation and a rule with which signatories must comply. The second provides, "it is prohibited to employ weapons, projectiles and material and methods of warfare of a nature to cause superfluous injury or unnecessary suffering."[16] This provision trembles in the face of the defiant passions of the states; it does not dare to prohibit decisively the use of total destruction arms, but resorts to the evasive stratagem of adopting a language which leaves the door wide open for the violence and injustice to which some states may be inclined. The St. Petersburg Declaration of 1868 may be said to constitute a greater restriction on the discretion of states because it requires that suffering should not exceed the limit necessary to render the enemy incapable of fighting.[17] I ask myself, "How did states muster the courage a century ago to include this restriction in the St. Petersburg Declaration as a desire or an aspiration, and then lose that courage when they were converting that Declaration into binding and mandatory legal provisions?"

I may be accused of ignoring international conventions that proscribe the use of certain arms of total destruction, such as the Geneva Protocol of 1925,[18] which prohibits the use of asphyxiating and poisonous gasses and germ and chemical weapons. A closer look at these conventions will show, however, that they were concluded to proscribe a weapon after it actually had been used to the detriment of humanity, or were most probably signed after the world had discovered a more powerful and deadlier weapon. Are we not witnesses today to a byzantine discussion about the proscription of nuclear weapons? No wonder, therefore, that article 36 of the First Protocol[19] should leave the desirability of using new weapons to the discretion of the signatory states. An actual agreement among states on such a matter is most improbable.

It is most probable that this problem was not of any concern to early Muslim jurists because it was not known to them. The weapons used in wars at the time lacked the technology which could qualify them as weapons of total destruction or as causing damages in excess of what is necessary to put the enemy out of action. However, later Islamic scholars did not miss this point completely. In fact, I have read that Khalil Al-Maliki, in his summary book on *Jihad* (holy war), said that a combatant is prohibited from using weapons capable of causing his opponent injuries that exceed the possible benefit achieved by the combatant. He gave an example which was consistent with the military thinking of his time, that the use of poisoned arrows was prohibited because such arrows could cause unjustified suffering to the victim. The rule in this connection is specific in condemning violence—it even specified the weapon concerned and proscribed its use.

The opinion of this scholar is supported by the general rules of Islam which prohibit excessive killing even when it is authorized. The Holy Verse says, "If anyone is killed wrongfully, we give to his next-of-kin authority but let him not be extravagant in killing." [17(33)] In this vein, Abu Huraira reports the following incident about the Prophet. When he dispatched Abu Huraira with a group of men to do battle, he said to the group, "If you come across so and so and so and so, burn them both." But when he was preparing to leave, the Prophet said, "I ordered you to burn those two, but God alone punishes with fire. So if you find them, kill them." This change of mind on the part of the Prophet from burning to killing constitutes in my opinion a tradition of proscribing injuring the enemy with a weapon that causes unjustified pain.

The Prophet's saying that "[f]airness is mandatory. If you kill, do it properly," is, in my opinion, a direct provision in this matter. Omar actually removed Khalid because the latter had killed the enemy excessively. He said, "Khalid's sword is indeed violent." He liked the way 'Amr Ibn Al-As fought because his battles resulted in less killing. Omar called 'Amr's war "a lenient war."[20] In a tradition of the Prophet reported by Ibn Hatim, Muhammad says: "If one of you fights his brother, let him avoid the face because God created Adam in His own image." Injury to the face is prohibited or at least disapproved, except in necessity, thereby preventing the excessive use of weapons beyond humanitarian limits.

In protecting the enemy from suffering, Islam has surpassed the achievements about which humanitarian western civilization is boasting. Let no one try to disprove what I have stated by alleging that Ali Ibn Abu Talib burnt a number of his own allies, the followers of Ibn As-Sa'uda Abd Allah ibn Saba who were Jewish, because they were saying that God had become incarnate in Ali, with the intent of misleading Muslims. This story cannot be found in history books, although of a group of people at the outset of Islam by Companions the Prophet who were virtuous Muslims is not an incident that would be ignored by historians or one that historians would fail to refute and totally overlook.

Islamic thought has another goal in connection with weapons, namely to prohibit their random use in a manner that would affect both combatants and noncombatants and hit military targets indiscriminately. The combatant has thus a twofold obligation: to distinguish the combatant from the noncombatant and to direct his weapon to the former; and to make a distinction between military and nonmilitary targets and confine his attacks to the former. The obligation of the Muslim combatant to make the first distinction is supported by a tradition according to which the Prophet saw people gathering after one of his battles and sent a man to find out the reasons. The man returned and told the Prophet that a woman had been killed, whereupon the Prophet said, "She certainly could not have been fighting." In another instance, some Muslims, acting like their enemies, killed a number of children. Angrily, the Prophet said, "Why is it that some people are so aggressive today as to kill progeny?" These comments on the part of the Prophet are clear indications of the necessity of making a distinction between combatants and noncombatants, and constitute disapproval of the random use of weapons against combatants and noncombatants.

The Muslim combatant is permitted to the point where he does not distinguish between combatants and noncombatants. In Islam, a combatant is a man fit for fighting, whether he takes part in the battle or not. Islam imposes on the Muslim combatant the duty to double his caution if there are noncombatant Muslims among the enemy in order to avoid hurting such noncombatant Muslims and incurring the ensuing disgrace or sin. It may help the enemy to distinguish the combatant from the noncombatant if combatants wear a special uniform or carry a particular badge. It is reported that the Prophet used to wear a special robe (Aba) during military marches. There is no evidence, however, that there was any organized effort during the lifetime of the Prophet to provide combatants with a uniform, except for a report that in the battle of Badr Muslims wore a distinctive sign consisting of a piece of wool. This led al-Tabari to state in his interpretation or exegesis, "Wool was used for the first time on that day," meaning the day of the battle of Badr.

Regarding the Muslim combatants' obligation to distinguish military targets from civilian targets, Ash-Shafi[21] stated that catapults could be directed against a fortress but not toward inhabited houses. The idea expressed by Ash-Shafi that inhabited dwellings be spared (unless these are too close to the fortress) can only be justified by an obligation to limit assaults to military targets. Let us not forget that destruction for the sake of destruction is prohibited in Islam, especially if, as in the majority of cases, the land would revert to Muslims after the conquest. Scholars have made a distinction between property acquired by Muslims by force and property acquired by chance or occupied as a result of a peace. In fact, assault against military targets without justification is a form of transgression prohibited by God, and a departure from justice ordered by the Almighty when He said, "My Lord has commanded justice." [42(15)] God declared His love for those who act justly when He said, "Allah loves those who deal fairly." [5(42)] To explain the meaning of justice, He said, "We shall place the balances of justice on the day of resurrection." [71(41)]

2. *The Treatment of the Enemy in Battle*

This may consist of actions directed at the enemy in combat or at the civilian population in the territory of the enemy. I shall begin with the combatant. The first precept of humanitarian international law may be that a combatant should refrain from killing, wounding, torturing or ill-treating the enemy, whenever the latter becomes incapable of combat, whether through surrender of his weapon or through surrender of his person.

This basic rule of humanitarian international law is recorded in article 23(c) of the Hague Convention of 1907[22] and confirmed by article 38 of the First protocol[23] and article 7 of Second Protocol[24] to the Geneva Convention. In fact, the humanitarian international law of Islam is extremely interested in this principle which is the object of many verses and traditions. God Almighty orders Muslims to act straight with their enemies when he says, "As long as they act straight with you, act straight with them; verily Allah Loves those who show piety." [9(7)] He also orders Muslims to be inclined to peace. "If they incline to peace, incline thou to it, and set thy trust upon

Allah." He also denies the Muslim combatant the right to injure his foe if the latter withdraws and ceases to fight. The Holy Qur'an says in this connection, "If then they withdraw from you and do not fight against you, but offer you peace, Allah has not opened for you a way against them." [4(90)] Hisham Ibn Hakim said, "I testify that I have heard God's Messenger say that God will torture those who torture people on this earth," The prophet also says "Cultivate the goodwill of people and treat them gently, do not attack them until you have called them (to embrace the faith). I would rather have you bring me any urban or nomad people having embraced Islam, than bringing me their women captives after having killed their men."

Islamic war is, therefore, instigated by kindness inasmuch as it prefers cultivation of goodwill to killing and does not allow killing without a pressing necessity.

The second rule, which is as important as the above-mentioned principle and is connected to it, prohibits a combatant from resorting to treachery in order to kill, injure, or capture his enemy. This rule is upheld by article 23(b) and article 24 of The Hague Convention of 1907[25] and dealt with in detail in article 37 of the First Protocol.[26] In this connection the rules of humanitarian international law make a distinction between ruse and treachery, and allow ruse but prohibit treachery, which is defined in the said protocol as "perfidy."

Islamic theory also upholds this distinction. The Prophet has described war as a ruse. Therefore, an enemy may be killed in surprise. The Prophet used to send his agents to infiltrate the ranks of the enemy and to spread defeatism and rumors among the enemy in order to undermine their morale. During the battle of the trench (Al-Khandaq), Na'im Ibn Mas'ud came to the Prophet and said, "O Messenger of God, I have embraced Islam but my people do not know that I have. Command me to do what you wish." The Prophet answered, "You are but one man if you stay with us, but go and dishearten the enemy if you can, for ruse is invaluable in war."

An interesting example of ruse is given by Ibn Shaddad in his book, "an-Nawadir as-Shultaniyah," where combatants put hogs on board ships instead of soldiers in order to mislead the enemy. In another example it is reported that Hajjaj Ibn Alat as-Salmi embraced Islam and fought with the Prophet at Khaybar. When Khaybar was conquered, he said, "O Messenger of God, I have property in Makkah with my wife Umm Shaybah daughter of Abu Talha, as well as assets with various merchants of Makkah, allow me O Messenger of God to go there." The Prophet gave him permission to go, whereupon he said, "O Messenger of God, I shall perforce have to lie there." The Prophet told him to say what had to be said. In other words, the Prophet's permission was sought by Hajjaj that he might resort to ruse with the inhabitants of Makkah in order to recover his property and assets. So, when he reached Makkah, his people asked him about news from Khaybar. He told them that Muhammad had suffered an unprecedented defeat and that his followers had either been killed or taken captive and that the people of Khaybar refrained from killing Muhammad but would send him to Makkah to be executed there in retaliation, whereupon the Makkans rejoiced. Hajjaj took this opportunity to ask them to help him recover his property so that he could return to Khaybar and buy some of the booty before other merchants arrived. They returned his property at an unheard-of speed.

According to An-Nawawi,[27] scholars are unanimous in allowing ruse in war with the unbelievers whenever this is possible, unless there is a covenant or an assurance of protection given to them. The Holy Verse says, "Do not violate oaths after their confirmation." [5(90)] Islam, however, does not permit treachery. The Prophet once said: "He who cheats us is not one of as." When Abu Jandal Ibn Suhayl fled to Medinah from the polytheists of Makkah, he heard that the prophet intended to return him to his people in execution of the prophet's covenant with the latter. Abu Jandal stood up among the Muslims and asked them if they would return him to the polytheists who would torture him to renounce Islam. The Prophet answered, "Treachery is not good for us, even to save a Muslim from the law of polytheists."

Similarly, it is reported that 'Umar Ibn al-Khattab heard that a Muslim soldier had said to a Persian combatant, "Do not be afraid," then killed the Persian. Thereupon Umar wrote to the commander of the army in these terms, "As God is my witness, if I hear of anyone who does that I shall cut his neck." In this connection, ash-Shafi' says, "Whatever is accepted by the Muslims and receives their consensus as being permissible in the land of Islam is not forbidden in the land of unbelievers, and whatever is forbidden in the land of Islam, is also forbidden in the land of unbelievers. He who commits a forbidden act will receive the punishment prescribed by God for his offense. The fact that the act was committed in the land of unbelievers shall not reduce his guilt."

An Islamic combatant is also forbidden to annihilate the enemy, threaten them with annihilation, or deny them the right to surrender. This same rule is laid down in article 40 of the First Protocol[28] and article 4(1) of the Second Protocol[29] in support of the text of article 23(d) of Hague Convention of 1907.[30] However, the Islamic rule on this matter predates all others. The precepts of Islam on the subject are included in the purport of the verses quoted above, whereby Muslims are commanded to incline to peace if the enemy inclines to it and are prohibited from killing an enemy who withdraws from the battle, surrenders his weapon and his person.

It has never been reported that any people were annihilated or killed as a group after the defeat of the enemy. The attitude of the Prophet toward the inhabitants of Makkah after it was conquered is the best evidence which can he adduced in this connection. The Prophet freed them all and they are known in history as "at-Tulaqa"—those who remained heathen until the surrender of Makkah and were set free. The Arabic word "Taliq" means freed or released. "Tulaqa" is its plural form.

Here a whisper may spread about the fate of Bani Qurayza. But the full story of these people disproves the suspicion it raises. We know that the Messenger of God entrusted Bani Qurayza with the protection of the Muslims' rear during the Battle of the Trench (al-Khandaq), that Muslims were in such distress in that battle that the Prophet offered the tribe of Ghatfan one third of the date crop of Medinah if they did not fight him and his companions, and that the Jews of Bani Qurayza did not hesitate to miss the opportunity to attack the Muslims after breaking their promise and joining forces with the polytheists. When the distress ended, the Prophet called Ali and gave him the command of the campaign against Bani Qurayza. When Ali drew near to their fortifications, he heard them insult the Prophet. Next morning, the tribe of al-Aws hurried toward the Prophet saying, "O Messenger of God, these are our clients and not those of the tribe of al-Khazraj, and yesterday you treated the clients of our brethren (meaning the tribe of Bani Qaynaqa' whom the Prophet had freed) well." This discussion ended and the Jews agreed to arbitration by the head of the tribe of al-Aws, Sa'd Ibn Ma'az, who decided their fate according to the precepts of their own religion and the rules set forth in their Book, namely that the men be killed, their property be divided, and their women and children be led into captivity. This incident is not a form of annihilation, but represents an award rendered in an arbitration requested by the party concerned and accepted by them as a judgment and as Law. This is in full agreement with the rules set forth in the Geneva Convention of 1949 with regard to prisoners of war and protected persons. The rule applied to Bani Qurayza is not Islamic, but an application of Deuteronomy, the enemy's Book.

This deed, attributed to Islam, was in fact a result of deference to the law of an enemy, an enemy who was excessively vindictive and very stubborn. How can we but praise the Muslims' attitude, knowing that when the temperature soared on that summer day, the Prophet said, "Do not add the heat of this day to the heat of the sword; defer their execution until they cool down," Furthermore, they refused to choose the Prophet for an arbitrator, and we know that his ruling regarding their neighbors, the tribes of Bani an-Nadir and Bani Quynaqa, affected their property but not their lives.

I shall relate a story reported by Abu Hurayrah because it confirms the Islamic ruling in this connection. Abu Hurayrah said that he had heard the Messenger of God relate the following parable. "An ant bit a Prophet whereupon he ordered the anthill to be burnt. Then God said to him, 'If an ant bites you, would you burn a whole community of ants who sing the praises of God?'"

As regards refuge, this is covered by an express Quranic text. God says, "If one of the polytheists asks thy protection, grant him protection until he hears the word of God, then see that he reaches his place of security; that is because they are a people who have no knowledge."[9(6)] Al-Awza'i[31] was once questioned about the verse: "And where is his place of security; do not think that if he says my place of security is in Constantinople, we should take him there?" Al-Awza'i answered, "If he reaches one of their fortresses or one of their strongholds, this would be his place of security." Al-Awza'i was then asked, "What if the polytheists are met by a Muslim patrol in their country before they reach their place of security?" Al-Awza'i answered, "The patrol should not stand in their way." He was then asked about the enemy who enters Muslim land under a safe conduct which is valid until his return and, on the way back to his country, climbs a mountain within his own territory but is forced by strong winds to return to Muslim land. If the enemy then says, "I am here under safe conduct, what should be done?" Al-Awza'i answered, "I am of the opinion that he is entitled to remain protected by the safe conduct."

The verse leads to a brief comment on "safe conduct" or "assurance of protections." This is one of the generous Islamic systems that characterize Islamic law and distinguish it from other laws. "Assurance of protection" prohibits slaying, enslavement, and the taking of property, providing the protection was given voluntarily by a sane Muslim. It is valid when it is given by a private citizen, as well as when it is given by an *Imam* or an *Amir* (ruler). Assurance of protection—whether given by a free man or a slave, by a man or a woman—usually covers a small number of people. According to scholars it applies to not more than ten individuals, a small caravan, or a fort. So, if a Muslim says to his adversary, "Lay down your weapon first and fear not," he has given him an assurance of protection. And if the enemy leaves his fort on the basis of a signal of assurance of protection, he may not be killed and must be retuned to his place of security. I would say more about the rules governing "assurance of protection" but for my desire to cover the topic of the topic of this article.

The Islamic combatant stay does not inflicts collective penalties, especially those tinted with vengeful deterrence. This rule is implied by the provisions of article 46 of the First Geneva Convention,[32] article 47 of the Second Geneva Convention,[33] article 20 of the First Protocol[34] and article 15 of the Second Protocol.[35] All these texts prohibit acts of deterrent vengeance against the wounded, the sick and the shipwrecked, as well as against individuals, ships, or material protected by the conventions.

The international community may have felt that its human endeavors in this were held deficient when the United Nations organization formulated the Treaty of 1948 on the crime of collective annihilation and genocide.[36] Article 2 of the Treaty defined the crime of collective annihilation as: (1) killing the members of a community; (2) causing grievous physical or mental injury to the members of a community; (3) willful imposition of living conditions capable of destroying or breaking the life of the whole or part of the community; (4) imposition of regulations intended to prevent procreation in the community; and (5) moving the children of the community to another community by force.[37]

Prohibition of collective punishment in Islam is of general application. It is not restricted to any particular class or group and makes no discrimination. The general rule in Islam is that "[n]o burden bearer bears the burden of another" [53(38)] and that "God lays not upon anyone more than he has capacity for; what he has gained stands to his credit and what he has piled up stands against him." I do not hesitate to say that the detailed provisions of the convention on the crime of annihilation are covered by the injunction and prohibitions of the Islamic theory and may be regarded as an explanation and expounding of its precepts.

As regards vengeful deterrence, there are verses in the Holy Qur'an that set forth the principle of punishment. "The recompense of any evil deed is an evil like it." [53(31)] "As for those who have piled up evil deeds, the recompense of an evil deed is its like." [40(40)] "If you take vengeance, take it only in the measure that vengeance was taken from you; but assuredly if you endure patiently, it is better for those who patiently endure." [42(40–44)] "The sacred month for the sacred month, things sacred being subject to the law of retaliation; so if any make an attack upon you, make a like attack upon them; show piety toward God and know that God is with those who show piety." [2(195)] By their clear implication, these verses establish the principle of reciprocation in punishment. One may imply from these verses that they permit Muslims—in reciprocation—to practice vengeful deterrence against the enemy, if the latter practices it against them.

This inference, however, can be criticized on two counts. First, vengeful deterrence, in its modern meaning intended in the articles of humanitarian international law conventions, is an illegitimate action taken by a state in vengeance against another state with the intent to force the latter to accept the settlement of a dispute which had resulted from a previous illegitimate action taken by that latter state. Consequently, vengeful deterrence is an illegitimate action in retaliation for an illegitimate action. It is inconceivable, however, that Muslim forces who abide by the precepts of Islam would take illegitimate actions against the enemy which would justify acts of vengeful deterrence against them by the enemy. It ensues from the foregoing that the hypothetical case given lies beyond the scope of the proper application of Islamic precepts.

Second, the application of the rule of reciprocation, posed above, is, in Islam, subjected to an important limitation, namely, that a Muslim is not allowed to follow the example of the enemy in their misdeeds. Some people may wonder that virtue should rule in the midst of swords where the taking of human life is permissible. Indeed, where permission is given, no prohibitive restriction remains. But it is the war waged by virtue against transgressive vice, and it is illogical that war in defense of virtue should be waged in the field in a manner that violates the precepts of virtue in order to keep pace with the aggressors. War by Muslims is, therefore, restricted by virtue and never transgresses its limits even though the aggressors may transgress those limits. If the enemy mutilates the bodies of dead Muslims we do not do the same with their dead because the Prophet said, "Be careful not to mutilate the dead." When the polytheists killed Hamza Ibn Abd al-Muttalib in the battle of Uhud and ferociously mutilated his corpse, the Prophet was deeply affected by their action because Hamza was his uncle and the relative he loved most. Nevertheless, he never thought of mutilating the dead body of an enemy in subsequent wars. Even if the enemy keeps prisoners of war hungry or lets them die of thirst, the army of virtue does not act like the enemy in this matter because the Almighty has commanded that prisoners be treated well and the Prophet prohibited that any man condemn another to die of thirst.

The rules of humanitarian international law prescribe that the wounded and the sick be respected and be given humanitarian treatment. For this purpose medical organizations were given special consideration; it is from this concept that many of the rules imposed by the Geneva Convention of 1949 and their two protocols with regard to the wounded, the sick, the shipwrecked and medical organizations, were derived.[38] To show the extent of the respect with which Islam treats the wounded and the sick enemy, I merely recall the story about Salahuddin al-Ayyubi and Richard Coeur de Lion, when the latter was taken ill. Salahuddin covertly went to his enemy's camp and treated him until he recovered, although Richard was the strongest and the fiercest Crusader. The story shows that Muslims not only take care of the wounded and the sick who are in their care but also extend their care to include the wounded and the sick in their enemy's camp. Whatever the motive of such action may be, Salahuddin would not have acted as he did if the action was contrary to the teachings of Islam.

I do not think I would he wrong to say that the commission of an illegitimate act against the wounded, the sick, or others who are protected by temporal conventions cannot be accepted by the Islamic theory within the scope of the foregoing explanations.

It is worthy of mention here that the traditional Islamic theory did not deal in detail with the case of the shipwrecked at sea because the early Muslims concern with naval warfare was limited. Nevertheless, they regarded a ship as a fort and applied to her and to those on board the same rules that they applied to an enemy fort. I reiterate here that the rules set forth in humanitarian international accords in this connection constitute, in their entirety, details of the Islamic theory and are consistent with the practical application of its rules.

I shall now deal with the personal relations of combatants. Two major statements were made on the subject by the Prophet and by his first successor, Abu Bakr as Siddiq. The Prophet commanded, "Go forth in the name of God and with the blessing of the Messenger of God, but do not kill a very old man, nor a child, nor a woman, and do not be treacherous. Gather your prizes, set things right and do well, for God loves those who do well."

According to the two statements, the Muslim army is prohibited from killing an old man or a man suffering from incapacitating chronic disease, unless either has a say or counsel in the war. In the latter case they become leaders of atheism, about whom the Qur'an says, "[f]ight the leaders of unbelief, no oath will hold in their case, mayhap they will refrain." [9(12)] The truth is that this verse of general application came down in connection with the polytheists of Quraish. These were the people meant by Abu Bakr when he told the soldiers that they would meet people who had shaved the middle of their scalp. Abu Bakr counselled the soldiers to strike down with their swords those who served as strongholds of the devil.

The statement also prohibits the Muslim combatant from killing a child or a woman. Some Muslim scholars, holding views similar to those embodied in the rules of Western, humanitarian international law, maintain that immunity for a woman or a child is conditional upon their taking no part in military action. However, when Malik was asked whether Muslims should kill enemy women and children who stand on the ramparts and throw stones at the Muslims and cause confusion in their ranks, he answered, "The Prophet has forbidden the slaying of women and children." When Al-Awza'i was asked about women and children capable of guiding the enemy, he said that they were not to be killed on suspicion, but only if they actually acted as guides.

The killing of craftsmen, wage earners, and farmers who do not do battle, or those who follow the army but do not participate in the hostilities, such as merchants, is also prohibited by the statements. All of these people are given immunity because they are builders of prosperity who devote their efforts to civic matters; Islamic war does not have for its object the destruction or undermining of civilization and prosperity. Similarly, Islamic combatants may not kill monks, including all non-Muslim priests who live in cells or as hermits and are from the people of the book (Christians). This immunity is conditional upon monks or hermits remaining in their churches or cells.

I now must turn to the matter of depriving civilization and the civilian population of necessary food and water with the intent of starving them or forcing them to leave. Islam prohibits the slaughter of animals unless it is necessary for food. Islam prohibits the killing of animals by burning lest their economic value should be unjustifiably wasted. The Prophet has indeed prohibited the slaughter of any animal in captivity except for military necessity, as in the case where an animal can be used to strengthen the enemy. Also, if the Muslims go out on a campaign and do not find food to buy for a price, or if people refuse to sell food to them, they can take it by force to meet their needs. When Islam permitted water to be cut off from the enemy or polluted by blood, filth, or poison, it was aimed at combatants and not civilians. Permission for such acts was limited by necessity.

If Muslims depart and leave food that they do not need, they shall not burn it unless it would strengthen the enemy. This means that they are not allowed to destroy food except for military necessity. In Year 6 of the *Hijrah*,[39] Thumamah, Chieftain of Yamamah, decided to withhold supplies from Makkah, whose inhabitants depended on his tribe's grain, in order to force the Makkans to embrace Islam or until the Prophet ordered Thumamah otherwise. When Makkah was threatened with famine, its inhabitants asked that the embargo be removed, and the Prophet wrote to Thumamah to remove it. The Prophet even sent ripe dates to Makkah, while hostilities were at their peak, and he gave a big amount of money. Needless to say, Makkah was at war with the Prophet from the time he left it to emigrate. His ruling to prohibit destruction, which I shall deal with later, supports and complements my statement.

I now move to the subject of a combatant's obligation as regards the property of his adversary. Very briefly, I would say that the basic obligation here consists of distinguishing between military targets and civilian property so that the latter can be saved from destruction. Abu Bakr's commandment expressly prohibited destruction and who better knew about the Prophet's true guidance than his close companion who was with him in the cave.

Some scholars, however, held that it is permissible to destroy buildings and to cut down trees. These scholars looked to the Quranic text that says, "The offshoot in fruition which you cut or left standing on its trunk, it was by leave of God." [59(5)] They likened the "offshoot in fruition" to the "palm tree." They also drew support for this view from the fact that the Muslims had struck the dwellings of Bani an-Nadir on the orders of the Prophet, and the report that the Prophet had ordered the burning of the palace of Malik ibn Awf, the army commander of Tayif, and ordered the destruction of the catapult of the fortress of Thaqif, and the cutting down of their orchards.

A first glance at these reports shows us that they do not allow destruction in an absolute mannner, because a "tendershoot in fruition" did not mean a "palm tree," but the fruit of a palm tree. The Quranic text, "the offshoot in fruition which you cut or left standing on its trunk, it was by leave of God," cannot mean the trunk of the palm tree but only the fruit standing on such trunk and cutting fruit does not constitute destruction. Furthermore, Abu Zahrah explains the destruction of the houses of Bani an-Nadir as follows:

This was done because they had used them as forts in which they took shelter and caused injury to the Muslims, so it was imperative to destroy those homes or to try to do so to protect the Muslims against injury. The companions of the Prophet did only what was necessary, but when the Jews realized that they would hand over their houses to the Muslims and leave, they destroyed them completely.

This sense is clear in the Holy Verse because the destruction was not the work of the believers alone; the Jews themselves participated in it. "They made their houses desolate with their own hands and the hands of the believers." [59(12)] As for the artillery assaults on the forts, this was permissible because they represented strongholds of a powerful and rough people and because destruction of forts is intended to weaken the enemy. The threat to cut down the orchards of Tayif was made because the fruit was used to make wine. It should be noted, however, that in order to encourage the enemy to surrender and to reduce the bloodshed, the Prophet did not carry out his threat. I would say that we should add to the foregoing that when Al-Aswad, a slave belonging to a Jew surrendered to the Prophet with some cattle belonging to his master during the battle of Khaybar, the Prophet said to him, "Go somewhere else and send them toward their owner."

C. The Treatment of War Prisoners

Divine guidance has provided precepts on this subject which modern international covenants and customs have not been able to equal. The starting point in determining the legal status of a prisoner of war is that the enemy state is responsible for his safety; he is not under the control of the combatant who captured him. Islam has made this point quite clear in the Holy Qur'an which says, "Therefore, when you meet the unbelievers (in battle), smite their necks; at length when you have thoroughly subdued them, bind them fast, and then either freely or by ransom (sent them free) until war lay down its burden." [47(4)]

This Holy verse orders Muslims to fight until they subdue the unbelievers and achieve victory over them, then to bind them fast and take them prisoners. Once the enemy is in captivity, the fighting ends and there only remains one alternative: to free the captives out of generosity or for a ransom. The Islamic rule is that the order to fight has for its object the capture of the enemy. The option thereafter is left to the *Imam*. Consequently, the prisoner of war is in the custody of the *Imam*, who is responsible for his safety, until he decides his fate. This is why the Prophet said, "[l]et no one interfere with his brother's captive and then kill him." Abd Allah Ibn Amir[40] is reported to have sent to Ibn Umar a captive so that he might kill him. Ibn Umar said, "By God I swear that I shall not kill a bound man," meaning that he did not have the right to kill the man after he was taken prisoner and bound fast because the man's fate was then up to the *Imam*.

Scholars are unanimous that the captor is answerable for the killing of his captive, but they differ about the penalty. Al Awza'i says that if the captor kills his prisoner before reporting to the *Imam*, he shall be punished, and if he kills the prisoner after reporting to the *Imam*, he shall be punished and ordered to pay a fine equal to the price of the prisoner. Ash-Shafi'i, in contrast, holds that no fine is due unless he has killed a child or a woman.

Captivity does not, however, divest the prisoner of his status as a combatant. He is a combatant who has become incapable of fighting because he has fallen captive in our hands. Therefore, this status must be terminated by some action. The majority of scholars hold that in terminating captivity, the *Imam* has four options: generosity, ransom, killing, or captivity. The verse quoted above clearly states that the prisoner shall be freed either out of generosity or for a ransom. The two other options represent a doubtful addition.

I believe that freeing the prisoner out of generosity should be given first consideration by the *Imam*. And the *Imam* should not turn away from it unless the interests of Muslims dictate otherwise, because the Holy Verse mentioned that the former is to be given priority over the latter. God also says, "O Prophet, say to the prisoners who are in your hands, 'If God knows any good in your hearts, He will give you something better than what has been taken from you and will forgive you; God is Forgiving and compassionate.'" [8(70)]

Generosity may or may not be conditional. If it is, the prisoner will have to abide by the condition set forth in his case. The Prophet at the Battle Badr freed a poet called Abu 'Azzah after the latter had given a formal promise never to join anyone who is fighting the Prophet. But Abu 'Azzah joined the polytheists in the Battle of 'Uhud and was taken prisoner by the Muslims. He pleaded for mercy with the Prophet who said "I swear to God that you will not wipe your cheeks in Makkah saying that you had mocked Muhammad twice: A believer is never stung twice in the same burrow."

Ransom takes many forms. It may consist of money or property, military material, or something else. At Badr, for example, the ransom was to teach ten children. It is also reported that 'Umar Ibn Abd Al-'Aziz freed a hundred thousand prisoners in return for the city of Byzantium. If the ransom is the release of Muslim prisoners, this is called an exchange of prisoners. Islamic theory does not insist that the exchange should involve an equal number of prisoners on both sides and allows that a Muslim prisoner be the ransom for other Muslims. The Prophet ransomed al-'Uqaili, who had embraced Islam, for two Muslim men. Islamic practice also indicates the permissibility of allowing representatives of the enemy to visit the place where prisoners are held so that they may count them and make sure that their number is correct. Islamic practice also indicates that it is necessary to protect the means by which prisoners are transported, so as to reassure them during transportation thereafter.

Scholars differ on the execution of prisoners; some deny it and some allow it. It is reported from various sources that the Prophet killed prisoners. Ash-'Shai' and Abu Yusef[41] allowed killing if it benefited Muslims by strengthening God's religion and weakening its enemy.

In my opinion, the reports of the Prophet's actions are too simple. Instances in which the Prophet ordered that a captive be killed were limited and rare. Taken one by one, these precedents show that the death penalty was not inflicted upon the captive as such or in exercise of the *Imam*'s discretionary power to decide the captive's fate, but as a penalty for acts committed by the prisoners prior to captivity end outside the scope of the battle during which they were taken prisoner. It was a penalty for a crime perpetrated against the Prophet and against Islam, and not because they were captive. This situation is, in fact, envisaged and permitted by article 85 of the Geneva Convention on the prisoners of war, which states, "prisoners of war who are prosecuted under the laws of the Detaining Power, for acts committed prior to capture shall retain, even if convicted the benefits of this Convention."[42]

In case the prisoner had not committed any criminal act before captivity, the *Imam* would have no authority to order his execution, as one of the options he has in dealing with the prisoners. The objection that the public interest of Muslims may dictate the prisoner's execution is unacceptable inasmuch as the interest of the Muslims cannot be harmed by the freeing of a prisoner who is not known to have threatened Islam or Muslims. If there is a necessity calling for the execution of a captive, this would be a matter of expediency on the strength of the principle accepted by civilized states that "necessity knows no law." These distinctions most probably never occurred or may not have been very clear to the scholars who allow execution of prisoners.

In making this distinction, I am relying on the fact that fighting is not a crime as long as it stays within the rules and limits set for it, and captivity is not a penal procedure, but is a means of detaining a combatant so that he may not be able to continue fighting. God did not permit that a combatant be killed except in battle and for no other reason. The Holy Verse says, "If they fight you, slay them." [2(191)] The penalty here was not prescribed as a punishment that can be inflicted upon a prisoner, but as a punishment for an act committed by such prisoner prior to captivity, the latter being just the occasion which placed the criminal in the hands of the Islamic State and made him subject to its sovereign power. I would quote in this connection this statement made by Abu Yusef. He said, "If a combatant is in custody and thus cannot harm Muslims, he will not he blamed for his actions in war, unless he had committed an act before, which will then be held against him."

This is why the Prophet forbade the execution of Abu an-Najtari Ibn His-ham, because the latter was the least aggressive. As for 'Uqbah Ibn Abu Mu'ayt, he asked the Prophet when the latter ordered his execution, "Will you kill me O Muhammad out of all Quraish tribe?" And the Prophet answered: "Yes. Do you know what this man did to me? He came upon me as I was prostrate in prayer behind the shrine of Abraham, placed his feet on my neck and pressed, and he did not remove them, until I thought my eyes would bulge. And another time he brought the gestation sac of a ewe and threw it on my head when I was prostrate in prayer, and Fatimah came and washed if off my head." The singling out of 'Uqbah from among the captives and his execution did not constitute a precedent as regards the *Imam*'s right to execute prisoners, but was a punishment for his previous transgressions against the Prophet. An-Nadr Ibn al-Harith was among the worst men and a most stubborn infidel. These two were the only prisoners killed among the captives taken at Badr. Some of these captives were freed without ransom, including Abu al-'As ar-Rabi' al-Amawy and Abu 'Azzah the poet. I can even say without risk of exaggeration that such prisoners as were executed had committed acts regarded by Islamic jurisprudence as war crimes and crimes against humanity.

Scholars held varying views on the slaying of prisoners, detailed above, they were unanimous that polytheists who were taken prisoner and who embraced Islam were spared.

It behooves me to comment here on enslavement, because this is a topic that is sometimes associated with imprisonment and toward which Islam's attitude is often misunderstood. It is difficult to reconcile the adoption of slavery by Islam with the Quranic report that angels kneeled before Adam the man. Moreover, it is an uncontested principle of Islam that men are free and equal. An Arab or a white man does not have more merit than a non-Arab or a black man except by reason of piety. Another principle in Islam is that there is no coercion in religion, and argument should only be conducted in good spirit.

Enslavement found its way into Islamic thought through a back door opened in an era of human decadence. In fact, the Holy Qur'an always speaks of enslavement in the past tense. This back door represents the international state of mind at a given time in history when slavery was a current practice from which Muslims had suffered greatly, because Muslims, taken prisoner by their enemies, were enslaved and sold in slave markets. In lbn Jubayr's description of his journey, he reports having seen Muslim women and children in great hardship being offered for sale in the Italian slave markets. So, Muslims had no alternative but to reciprocate by also allowing enslavement. The humanitarian quality of slavery in Islam, however, was a far cry from the barbarism of the enemy.

Where slavery was permitted, Islam surrounded it with a protective fence of humanity and tenderness that raised the slave to the level of his master He was never called a slave, but a "lad" or "servant." The Prophet used to advise Muslims against saying "my slave or my handmaid." He told them to call their slaves "my lad or my lass." The Holy Qur'an says, "[O]f these whom your hands possess, believing maid-servants." [4(25)] And slaves can validly lead Muslims in prayer. 'Aishah, wife of the Prophet, had a slave who used to lead her in prayer.

Abu Dharr[43] was once asked why he would not take his slave's garment, which was of a better quality than his own, and give the lad another garment. He answered,

> I have heard the Messenger of God say, "They are your brethren whom God has placed under your care. So whoever has a brother under his care, let him feed that brother of the same food he eats and clothe him of the same material he wears, and refrain from asking him to perform works which is beyond his power, but if you do then help him out."

Islam has prohibited harming a slave. The expiation of unjust treatment of a slave is the manumission of that slave by his master. Slaves have also been allowed to purchase their freedom from their masters by agreement. Islam laid down the rules for such a purchase in a manner that almost imposes the will of a slave on his master. The Holy Verse reads as follows: "And if any of your slaves asks for a deed in writing [to earn their freedom], give them such a deed, if you know any good in them." [24(33)] The female slave who bears a son becomes a free woman upon the death of her master. She is emancipated by her progeny.

Slavery in Islam cannot be dealt with in a few lines, and detailed study of the system is beyond the scope of this article. My intent is merely to show that slavery is foreign to Islamic theory and that Islam absorbed the system with a true humanitarian sprit and molded it into a noble and gentle form. Even the term "slavery" (*Riq*) seems to derive from the Arabic word for "gentleness" (*Riqqa*) rather than from the Arabic word for "enslavement" (*Istirquq*). No wonder, therefore, that the Prophet should remember slaves on his deathbed and enjoin his nation saying, "Show piety to God in your treatment of the weak: women and slaves."

Indeed, slavery is foreign to Islam and it was natural that it should disappear with the disappearance of its causes. Now as the international community today condemns slavery, there is no doubt that slavery is no longer an option open to the *Imam* in dealing with prisoners of war. Muslims are therefore not allowed to enslave their prisoners, because in so doing they would be breaking the rules of their own religion.

Abu Yusef recommends that prisoners be treated well and be given food and clothing at the expense of the State, according to the Quranic Verse which says, "We feed you simply for the favor of God, desiring from you neither recompense nor gratitude." As a way of honoring the captive, the Holy Qur'an says, "They give good for His love to the poor, the orphan and the prisoner" [76(8)] And the Prophet says in this connection, "Recommend to one another that prisoners be well treated." In fact, Muslims were so courteous to the prisoners taken at the Battle of Badr, that they fed them ripe dates and bread. Salah ud-Din al-Ayybui set free a large number of crusaders when he did not have enough provisions to feed them, even though the release of such a large number of enemy combatants represented a menace to Muslims if they rejoined their own forces.

Now, as the *Imam* may not make a decision on the fate of a prisoner before the lapse of a certain period of time, the latter needs certain guarantees to protect him during the said period. It may be desirable that I should cover these guarantees briefly below. The first and foremost of these guarantees is respect for the person and honor of the prisoner, thus it is not permissible to torture him. The Prophet is reported to have said, "God will torture those who torture people on earth." He also forbade mutilation of the dead, even of a rabid dog. His disapproval of torture is shown in the case of Sahl Ibn 'Umar al-Amiri, who was an eloquent orator who devoted his talent to attacking the Prophet and his cause. When Umar Ibn Al-Khattab asked the Prophet to allow him to extract Suhayl's incisors so that the latter could no longer attack the Prophet, Muhammad said, "I will not disfigure him, lest God should disfigure me, even though I am a Prophet."

Humanitarian principles also dictate that the unity of the family be preserved as much as possible in case of captivity. Hence, scholars are unanimous in stating that it is not permissible to separate from a mother a child who has not changed his teeth or is not yet seven years old. Some scholars, however, allow the separation of spouses in the division of prizes and in case of sale. A prisoner is entitled to correspond with his family if he wishes to do so. The guarantee of correspondence is derived from the guarantee established in favor of messengers or emissaries.

Discriminatory treatment of prisoners is also not permissible for any reason whatsoever. Islam is clear on this point, for we are all descendants of Adam, and Adam was made of clay. However, equality of our human nature does not mean equality of social conditions. References in the Qur'an are numerous to this effect. "Do not covet what God has bestowed in bounty upon one more than upon another" [14(32)]; "To some of these messengers we gave pre-eminence over others" [2(253)]; "That God should send down part of His bounty upon whomsoever of His servants He wills" [2(190)]; "And have given them great preference over many of those we have created."[16(71)]

The objectivity of Islam indeed does not allow us to indulge in fantasy and to put all prisoners on the same footing, regardless of rank and social status, provided that we have given each the treatment dictated by humanitarian considerations. When the daughter of al-Maqawqas was taken prisoner, al-Maqrizi said, "Daughters of kings deserve special regard that need not be accorded to others."

The Prophet is reported to have said, "Be kind to a dignified man who has lost his status." Ibn Asakir quotes the Prophet saying, "If a nobleman falls into your hands, treat him well." It follows that Islamic theory favors that amenities be commensurate with the status of the captive, as long as the minimum human consideration is assured. The prohibition of discrimination was, in the early stages of humanitarian intentional law, restricted to discrimination on account of nationality. And while the criteria for the prohibition of discrimination have since acquired a wider range, articles 44 and 45 of the Geneva Convention on Prisoners of War[44] provide that officers and other prisoners having the same status as officers must be treated with due regard for their respective rank and age.

Finally, it should be noted that if a prisoner escapes and reaches his place of security, he becomes free, unless he is bound by a promise. If he is bound by a promise, he shall be under obligation to fulfill that promise because Islam rejects treachery. The Holy Book says, "Verily, God loves not the treacherous." [8(58)]

III. CONCLUSION

This is but a very small amount of the abundance of rules pertaining to humanitarian international law in Islam. These rules are in the nature of rules of public policy. A Muslim cannot break these rules on the pretext that he was under orders from his superiors, for the rule in Islam is that a combatant is held personally responsible for compliance with the previsions of humanitarian international law, for obedience is owed to no man who orders another to commit a sin. It is reported that Alquamah Ibn al-Majazzaz had been ordered to pursue the enemy after the battle of Dhul-Qird, but the prophet recalled him with part of the troops and sent off the rest under the command of Hudhafa ash-Shami. On the way, the latter built a fire and said to his men, "By virtue of my rank, I order you to jump into the fire." But when some of the men moved to obey his command, he laughed and said, "Stay where you are, I was only joking." Then the incident was reported to the Prophet, the latter commented, "If any one orders you to do an objectionable thing, do not obey him."

NOTES

This chapter is adopted from an article in 7 Mich. Y. B. Int'l Legal Stud. 189 (1985). Copyright (c) 1985 Michigan Journal of International Law. Reprinted with permission of the journal.

1. *Shari'ah* literally means the path that the believer must tread. As a religious and legal term it means the totality of God's commandments or the canon law of Islam. *See generally* ENCYCLOPEDIA OF ISLAM (M. Houtsma, T. Arnold, R. Bassey & R. Hartmann 1st ed. 1913).

The Background notes in this article were added by the editors for the convenience of those readers unfamiliar with Islam. Unless otherwise noted, they are based on the appropriate listing in the first edition of ENCYCLOPEDIA OF ISLAM.

2. All citation to the *Qur'an* refers to the standard Arabic chapter and verse numbering. For further reference, English speaking reader may with to look to Koran (N. Dawood trans. 1956) or THE MEANING OF THE GLORIOUS KORAN (M. Pickthall trans. 1956), two of the best known English translations of the Qur'an.

3. The saying or the traditions of the prophet Muhammad discussed in this article are not specifically cited herein. These traditions were complied by various Muslim jurists and make up many volumes of reference materials. For information regarding the role of those traditions in Islamic law, See M. Coulson, A HISTORY OF ISLAMIC LAW 41–43, 62–65 (1964).

4. Pictet, *The Principles of International Humanitarian Law.* 1966 Int'l Rev. Red Cross, 455, 462.

5. Henri Dunant (1828–1910), A banker from Geneva and the founder of the international Red Cross, was a leading force behind the conclusion of the Geneva convention for the Amelioration of Conditions of the wounded in armies in the field, Aug. 22, 1864, Stat. 940, T. S. No. 377, 1 Bevans 7.

For convenient collection of convections and international agreements on international humanitarian law, see INT'L COMM. OF THE RED CROSS, INTERNATIONAL RED CROSS HANDBOOK (12th ed.).

6. Protocol Relating to the Protection of Victims of Non-International Conflicts, June 8 1977, preamble, U.N. Doc. A/32/144 Annex 2 (1977) [hereinafter cited as Protocol II].

7. Al-Mawardi (d. 450 H/1058 A.D.) was a leading *Shafi'i* jurist who often taught in Basra and Baghdad. The dates of death given in this and subsequent notes are from the Islamic calendar.

8. The author in this section draws on the works of Al-Mawardi and Abu Ya' li and who agreed with these jurists.

9. *See generally* I. GOLDZIHER, INTRODUCTION TO ISLAMIC THEOLOGY AND LAW 170–74 (A. Hamori & R. Hamori trans. 1981).

10. *E.g.* Geneva Convention for the Amelioration of the Condition of the Wounded and Sick in Armed Forces in the Field, Aug. 12, 1949, art, 3, 6, U.S.T. 3115, T.I.A.S. No. 3362, 75 U.N.T.S.31 [hereinafter cited as 1949 Geneva convention I]. The three other Geneva Conventions of 1949 are the Geneva Convention for the Amelioration of the Condition of Wounded, Sick and Shipwrecked Members of Armed forces at Sea, Aug. 12 1949, 6 U.S.T. 3219, T.I.A.S. No. 3363, 75 U.N.T.S. 85 [hereinafter cited as 1949 Geneva Convention II]; The Geneva Convention Relative to the Treatment of Prisoners of War, Aug. 12, 1949, 6 U.S.T. 3317, T.I.A.S. No.3364, 75 U.N.T.S. 135 [hereinafter cited as 1949 Geneva Convention III]; and Geneva Convention Relative to Protection of Civilian Persons In Time of War, Aug. 12, 1949, 6 U.S.T. 3517, T.I.A.S. No. 3365, 75 U. N. T. S. 287.

11. Protocol II, *Supra* Note 6.

12. Abu-Bakr aSiddiq (d. 13H/637 A.D.), 'Umar Ibn al-Khattab(d. 35H/656 A.D.), 'Uthman (23H/644 A.D.) and Ali Ibn Abu Talib (41H/ 661 A.D.) were four of the Prophet Muhammad's most closely trusted and devout companions. Following the death of the Prophet, they succeeded each other as the first four *Caliphs* (successors) to the religious and political leadership of the Islamic community.

13. Declaration of St. Petersburg of 1868, 58 British and Foreign State Papers 16 [hereinafter cited as St. Petersburg Declaration of 1868].

14. Protocol Relating to the Protection of Victims of International Armed Conflict, June 8, 1977, art. 35, U.N. Doc. A/32/144 Annex 1(1977) [hereinafter cited as protocol I].

15. *Id.* at art. 35(1).

16. *Id.* at art. 35(2).

17. *See* St. Petersburg Declaration of 1868, *Supra* note 13.

18. Protocol Prohibited the use in war of Asphyxiating, Poisonous or other Gases and Bacteriological Methods of Warfare, June 17, 1925, 26 U.S.T. 571, T.I.A.S. 8061, 94 L.N.T.S. 65 (entered into force for the U.S., April 10, 1975).

19. Protocol I, *Supra* note 14, at art. 36.

20. Khalid Ibn Walid (d. 21H/641–42 A.D.) and Amr Ibn Al-As (d. 42H/663 A.D.) were contemporaries of Muhammad who converted to Islam while Muhammad was in Medina. The two were among the most successful Military Leaders in early Islamic history.

21. There are four Major Schools of Legal though dominating Islamic Jurisprudence today. They are named after Imam Ash-hafi' (d. 204 H/820 A.D.), Malak Ibn Anas (d. 179 H/795 A.D.), Abu Hanifa (d. 150 H/676 A.D.), and Ahmed Ibn Hanbal (d. 24 H/855 A.D.), leading Islamic jurists of their day. These schools differ in their view of the role of human reason in interpreting law from the *Qur'an* and the traditions of the prophet. The *Al-Malaki* school places primary emphasis on consensus among Muslims jurists (Ijma'a). The *Al-Hanbali* school defines legal rules on the basis of Quranic passages and the practice of the prophet only. Followers of Ash-Shafi' take a view somewhere in between the *Al-Hanbali* and *Al-Malaki* schools. They supplement divine inspiration through the Prophet's actions with consensus and reasoning. See N. COULSEN, A HISTORY OF ISLAMIC LAW 70–73 (1964).

22. Convention Respecting the Laws and Customs of War on Land, Oct. 18, 1907, art. 23©, 36 Stat. 2277, T.S. No. 539 [hereinafter cited as Hague Convention].

23. Protocol I, *Supra* note 14, at art. 41.

24. Protocol II, *Supra* note 6, at art. 7.

25. Hague Convention, *Supra* note 22, at arts. 23(b), 24.

26. Protocol I, *Supra* note 14, at art. 37.

27. An-Nawawi (d. 676H/127 A.D.) was a highly respected Syrian jurist of the *Shafi'* school.

28. Protocol I, *Supra* note 14, at art. 40.

29. Protocol II, *Supra* note 6, at art. 4(1).

30. Hague Convention, *Supra* note 22, at art. 23(d).

31. Al-Awza'I (d. 157H/774 A.D.) was a Muslim jurist who lived primarily in Damascus and Beirut.

32. 1949 Geneva Convention I, *Supra* note 10 at art. 46.

33. 1949 Geneva Convention II, *Supra* note 10 at art. 47.

34. Protocol I, *Supra* note 14, at art. 20.

35. Protocol II, *Supra* note 6, at art. 15.

36. Convention on the Prevention and Punishment of the Crime of Genocide, Dec. 9, 1978, 78 U.N.T.S. 277.

37. *See Id*. at art. 2.

38. 1949 Geneva Convention I, *Supra* note 10; 1949 Geneva Convention II, *Supra* note 10; Protocol I, *Supra* note 14, at arts. 8–34; Protocol II, *Supra* note 6, at arts. 7–12.

39. The *Hijra* was the emigration of Muhammad and his Followers from Mecca to Medina in 622 A.D. and represents the beginning of the Islamic calendar.

40. Abd Allah Ibn Amir (d. 59 H/680 A.D.) was a military leader and governor of Basra during the Caliphate of Uthman.

41. Abu Yusef (d. 182 H/798 A.D.) was a Hanfi jurist and chief *Qadi* (judge) of the Caliphs al-Mahdi and Harun al-Rashid.

42. 1949 Geneva Convention III, *Supra* note 10, at art. 85.

43. Abu Dharr al-Chifari (d. 31 H/651–652 A.D.), a companion of Muhammad, was highly respected for his piety and asceticism.

44. 1949 Geneva Convention III, *Supra* note 10 at arts. 44, 45.

4

Principles of Islamic Contract Law

Noor Mohammed

Heightened awareness in the United States about Islam and Muslims presents an opportunity to explore issues in Islamic law, and particularly to examine the concepts that underlie Islamic law. This study is an effort to present briefly the controlling principles of Islamic contract law. In view of the monumental growth of trade between western and Muslim worlds and projected increase in the coming century, the subject should continue to be of particular interest.

The doctrinal basis of Islamic law is the point of departure for this study. A brief historical sketch reveals the doctrinally-based components that have evolved into Islamic law.[1] Islamic belief begins with the Prophet Muhammad, the messenger of God (Allah). The Prophet Mission was to establish an order in this world based on divine revelations made to him by God (Allah). These divine revelations are recorded in the *Quran*, the sole Scripture of the Muslims. The spiritual and secular practices of the Prophet came to be known as Sunna. These two sources constitute the main guidelines for spiritual as well as temporal Muslim conduct in this life as preparation for the hereafter, and are called *Sharia*. The word *Sharia* means the highway for the good life. Over a period of time two additional sources of *Sharia* came into existence. They are: (1) *Qiyas*, or analogical reasoning, and (2) *Ijma*, or consensus of the Islamic community on a point of law. According to *Sharia*, sovereignty vests in God (Allah), requiring the state to act within the limits of divine law, or Sharia. This sovereignty is recognized by incorporation of *Sharia* into the Islamic legal system and community. In this sense *Sharia* is the constitutional law of Muslim society.[2]

The umbrella of *Sharia* in Islamic society covers the entire spectrum of

Islamic life and ethical values in both temporal and spiritual activity. *Sharia* addresses itself to spiritual (*Ibadat*) matters as well as the temporal (*Muamlatt*) transactions. In the field of spiritual (*Ibadat*) life, the control of *Sharia* is unfettered. But its role in temporal transitions (*Muamlatt*) is less pervasive, but still vital.

Like other legal systems, *Sharia* classifies human conduct into three categories—Mandatory, Prohibited, and Permitted. The last category is further subdivided by Sharia as (a) Praiseworthy, (b) Repulsive, and (c) Permitted.[3]

Sharia becomes of importance when temporal transactions are caught within its prohibitions or come under its disapproval. In brief, *Sharia* requires the accomplishment of a number of collective duties by Muslims. This can be summarized as "enjoining the good and forbidding the evil": "Ya amroona bil-maruf way a-nahoona an al-munkar."[4]

SHARIA AND CONTRACT

The Initial source of Islamic contract law is apparent through the Quranic revelation in these words:

> O ye who believe!
> Fulfill (all) obligations.[5]

This Quranic verse is the basis of the sanctity of a wide variety of obligations. The Arabic word *'uqud'* converse the entire field of obligations, including those that are spiritual, social, political, and commercial. In the spiritual realm *'uqud'* deals with the individual's obligation to Allah; in social relations the term refers to relations including the contract of marriage; in political arena it encompasses treaty obligations, and similarly, in the field of commerce, it covers the whole spectrum of obligations of parties in regard to their respective undertakings. Hence, the generic word *'uqud'* forms the foundation of contract and attendant liabilities.[6]

This short background of *Sharia* as the root principle of Islamic law must be kept in mind for an analysis and understanding of Islamic contract law. In contrast to Islamic law, the western common law of contract, which developed during the eighteenth and nineteenth centuries, grew out of the economic and legal theories of the period in which it was formulated. In its nascency it was formulated by natural law theories and later by laissez faire economic theory. Both these theories have undergone considerable revision over time.[7]

Islamic contract law, by contrast, started taking its shape in the seventh century. It is fair to assume that at this time in human history commerce was limited to market overt and that goods consisted of surplus farm products and handicrafts. Islamic law of contracts reflects and addresses the transactional reality of this period. The Anglo-Saxon common law of contracts was reshaped in the wake of the industrial revolution of the eighteenth centuries. The Muslim world in general did not experience the challenges of the industrial revolution. But in recent years the sudden oil-based prosperity of some Islamic lands has put the Islamic law of contract in full gear. We find that through its history its responses are reminiscent of the common law tradition. Hence its growth should also be responsive to changing needs and times, as has been the common law.[8]

THE TWIN DOCTRINES OF *SHARIA* AND CONTRACT

It has been recorded that in the immediate pre-Islamic era life in Mecca was decadent and this decadence was reflected in trade practices as well. The Prophet was himself a merchant before he embarked upon his career as the messenger of God (Allah). Mecca was a trade center and reforming trade practice was a natural focus of his attention. To redress the unconscionable and abusive commercial practice of pre-Islamic times, he insisted that transactions be required to comply with the evolving principles of *Sharia*.[9]

Two cardinal Sharia doctrines have held sway in the development of Islamic contract law through history. These are: 1) riba 2) gharar. Looking at these doctrines and their juristic interpretations enables us to understand the past and to project the future of Islamic law of contract.

DOCTRINE OF *RIBA* IN ISLAM

Muhammad's monotheism was linked with a humanism that had as its goal, social and economic justice.[10] The Prophet seemed to insist: One God—One Humanity. The Objective of economic and social justice presupposes the existence of oppressive economic practices. The *Quran* in one of the earliest revelations insists that "God hath permitted trade and forbidden usury."[11] The Arabic word in the *Quran* referring to the prohibited act is *riba*, which roughly translates to "usury." Yusuf Ali in his commentary explains that *riba* is any increase sought through illegal means, such as usury, bribery, profiteering, and fraudulent trading.[12] It includes economic selfishness and many kinds of sharp practices, including those that are individual, national and international in character. Irving in his remarkable commentary on the *Quran* translates a verse on usury:

You who believe, do not live off usury which is compound over and over again. Heed God so that you may prosper: Heed the fire which has been prepared for disbelievers; obey God and the messenger so you may find mercy.[13]

Through centuries of juristic interpretations, the prohibition of *riba* has maintained broad vitality except that different schools of interpretation have continued to interpret it differently. A contemporary commentator has brought together various strains of thought by the leading jurists and explains the term *riba* in its *Sharia* context as follows:

An unlawful gain derived from the quantitative inequality of the countervalues in any transaction purporting to effect the exchange of two or more species . . . which belong to the same genus, and are governed by the same efficient cause. Deferred completion of the exchange of such species, or even of species which belong to different genera but are governed by the same (efficient cause)[14] is also *riba*, whether or not the deferment is a companion by an increase in any one of the exchanged countervalues.[15]

Usurious transactions were classified by the jurists into two classes: (1) *riba al-fadl*, which produced unlawful excess in exchange of countervalues in a contemporaneous transaction, and (2) *riba al-nasi'a*, which produced unlawful gain by deferring the completion of exchange of countervalues, with or without an increase in profit. A third category was also added by some scholars called *riba al-jahilyya* or pre-Islamic *riba* exemplified by the lender asking the borrower at maturity date if he will settle the debt or increase it. Increase occurred by charging interest on the debt initially accrued.[16]

Riba al-Jahilyya relates to pre-Islamic riba also described as usury.[17] But *riba al-fadl* and *riba al-nasi'a* apply to the exchange (whether concurrent or deferred) of two precious metals (gold or silver) and four commodities (wheat, barley, dates and salt). The application of the doctrine of *riba* to these articles is based on the Prophet's tradition. It was further extended by analogy (*qiyas*), to the products of these six articles if their present or future exchange could have the smell or taint of *riba*.

It is not difficult to imagine that the seventh century economy was not monetized and that trade mostly consisted of face-to-face exchange as a result of some negotiation called contract or barter. Islamic law did not permit exchange of unequal values of the enumerated articles and by analogy to a variety of their products. These articles happened to be the basic necessities of life and were a convenient means of exploitation. The promises for future performance were clearly forbidden if goods comprised the enumerated articles as the transactions were suspected to contain *riba*.[18]

Over the centuries the concept of *riba* has held a firm ground in Islamic contract law, but its interpretation has continued to be revised under the changing economic setting. By the turn of the century, the leading Islamic scholars Abduh and Rida held the view that *riba al-Jahilyya* (pre-Islamic *riba*) was manifest *riba* and hence forbidden and made the transaction void.[19] But *riba al-fadl* and *riba al nasi'a* are under a rebuttable presumption of prohibition. In other words the extension of the time of payment on the maturity of a loan, conditioned on an additional increase, was manifest *riba* and forbidden. But it could be deemed lawful under extreme necessity. As to *riba al-fadl* and *riba al-nasi'a*, they held that these be looked at with aversion and are not prohibited. Their thinking helped open the door for sale of unequal quantities of the enumerated articles or their product.

Contemporary thinkers have examined further the time-honored Islamic Law of *riba*. Daoualibi, a noted commentator, holds that *riba* applied to unproductive loans borrowed in the Prophet's time by the needy for subsistence. But today people borrow money to make money. Hence, Islam should make a distinction between productive and unproductive *riba* (interest) and allow the former.[20]

Yet another process underway in Islamic societies is the direct effort to abolish the role of interest in Islamic economy[21] and thus devitalize *riba*.[22] Several Islamic countries have mounted efforts in this direction. Two in particular should be noted: Pakistan and Iran. These countries are attempting to establish an interest-free Islamic economy through Islamic banking.[23]

DOCTRINE OF *GHARAR*

Along with the doctrine of *riba* the other pervasive principle affecting the validity of contract is *gharar*. The relevant verses in the *Quran* dealing with the prohibition of *gharar* are Sura II verse 219 and Sura V verse 93 & 94.[24] These verses refer to gambling. The Arabic word *"maisir"* literally means getting something too easily, getting a profit without working for it, hence gambling. The initial prohibition against gambling in the light of the Prophet's tradition of cleansing commerce of unconscionable practices, gives a wider meaning to the principle. This expanded scope has been ably summarized:

> This idea of protecting the weak against exploitation by the strong led to the elaboration of a rule of general application, commanding that any transaction should be devoid of uncertainty and speculation, and thus, according to learned men and legal scholars, could only be secured by the contracting parties' having perfect knowledge of the countervalues intended to be exchanged as a result of their transaction, otherwise there is an unacceptable degree of *gharar*. Thus, what was intended to be a religious precept was transformed into a worldly rule which affects a great proportion of secular transactions.[25]

Thus, *gharar* prohibition applies to a whole range of commercial activities involving speculative activities and aleatory contracts. The doctrine becomes applicable if the subject matter of contract, the price, or both are not determined and fixed in advance.[26] Thus, in a stroke, the doctrine strikes at the very root of common law exchange of promise for future performance.

Muslim jurists continued to interpret the concept in the light of commercial reality.[27] In its early development the concept was applied to transactions where the goods were not in existence at the time the parties were contracting for them. In other words future goods could not be made a subject of sale under the doctrine. But the leading jurist Ibn Qayyim explained the concept applied to uncertainty of availability of the subject matter and not merely to nonexistence at the time of contract.

Later, lack of knowledge about the existence or nonexistence of the subject matter, or concerning its quality, quantity, or date of performance, was held to trigger *gharar*.[28] One jurist came up with a list of ten cases which constituted as examples of *gharar*.[29]

Ibn Rushd[30] gave a helpful formula for the application of *gharar*. According to him material want of knowledge in either the subject matter or in price can produce *gharar*. But if the subject matter could be adequately described and price could be clearly fixed then it would eliminate the speculative risk and hence, *gharar* would become inapplicable.

Contemporary thinking on *gharar* in contracts has been summarized as follows:[31]

1. There should be no want of knowledge (*jahl*) regarding the existence of the exchanged countervalues.
2. There should be no want of knowledge (*jahl*) regarding the characteristics of the exchanged countervalues or the identification of their species or knowledge of their quantities or of the date of future performance, if any.
3. Control of the parties over the exchanged countervalues should be effective.[32]

The ongoing refinement of the doctrine of *gharar* has continued over time and has been narrowed down to the presence or absence of uncertainty about future performance and not to the existence or nonexistence of the subject matter at the time of contract. It does not apply to business risk. But it applies to speculative or unconscionable risk. If the nonexistent article or subject matter is certain to be delivered or performed at a future date the prohibition of gharar does not apply. The risk in such transactions is minimal and does not attract the prohibition imposed by *gharar*.[33]

It must be pointed out that the concept of *riba* has held sway in Muslim societies from inception. Since *riba* typically applied to deferred transactions, any contract dealing with future performance was suspected to have the double taint of *riba* and *gharar*. The effectiveness of these two concepts have been moderated under the overriding doctrine of necessity; however, they continue to be alive and well and a subject of debate for Muslim scholarship.

The stage is now set for us to look at the contract prototypes developed in early Islamic society described by some commentators as "nominate contracts."[34] These nominate contracts comprise the following:[35]

1. *bay'*—sale is transfer of the corpus for a consideration.
2. *hiba*—gift, is the transfer of the corpus without a consideration.
3. *I'jara*, or *hire*, is the transfer of the usufruct for a consideration.
4. *'ariyya*—loan, is the transfer of the usufruct without a consideration.

We shall limit our inquiry to the contract of sale. We have already seen the pervasive hold of *Sharia* both in spiritual and secular matters. In the realm of commerce the twin concepts of *riba* and *gharar* were at work to confront the unconscionability and commercial overreaching. These principles laid down what was a valid contract of sale. Thus, contract required a concurrent[36] sale (*bay'*) and exchange for a fixed price in cash or kind. The delivery of the goods could not be postponed. It seems that transaction was akin to barter. But it had the merit of preventing *riba* (usurious price) and *gharar* (speculative uncertainty). It has been ably commented[37] that although consensual, the Islamic contract is not promissory. It is not formed by an exchange of promises but by an exchange of grants. The prohibition of aleatory contracts in Islamic law confirmed this tendency to confine transactions as much as possible to the here and now.

In its purity a completed exchange not in violation of *riba* principle is a prototype contract envisaged by *Sharia*. But soon the necessity of life began asserting themselves. Thus we notice the development of *Bay' salam* or the sale of subject of contract matter not available at the time the parties entered into contract. According to the Prophet's (*Hadith*) statement, "whoever pays money in advance for dates (to be delivered) later should pay it for known specified weight and measure of the dates."[38] It is obvious that the transaction departs from the earlier *Sharia* principle of contemporaneous exchange, but it developed as a modification of the *Sharia* by the Prophet and as such it is firmly in place. In a typical *salam* transaction the buyer was required to pay in advance in return for the promise of the seller that the goods would be delivered at some future date. At the time of sale these goods did not exist and hence, to avert gharar, a description of the goods was required. *Salam* dealt with goods such as fruit or crops. Along with *salam* came *istisna*, or contract of manufacture. *Istisna* contract is a contract by a laborer or artisan to manufacture an article for an agreed price. In *istisna* payment and delivery had to await until the product was ready. This form of contract was subject to a right of inspection. But once the goods were made the contract could not be revoked. *Istisna*, like *salam*, was upheld during the time of the Prophet and justified under the rule of necessity.[39]

The development of *salam* and *istisna* responded to the commercial need of the time and is a short step away from the transactional realities of our present age. This development brings us to the basic questions: How does the common law of contract formation fare on the scale of Islamic law or *Sharia*? and, Is Islamic law malleable enough to encompass changing contractual and business relationships in the modern commercial world?

PRINCIPLES OF INTERPRETATION OF *SHARIA*

A brief mention of the development of the principles of *Sharia* interpretation[40] will help our study further. The first forty years of Islam, from 622 to 661 A.D., is regarded as the spiritually golden era of Islam. During this period from 622–632 A.D. the Prophet set up an Islamic city of Medina in which Islam developed as a sociopolitical force. It also became the backdrop of Quranic revelations of the principles along with the Prophetic traditions on spiritual and secular matters. These revelations and practices became the doctrines and sources of further application and development of laws during the regimes of the first four Caliphs, from 632 to 661. These four Caliphs are regarded by Muslims as rightly guided. After the fourth Caliph, the Umayyad Dynasty took over the leadership of Islam under Muawiyah, a dynamic statesman. But this Dynasty departed from Islamic Ideals resulting in soul-searching by leading Muslim scholars who launched an effort to study *Quran* and the tradition of the Prophet to lay down a comprehensive text of Islamic Sharia for Muslims to follow. After the fall of Umayyad (661–750), the mantle of Islamic leadership was taken by Abbasid (750–950) who gave renewed vigor to this effort, which began in the eighth century and continued through the tenth century. During the two centuries Muslim scholars set up schools of law at major Islamic centers and developed Islamic law. Islamic law, unlike the common law, developed[41] through scholarly writing and polemic and not through judicial decision. In the tenth century, Muslim scholarship came to a consensus that Islamic law or Sharia was finalized as laid down in juristic writings. The task of the forthcoming generations was to follow these laws. This Consensus also announced that further individual, independent reasoning or personal interpretation would not be necessary or permissible. The doors of *Ijtihad* (independent or personal interpretation) were henceforth closed.

The ban on *Ijtihad* may have served well in a medieval, static and agrarian economy with relative political stability and prosperity. But it was not to survive for long. We come across great Muslim[42] scholarship pursuing *Ijtihad* through the centuries to ensure that Islamic law ideals of *Sharia* are applied to the changed sociopolitical and economic circumstances. The question has arisen whether the Islamic law of contract under *Sharia* covers the vast varieties of commercial contracts of the present day and age or permits only the types of contracts (nominate) noted earlier and practiced in early Muslim societies.

We have seen above that Islamic law or *Sharia* developed systematically through the efforts of Muslim jurists laying out detailed texts explaining conduct which conforms to the Islamic ideal. In this effort they were guided by the doctrines of *Sharia* noted earlier.

The questions to be asked are: (1) Whether Islamic scholarship would have remained mute in earlier periods had Muslim lands gone through industrial revolution? and (2) How should Islamic scholarship face the commercial realities of the marketplace of present day and age? It can be argued that scholars who gave the principles of the Sharia if confronted with the present day commercial problems would have developed a timely theory of contract. Islamic jurists through history followed the principle of *al-masalih al mursala* (wherever and whenever the interest of the people exist, it should be considered).

In his effort to outline a general theory of contract, Musa has argued that the theory of contract should be guided by the state of the time, public interest and overriding spirit of Islamic law or *Sharia*. This makes Islamic law adaptable to transactional realities and yet keeps it within the limits of Islamic ideals. It would free transactions from conforming to strict forms which have no relevance to current world trade or commerce.[43]

In western legal thinking two concepts have played a role in contract formation and have been applauded for their contribution in facilitating contracts. These are: (1) the autonomy of the will and (2) freedom of contract. The first deals with the idea that everyone is perfectly free to enter into a contract for the transfer of whatever one wishes. The second means that one is perfectly free to enter into a contract with whomsoever one wishes. Under *Sharia* the autonomy of will is subject to the Islamic prohibition against *riba*, *gharar* and dealing in certain articles specifically forbidden in *Quran*, such as wine and pork. Thus the concept of freedom of contract operates as it does in common law except that autonomy of will is modified by the requirement to comply with limits set by Islam. Within these limits one is free to enter into a contract with whoever one wishes.

As to the enforceability of contracts in general, another well-known juridical principle to be considered is: *Al-Ibah asalan fil ashya*:[44] "lawfulness is a recognized principle in all things." Expressed in more western fashion, this means that everything is presumed to be lawful, unless it is definitely prohibited by law.

According to Ibn Taymiya, a creative and liberalizing Islamic thinker,

> if . . . demands . . . made by men of good sense are introduced into contract, and
> if they are as suitable as they ought to be, they are never in vain and are not
> directly wasted; for example, credit, certain qualities in the commodities sold. [45]

In developing general theory of contract under *Sharia*, Musa points out
the traditional positions held by followers of Zahiris, a literalist school which
would not permit any contract not mentioned in the *Quran* and the *Sunna*,
and by other schools of the middle ground represented by Shafi and Maliki.
Then he points to the liberal position held by Hanbali School further developed by Ibn Taymiya.

The Hanbali School's position has promoted the recognition of transactional reality. As noted earlier, al-maslih al-mursala, or the principle of public interest of the people in the field of Muamlat transaction, has kept Islamic
law of contract responsive to the changing commercial reality. It is not limited to nominate contracts. [46] As Musa suggested, then, there is in existence
an outline of theory of contract under Islamic law. It is not based on western
principles of economics but on those of *Sharia*. Under these principles we
find that trade or commerce has been blessed. But the parties to pursue the
trade must keep in mind certain prohibitions. Outside these prohibitions,
the transaction could be either:

1. Contemporaneous exchange of goods and payment of price, called
   bay,' or
2. Contemporaneous exchange of promises for promises for performance
   at some future date.

It is the absence of the second form of transactions or exchange in the
early and medieval scene which has generated disillusion and hasty comments. Despite the absence of the promises for future performance under
Islamic law, we note that this new reality was not ignored. *Majalla*, the Otto-
man civil code, included the Islamic law of contract in the mid-nineteenth
century. It defined "contracts" as "the obligation and engagement of two
parties with reference to particular matter. It expresses the combination of
offer and acceptance. In the conclusion of the contract both the offer and
acceptance are inter-related in a legal manner, the result of which is seen in
their mutual relationship." [47]

In recent times the definition of "contract" in the Egyptian Civil Code
deserve mention: "a contract is created, subject to any special formalities that
may be required by law for its conclusion, from the moment that two persons have exchanged two concordant intentions." [48]

Also of interest is the definition in the Iranian Civil Code (as amended 1983) which states that a contract is an "agreement between two or more persons concerning certain subjects to which they consent."[49] Offer and acceptance, therefore, can be expressed in any form.

The government of Bahrain enacted the contract law in 1969. In defining "contracts" it stated in section 12: "all agreements are contracts if they are made by free consent of parties, competent to contract, for a lawful consideration and with lawful object, and are not herby declared to be void."[50]

EXPRESSED AND IMPLIED CONTRACT[51]

Islamic contract law recognized both express contracts as well as what has been described in common law as contract by conduct. It presupposes the making of an offer either orally or by writing or by conduct. The acceptance of the offer creates the contract. The parties entering into contract are also required to be competent.[52]

CONSIDERATION[53]

As in the common law there is a requirement of consideration under Islamic law. Consideration has an analogous meaning and implies what the parties give in exchange for or in performance of their promise. The concept of consideration implies a bargain, or value given in return for value received. But consideration is required to be lawful under *Sharia*. This would make exchange of forbidden goods and services illegal and unenforceable. Examples of such exchanges are sale of alcohol, pork or lending money which has an implication of *riba*.

CONCLUSION

Our study attempts to outline for the reader the underlying concepts or doctrines governing Islamic law of contract under *Sharia*. One is heartened to find that its objectives are the same as those of the common law or civil law, namely the enforcement of promises. But Islamic law prohibits contract which *Sharia* disallows. Its evolution has continued with the progress of Muslim societies in the field of commerce and industry. It would be a vain exercise to look for a doctrinal facsimile of the Western law of contract while studying Islamic law. But the refinement and development of the law of Islamic contract has kept pace suiting the transactional needs of the times.

Berman points out that the Western law of contract has originated from moral theology going back to Christian and pre-Christian eras.[54] Its moorings were cut off from the past, however, in the eighteenth and nineteenth centuries were supplanted by the secular theories of autonomy of will and considerations of social utility. Berman's remarkable study helps us to understand the foundational kinship between Islamic and Western laws of contract. As Berman has commented elsewhere: "society moves inevitably into future. But it does so by walking backwards, so to speak, with its eyes on the past."[55] In the field of *Muammlat* transactions Islamic law will continue moving onward while keeping in the view the historic themes of Islamic morality.

It is safe to say that the overriding principles of *Sharia* will continue to guide the general direction of Islamic contract law. The doctrines of *riba* and *gharar* discussed earlier have continued to draw lively debate in Islamic societies and will continue to be asserted if a matter in dispute happens to come before *Sharia* Courts. Both Saudi Arabia and Iran have *Sharia* Courts which abide by these substantive principles. It is possible to suggest that a *Sharia* Court in adjudicating a contract dispute which also has an element of *riba* in it will limit the enforcement of the contract. It will grant recovery due on the contract except for the amount of recovery ascribed to *riba*. Similarly the contracts of *gharar* would not be enforced by the *Sharia* Courts. But if the parties resolve their dispute outside the *Sharia* forum, the *Sharia* courts will not interfere with the parties' private settlement.

NOTES

This chapter is published with the permission of *Journal of Law and Religion*. The original citation is, 6 J. L. & Religion 115 (1988).

1. Readers unfamiliar with Islam will find useful a chapter by the author entitled *Introduction to Islamic Law*, V MODERN LEGAL SYSTEMS CYCLOPEDIA 681–92 (Redden ed. 1985).

2. F. RAHMAN, ISLAM 100 (1979).

3. Badr, *Islamic Law: It's Reaction to Other Legal Systems*, 26 American Journal of Comparative Law 183 at 189.

4. Al-Quran, 9:71.

5. *Id.*, 5:1.

6. A. Y. Ali, The Holy Quran (1946), Note 682. *See also* S. H. Amin, REMEDIES FOR BREACH OF CONTRACT IN ISLAMIC & IRANIAN LAW 11–12 (1984); ABDUR RAHMAN I. DOI, SHARIAH THE ISLAMIC LAW 355–56 (1984).

7. P. S. ATIYAH, THE LAW OF CONTRACT 1–19 (1961). *See also* H. C. HAVINGHURST, THE NATURE OF PRIVATE CONTRACT (1961).

8. Makdisi, *Legal History of Islamic Law & English Common Law; Origins & Metamorphosis*, 34 CLEV. ST. L. REV. 3–18 (1985–1986).

9. F. RAHMAN, ISLAM 14 (1979).

10. *Supra* note 9, at 13. *See also* SAHIH AL-BUKHARI, XXXIV, Sales, chapter 24–26.

11. The Holy Quran 2:274.

12. *Supra* note 6, *A. Y. Ali*, footnote 3552:

The term *riba* in Arabic language connotes increase or augmentation. In Islamic legal jurisprudence, it is often defined as increase which has no consideration, as stipulated in loan transactions or in the exchange of goods of the same kind. Riba was commonly practiced in pre-Islamic Arabia mainly in the form of extension of loan repayment periods against the doubling of the principle amount of the loan. This particular form was prohibited by the Quran (Surat Al-i-Imran, III, verse 130) before the general prohibition of all *riba* was established (Surat the Cow, II verses 278–281) and elaborated on in the Prophet's last address in his farewell pilgrimage. Subsequent jurisprudence distinguished between the *loans' riba* (known also as *riba an-nassi'a* and as *riba* prohibited by the Koran) and the sales' riba which takes the form of either the spot sale of one of six items (gold, silver, wheat, Barley, dates and salt) against an item of its own kind but with an increase in amount or value (riba al-fadhl) or the exchange of any goods with goods of the same kind or of another kind which serves the same purpose when the latter are delivered in the future in an augmented quantity or value (*riba an-nassi'a*). *See also* Ibrahim F. I. Shihata, Legal Aspects of Islamic World Bank, Concluding Remarks in International Conference of Islamic Banking & Finance, 26 September 1986. Dr. Shihata is Vice President & General Counsel, World Bank, Washington, D.C. A copy of his remarks could be obtained upon request.

13. T. B. IRVING, The Quran, THE FIRST AMERICAN VERSION, TRANSLATION & COMMENTARY 34 (1985).

14. "Efficient cause" is possibly the nearest English Translation for *Illa*.

15. N. A. SALEH, UNLAWFUL GAIN & LEGITIMATE PROPHET IN ISLAMIC LAW 12–13 (1986). A common *"illa"* should connect together two elements of analogy, namely the object of the analogy and its subject, in order to produce the analogical reasoning. The following example will throw more light on this method of legal reasoning: Drinking wine (khamr) is forbidden by Quranic injunctions; the drinking prohibition extended to all kinds of alcoholic drinks (nabidh) apparently by a Hadith but also by analogy because of the common *"illa"* of wine and alcoholic drink, which is the capacity to produce intoxication.

16. *Id.* 13. The author gives what appears as a final breakdown of *Riba*:

Riba: unlawful advantage by way of excess or deferment.

Riba al fadl: riba by way of excess of one of the exchange countervalues.

Riba al-nasi'a: riba by way of deferment of completion of an exchange.

Riba al-jahiliyya: pre-Islamic riba.

Mal ribawi: property susceptible of riba.

17. *Id.* 14.

18. *Id.* 14–27, the author very ably collects the position of all the different schools on the issue of present or deferred exchange of goods.

19. *Id.* at 28.

20. *Id.* at 29.

21. S.N.H. NAQVI, ETHICS & ECONOMIC, AN ISLAMIC SYNTHESIS (1981).

22. M. N. Siddiqi, Muslim Economic Thinking, A Survey of Contemporary Literature (1981). See also by the same author, Issues in Islamic Banking (1983); *S. H. Homoud*, Islamic Banking (1985).

23. Z. Igbal & A. Mirakhor, International Monetary Fund, Islamic Banking (unpublished and undated research paper).

24. A. Y. Ali, *Supra* note 6 at 86, footnote 241. *See* also *Supra* note 13, at 18 and 60.

25. *Supra* note 25, at 49.

26. *Id*. 50.

27. *Id*. 50.

28. *Id*. 51.

29. *Id*. 51. Ibn Juzay's list is as follow:

    (a) Difficulty in putting the buyer in possession of the subject-matter; such as the sale of a stray animal or the young still unborn when the mother is not part of the sale.

    (b) Want of knowledge (jahal) with regard to the price or the subject-matter, such as the vendor saying to the potential buyer: "I sell you what is in my sleeve."

    (c) Want of knowledge with regard to the characteristics of the price or of the subject-matter, such as the vendor saying to the potential buyer: "I sell you a piece of cloth which is in my home" or the sale of an article without the buyer inspecting or the seller describing it.

    (d) Want of knowledge with regard to the quantum of the price or the quantity of the subject-matter, such as an offer to sell "at today's price" or "at the market price."

    (e) Want of knowledge with regard to the date of future performance, such as an offer to sell when a stated person enters the room or when a stated person dies.

    (f) Two sales on one transaction, such as selling one article at two different prices, one for cash and one for credit, or selling two different articles at one price, one for immediate remittance and one for deferred one.

    (g) The sale of what is not expected to revive, such as the sale of a sick animal.

    (h) *Bay' al-hasah*, which is a type of sale whose outcome is determined by the throwing of a stone.

    (i) *Bay' al-munabadha*, which is sale performed by the vender throwing a cloth at the buyer and achieving the sale transaction without giving the buyer the opportunity for properly examining the object of the sale.

    (j) *Bay' mulamasa,* where the bargain is struck by touching the object of the sale without examining it.

30. *Id*. 52.

31. *Id*. 53.

32. *Id*. 79–80.

33. *Id*. 52–78.

34. S. H. AMIN, REMEDIES FOR BREACH OF CONTRACT IN ISLAMIC LAW AND IRANIAN LAW 11 (1984).

35. J. J. COULSON, COMMERCIAL LAW IN THE GULF STATES 11 (1984).

36. *Id.* 19–20.

37. Zysow, *The Problem of Offer & Acceptance: A Study of Implied in fact Contracts in Islamic Law & the Common Law*, 34 Cleveland St. L. Rev. 69 at 77.

38. Sahih-Al-Bukhari, Vol. 3, pp. 243–250.

39. *Supra* note 15, at 61–62. *See* also *Supra* note 35, at 21.

40. J. L. Esposito, Islam & Politics 3–15 (1984).

41. *Id.* 15–19.

42. *Id.* 19–57.

43. Musa, *The Liberty of Individual in Contracts and Conditions According to Islamic Law*, 2 ISLAMIC QUARTERLY 70 (1955).

44. *Doi, A. R. I., Shari'ah, The Islamic Law 406* (1984).

45. *Supra* note 43, at 263.

46. *Id.* 79–80, 251–263.

47. S. H. AMIN, REMEDIES FOR BREACH OF CONTRACT IN ISLAMIC LAW AND IRANIAN LAW 12 (1984).

48. *Id.* 13.

49. *Id.* 13.

50. Govt. of Bahrain, The Contract Law 1969, Section 12 at p. 4.

51. *Supra* note 44, at 356–357.

52. *Id.* 357–358.

53. *Id.* 356–357.

54. Berman, The Religious Sources of General Contract law: A Historical Prospective, 4 J. LAW & RELIG. 103–124.

55. H. J. BERMAN, LAW & REVOLUTION 41 (1983).

5

Marriage, Divorce, and Inheritance in Islamic Law

Mahmoud Hoballah

In the following a brief outline will be given of one of the most important parts of Islamic law which made a very strong imprint on the life of the Islamic people, the law of family relationship and inheritance. It is plainly impossible to present a comprehensive picture of such a voluminous and controversial subject in a brief space and this paper will therefore be confined to a general outline of the basic principles of this field of Islamic law.

Islam is a way of life. It covers man's whole field of activity and regulates the spiritual and personal aspects of his life as well as the physical and social ones. The spiritual aspects are technically termed *devotions* and the social aspects are termed *transactions*. Although distinguished from one another, devotions and transactions arc not exclusive of one another. Their ultimate ends and functions are the same, namely, to promote man's welfare. Devotions and transactions in the concept of Islam are so interconnected, so interwoven, that it is hard to determine where the sphere of the one ends and that of the other begins. A man cannot be socially good unless and until he is spiritually good. The inner and the external life of man have thus been intimately blended so that neither of them can be enriched or reach its ultimate perfection without the other. That which truly helps one of them must thereby help the other.

I. MARRIAGE

Marriage is a civil contract, but it also has its spiritual content. The Prophet of Islam has said, "He who marries perfects half his religion. Let him therefore take care of the other half." Marriage has a deeper sacred content than other contracts because it touches upon the very foundation of mankind and entails a closer relationship between the parties than any other contract.

Since marriage is a civil contract between husband and wife it ought to satisfy all the basic requirements of a contract. The conditions prerequisite for the validity of the marriage contract can be summarized as follows: The contracting parties must be mature in age and mind and be free to act. There should be no circumstance that would make it illegal for the couple to marry one another. The contract itself should not be limited in time, and it should be made public or at least two witnesses should he present during the marriage ceremony. Lastly, the wife should be given a dowry. If any of these conditions except the last is not satisfied, the contract is null and void. Failure to grant a dowry will neither vitiate the contract nor will it deprive the wife of her right to a dowry. If the dowry was neither determined nor mentioned the wife has the right to claim from her husband the dowry of her equals and the husband will be obliged to pay the same. Since in principle Islam grants women the same rights as men, women are parties to the marriage contract and not mere objects of the contract.

No specific age for marriage was mentioned either in the Quran or in the traditions of the Prophet. It is true that the Holy Quran speaks about "the age of marriage," but it does not determine any particular age, and so leaves its determination to circumstances and climatic conditions. Every community is thus given the right to determine the age of marriage deemed fit and suitable for the growth of its individuals. As for minors, it is said by some schools that they can be given in marriage by their guardians, but they will have the option of confirming or repudiating the marriage contract when they reach majority. Some schools, however, say that such option can only be exercised if the guardians are not the fathers or grandfathers.

There are certain persons who are not allowed to marry one another. One may not marry any of his ascendants, descendants, brothers or sisters, whether they are consanguine, uterine, or full, nor their descendants. Nor may one marry any of the following: the brothers or sisters of his or her ascendants; the foster mother or the foster father or any of their relatives who would be prohibited if the relation were that of blood; the mother-in-law or father-in-law; the step-son or step-daughter. Lastly, it is prohibited to have as co-wives women who are sisters or who would be otherwise prohibited from marrying each other if one of them were a man.

Marriage may be contracted for one or all of the following purposes: the propagation of the human race; the unification of different people so as to create between them a bond of relationship which is not less if not more important than that of blood relationship; to cherish in man and woman a sense of responsibility which is particularly essential for human stability and progress; to develop in man and woman the feeling of respect and love, and to keep the character of both man and woman pure and clean. But the more often repeated purpose in the Holy Quran is to the end that each one of the couple should find "comfort," "peace of mind," "ease of mind," and "tranquility and quietude in the other." We read in the Quran, "And one of His signs is that He created mates for you from yourselves that you may find quiet of mind in them and He put between you love and compassion." That "ease of mind" is not likely nor is it usually achieved unless a man marries only one wife. The religion of Islam, however, is alive to the fact that, in some cases and among some communities, plurality of wives may be absolutely essential and monogamy would be disastrous to the social progress of the society and undermine its very existence. Therefore plurality of wives which was allowed in Arabia without restriction in pre-Islamic times is permitted with certain limitations. It was not, however, primarily intended for the satisfaction of anyone's sexual desires but rather as a solution to certain social problems which could not otherwise be solved. This is shown by the fact that polygamous marriages have been subjected to a number of conditions to limit their practice. Chief among these conditions is the requirement that the husband must treat his wives equally. It is illegal for him to show any preferences. It would be permissible for a Muslim government to limit polygamous marriage even further as long as there is no direct contradiction of Islamic principles.

II. DIVORCE

Despite the fact that the marriage contract is supposed to be a permanent one, and despite the sacredness which is attached to the marriage tie, the religion of Islam recognizes the necessity of keeping the way open for its dissolution if the parties concerned have made their decision that they can no longer live together as husband and wife. Nothing is more harmful to the individual and society than the forcing of such a couple to live under the same roof under the pretense that they are finding "ease of mind" in one another. Divorce, thus recognized as a necessary evil, is a preventive measure to avoid tensions which may prove more dangerous and more evil than the dissolution of the marriage. It ought not to be resorted to before all means to effect reconciliation have been exhausted. If the couple cannot live together and all means of reconciliation have utterly failed, divorce will be, then, the best alternative.

Here we find a very expressive and instructive verse of the Holy Quran. It is stated (Sura IV, 39) "If you fear a breach between them [man and wife], appoint two arbiters, one from his family, and the other from hers; if they wish for agreement, God will cause their reconciliation." Thus it is here enjoined upon the Muslims to try to effect reconciliation before resorting to divorce. Again we read (Sura IV, 24), "If you hate them [your wives], it may be that you dislike a thing in which God has placed abundant good." Here men are told not to be hasty about divorce, for the wives whom they want to divorce may be the source of blessings to them. It was often repeated by the Prophet that divorce is the most hateful of all things permitted. The traditions of the Prophet have also here laid down various conditions, designed to make the repudiation of the wife more difficult, and to leave the door open for reconciliation. Here again if a Muslim government or a Muslin community deems it necessary to lay down rules for the procedure of divorce and to place such limitations upon the husband as are not inconsistent with the principles laid down by the Holy Koran, such regulations will be acceptable. In general, Islamic law does not require specific grounds for divorce on the part of either the husband or the wife. Limitations, however, lately contemplated in some Muslim quarters, were defeated due to the strong opposition which they encountered. But whether such limitations are introduced or not, the number of cases of divorce as well as of polygamy in Muslim countries is not proportionately alarming. Indeed, they are much less than one would rationally expect. Deeply conscious of their religious duties and obligations and faithful to their covenants and contracts, Muslims as a rule do not easily resort to divorce.

Although procedures differ, a wife has the same basic right to divorce as has her husband. If divorced, however, a woman cannot remarry any man other than her previous husband before some definite period of time elapses so as to be sure that there is no pregnancy from the previous marriage; since there is no similar problem in the case of the man he may remarry as soon as he is divorced. In case of a divorce the wife must return the dowry she received from her husband. The husband is strongly urged to take no more. The case of the wife of Thabit Ben Keise is a typical example. There the wife went to the Prophet and said, "I have no grudges or complaints against Thabit, but I cannot live with him as a wife." The Prophet said, "Would you give him back the orchard he has conferred upon you?" When the answer was in the affirmative, Thabit was called forth and the matter was immediately settled. But if the husband is the divorcing party or responsible for the divorce, the wife keeps all she has received from him and in many cases she may get either more or continued support, as is specified by the Islamic jurists. The subject should not be closed without a reference to a verse of the Holy Quran which explicitly provides that wives have rights upon their husbands equal to their obligations. It reads (Sura II, 228): "And their rights [the wives'] are equal to their obligations in a just manner."

The custody of the child whose parents are divorced is the right of the woman so long as the child can reasonably be entrusted to her. If she remarries, custody will go to her mother, or if not available or fit, to the mother of the child's father. In any case, the husband, if able to do so, has to support both the child and the person caring for the child.

III. INHERITANCE

Before going into the subject of inheritance, I should like to refer to some basic underlying principles. First, that property, although private and of private concern, has a social function and responsibility. During his lifetime the rich man has to maintain the poor and weak among his near relations. When he dies such relatives share the property from which they received benefit when he was alive and in the accumulation of which they somehow participated. The religion of Islam does not encourage the pre-Islamic practice that was universally prevailing—that is, the vast accumulation and concentration of wealth in one hand. The law of inheritance can be said to be based upon these various basic principles.

In Islamic law the distribution of the estate is determined by the law rather than by the will of the deceased. A person may dispose by will of one-third of his estate only, provided that no part of this one-third may he bequeathed to any of the legal heirs. All transactions or gifts made during the last illness are considered as bequests and thus are valid only within the limitation of this one-third of the estate. The estate itself is to be widely distributed among the heirs. Rather than handing it to the oldest son or to those who could smite with their spears, it is divided among the heirs so that the females as well as the weak and the infants become co-sharers with the rest. The wife also receives a share of her husband's estate in contrast to pre-Islamic times.

The heirs are wife or husband, descendants and ascendants, and collateral relatives. For the sake of simplicity they are divided by the Hanafi School into two groups: those whose shares are specified, and those who take the residue. The first group consists of four males and eight females—the father, the grandfather, the uterine brother, the husband, the wife, the daughter, the son's daughter, the mother, the grandmother, the sister, full, consanguine, and uterine. Those who take what is left are the males related by blood, such as sons and their sons, fathers and grandfathers, full or consanguine brothers, and their descendants. If none of either group is alive the property will go to the nearest relative extant and if there is no relative the inheritance will go to the treasury. The manner of the distribution of the estate can be summarized in this way: when a male and a female heir are of one and the same level, the male heir will get two shares, the female only one. The sharers and those who take the residue are not exclusive of one another; some of the sharers may also have the power to take as residuaries. In some cases women may be in the class who take the residue.

CONCLUSION

As can be seen from this brief outline, Islamic law has given careful consideration to the regulation of family relationships and inheritance and has built an intricate but not inflexible structure which caught deep roots in Islamic society and has caused these fields of law to remain relatively untouched by Western influence in many Islamic countries.

NOTE

This article was published with the permission of *George Washington Law Review*. It has been originally cited as 22 Geo. Wash. L. Rev. 24 (1953).

6

Gender Equality in Islamic Family Law: Dispelling Common Misconceptions and Misunderstandings

Hafiz Nazeem Goolam

INTRODUCTION

In a recent issue paper[1] on Islamic Marriages and Related Matters, the South African Law Commission states:

> The issue of greatest concern for any legislation recognizing aspects of Muslim Personal Law is the compatibility of such legislation with the Bill of Rights as a whole but particularly its compatibility with the guarantee of equality.[2]

There prevails, particularly in western circles, serious misconceptions on the issue of gender equality in Islamic family law. This article sets out to dispel these misunderstandings in four specific areas of the law, namely:

(1) divorce;
(2) division of property upon dissolution of marriage;
(3) custody; and
(4) inheritance.

Before such analysis, however, it is important to set out, albeit briefly, the Koranic and Prophetic foundations of the principle of gender equality, and to have a basic appreciation and understanding of the Islamic approach to scriptural interpretation.

The Koranic and Prophetic Foundations of the Principle of Gender Equality

The Holy Koran and the Sunnah (sayings of the Prophet Muhammad (peace be upon him)) are, of course, the primary sources of the Sharia (Islamic law). The Koran declares:

> They are your garments
> And ye are their garments.[3]

By stating that the two parties to a marriage contract complement each other, the implicit deduction is that neither spouse is inferior in status or dignity. Even more clearly, the Koran states: "And women shall have rights similar to the rights (men have) over them, according to well-known rules of equity."[4] Although in its specific context, this verse refers to rights attaching to divorce, its import may be extended to other areas of male-female relations and thus be elevated to the status of a general rule. The following two sayings or traditions of the Prophet Muhammad, inter alia, clearly support the Koranic foundations of gender equality. In his famous last sermon, delivered on Mount Arafat outside Makkah, he stated:

> Fear God in matters concerning women.
> Verily women have rights against you.
> Just as you have rights against them.[5]

In his sermon, the Prophet further stressed the importance of being kind to women and treating them well. He is also reported to have said: "The rights of women are sacred; ensure that women's rights are upheld and maintained."[6]

The Islamic Approach to Scriptural Interpretation

According to Kamali, Islamic jurisprudence is concerned with the way in which laws are derived from the Koran and Sunnah. Revelation, given to the human being in order to restore unity and help him to achieve a just and devout order in society, as well as in the soul, must be interpreted so as to render it practicable in every culture, while not betraying its spirit and immutable provisions.[7] To achieve this, Kamali explains, additional sources of legal authority are recognized, including consensus (ijma), analogical deduction (qiyas), public interest (maslaha) and local customary precedent (urf). In employing these mechanisms of interpretation, the jurist must guard the five principles that enshrine the objectives of Islamic law (Maqasid Al-Sharia), namely the right to life, intellect, faith, lineage and property.[8] The Sharia, on the whole, seeks primarily to protect and promote these essential values and validates all measures necessary for their preservation and advancement.

Justice (adl or qist) is also regarded as a principal objective and value of the Sharia, being mentioned no less than 53 times in the Koran. As a fundamental objective of the Sharia, adl—literally meaning to place things in proper place—seeks to establish an equilibrium between rights and obligations, so as to eliminate all excesses and disparities, in all spheres of life.[9]

Abu Ishaq Ibrahim Al-Shatibi (d 790 H—the Islamic era), who is regarded as the leading exponent of Al-Maqasid, wrote affirmatively of the need to respect and observe the explicit injunctions of Islamic law, but added that adherence to the text should not be so rigid or strict as to alienate the rationale and purpose of the text from its words and sentences.[10]

In the light of this brief exposition on the Islamic approach to scriptural interpretation, the common misconceptions and misunderstandings in the four areas of Islamic family law listed earlier—namely: divorce; division of property upon dissolution of marriage; custody; and inheritance can now be comfortably dispelled. However, attention must first be brought to an issue that precedes it, the taqliq or prenuptial agreement.

Taqliq or Prenuptial Agreement

The majority of Muslim women around the world are unaware of the taqliq or prenuptial agreement. A Muslim woman has the right to lay down certain conditions in the taqliq before signing the marriage certificate, in order to safeguard her welfare and rights. Furthermore, she may amend the taqliq or add further conditions at a later stage. For example, the woman may insert a clause stating that her husband allows her to continue working and that he understands the nature of her work. Another good example is to be found in the Jordanian legislation. Although this legislation imposes no express restrictions on polygamy, it permits the wife to stipulate in the taqliq that the husband shall not take another wife and enables the wife to apply for divorce if such condition is not complied with.[11] Similar provisions are found in Syrian and Iraqi legislation. In fact, the taqliq should be read to both parties at the marriage ceremony, so that they are aware of their rights and obligations, as well as the consequences of failing to fulfil such obligations. The prenuptial contract should be interpreted in the context and spirit of the Koranic verse: "O ye who believe, fulfil your obligations."[12]

DIVORCE

The Arabic word for divorce is talaq and means "freeing or undoing the knot." The most relevant Koranic verses appear in the chapter entitled Women (Al-Nisaa). They provide:

> A divorce is only permissible twice: after that,
> The parties should either hold together on equitable terms,
> Or separate with kindness/dignity[13]

> When ye divorce women, and they fulfill
> The term of their (idda),
> Either take them back on equitable terms
> Or set them free on equitable terms[14]

Commenting on the spirit and tenor of these verses, the late Professor Ahmad Ibrahim[15] states that, just as marriage takes place in an environment of love and understanding, so too divorce should occur in an environment of kindness and on equitable terms. He adds[16] that the Koran and the Sunnah of the Prophet Muhammad (on whom be peace) make it clear that divorce should not be pronounced at the whim and fancy of the husband, but should be effected only for good reason and where the marriage has broken down irretrievably. In this regard the Prophetic saying that "of all lawful acts, divorce is the most detestable to Allah" cogently sums up the spirit of divorce law in Islam.

A common misunderstanding in western thinking is that the right to divorce vests in the husband, but it may be "transferred" to the wife in certain instances. This means that the wife has no independent right to divorce her husband. If this were indeed the case it would be contrary to the Koranic and Prophetic foundations of the principle of gender equality, however, the Koranic verse that provides that: "And women shall have rights similar to the rights (men have) over them, according to well-known rules of equity."[17] This verse (ayah) refers specifically to divorce rights.

In the 1967 Supreme Court of Pakistan decision of *Khurshid Bibi v Muhammad Amin*,[18] the question of law that fell for consideration was whether a wife is entitled, under Islamic law, to claim judicial separation (khul'), despite the unwillingness of the husband to release her from the matrimonial tie. The classic example of khul' narrated in the ahadith (sayings of the Prophet) is the case of the wife of Thabit bin Qais. She complained to the Prophet that Thabit was repulsive and that she felt like spitting on him. The Prophet, convinced that the spouses could not live together in conformity with their conjugal obligations, advised the husband to release her. Relying on this example, Judge Rahman declared that it is consistent with the letter and spirit of the Koran, which place the husband and wife on an equal footing, that the wife can claim judicial separation (khul'), notwithstanding the husband's unwillingness.[19] It is thus clearly contrary to the spirit of the Islamic law of divorce for a man to refuse to divorce his wife where she so desires, for good reason, of course. For the parties are clearly enjoined in the Koran to remain together on equitable terms, or to separate with dignity, kindness and grace.

Analysing the nature of khul', the court referred to a leading medieval scholar and philosopher, Ibn Rushd. Born in Cordova in 1126, he expressed himself as follows:

> And the philosophy of khul', is this, that khul' is provided for the woman, in opposition to the right of divorce vested in the man. Thus if trouble arises from the side of the woman, the man is given the power to divorce her, and when injury is received from the man's side, the woman is given the right to obtain khul.[20]

In other words, if divorce takes place at the husband's behest, the wife retains the dower; if it occurs at the wife's behest, she returns the dower. The notion that the wife is hereby "paying" for her freedom is a misconceived one. It is interesting to note that where the husband dissolves the marriage before consummation, he nevertheless remains obliged to "pay"[21] his wife half of the dower.[22]

Over and above her right to khul', the wife may also apply for the dissolution of her marriage by the court. This is known as faskh or judicial divorce. The principal grounds on which she may apply for faskh are:

- injury or discord;
- failure to maintain;
- defect on the husband's part; or
- husband's absence sine causa or imprisonment.

Injury or Discord

Imam Malik and Imam Ahmad[23] state that the wife may apply for divorce where her husband has caused her injury, for example by beating or insulting, so as to make the continuation of their marital life impossible. On the other hand Imam Abu Hanifa and Imam Shafi state that other remedies, such as reprimanding the husband, are applicable in this case. The rules applicable are as follows:

- reconciliation is paramount, but if the judge cannot reconcile the couple, he should order an irrevocable divorce (talaq bain);
- if the wife cannot prove her case, the judge should appoint two arbiters to investigate and attempt reconciliation;

- if the arbiters cannot reach consensus the judge should order further investigation, failing which he shall appoint two other arbiters.

These rules are based on the Koranic verse which provides: "If ye fear a breach between them appoint two arbiters, one from his family, the other from hers. If they wish for peace, Allah will cause their reconciliation."[24]

The hadith of the Prophet that "there shall be no injury and no injury shall be remedied with any injury" (la darar wa la dirar) is also applicable in this regard. Injury includes cruelty (darar) and, in this regard, section 2(viii) of India's Dissolution of Muslim Marriages Act 1939 lists six grounds. These grounds have been reproduced verbatim in the Islamic Family Law (Federal Territory) Act 1984 in Malaysia. Section 52(1)(L) of the Act reads:

> That the husband treats her with cruelty, that is to say, inter alia: (i) habitually assaults her or makes her life miserable by cruelty of conduct; or (ii) associates with women of evil repute or leads what according to hukm shar'i is an infamous life; or (iii) attempts to force her to lead an immoral life; or (iv) disposes of her property or prevents her from exercising her legal rights over it; or (v) obstructs her in the observance of her religious obligations or practice; or (vi) if he has more wives than one does not treat her equitably in accordance with the requirements of hukm shar'i.

A striking and very flexible remedy is provided by Egyptian law, in its employment of the concept of "harm." Article 6 of Law 25 of 1929 reads:

> If a wife claims that her husband has caused harm to her in any manner whereby she can no longer live with him, she is permitted to seek divorce, in which case the judge will grant her an irrevocable divorce providing the harm is proved and that he is unable to reconcile the couple.

Failure to Maintain Finances

It is stated in the Koran: "For divorced women maintenance (should be provided) on a reasonable (scale). This is a duty on the righteous."[25] If Allah has made it incumbent to maintain divorced women, then how much more incumbent, one may ask, is it to maintain married women? Once again there is disagreement amongst the fuqaha (jurists) whether the failure to pay maintenance is a valid ground for judicial divorce. The Hanafis[26] say that it is not, whether the reason for such failure is insolvency or simply refusal. They base their argument on chapter 69, verse 7, which, they argue, covers the case of the indigent husband as well as the man of affluence. As for the affluent man, his property could be sold and the proceeds therefrom given to his wife. Another remedy is the imprisonment of the husband. Divorce should be resorted to only where all other avenues have been exhausted, since it is regarded as the most detestable of all lawful acts in the eyes of Allah. The other three Sunni A'immah[27]—Imam Malik, Imam Ahmad and Imam Shafi—state that failure to maintain is a grievous injury to the wife and thus she may file for divorce where her husband has no known property. Failure to maintain does not conform to retention with honour and is thus in con-travention of the Koranic verse that a woman must be retained in honour or released with kindness. They also quote the following hadith to support their case: "There shall be no injury, and no injury shall be remedied by another."

The Shafis further hold that if the wife asks for separation on grounds of the husband's inability to provide maintenance, then a judge should not comply with this request; rather he should instruct her to incur debts, that is to buy food on credit—the cost to be met from the money of the husband. This is in accordance with Surah 2, verse 228 and Surah 65, verse 7. The first of these clearly explains that a person who is in debt, but who is poor, should have his debts deferred until he becomes more prosperous.

Defect on the Husband's Part

The Imamiyah code allows judicial divorce on grounds of the husband's impotence, castration or mutilation. Imam Abu Hanifa and Abu Yusuf con-cur with the Shias, but Muhammad, a disciple of Abu Hanifa, adds insanity and leprosy as just grounds. The other three Sunni A'immah allow faskh by either spouse—Hanafis only permit the husband—with Malik regarding it as an irrevocable repudiation, and Shafi regarding it as a decree of annulment. The Egyptian Act gives the wife the right to apply for judicial divorce on the fulfilment of three conditions:

(1) that the defect is long-standing and incurable;
(2) that such injury or defect will affect her and her offspring;
(3) she was unaware of the defect at the time of marriage.

Husband's absence sine causa or imprisonment

According to Imam Malik and Imam Ahmad, these are valid grounds for a wife applying to court for a divorce. They say that the absence or impris-onment must cause actual, rather than anticipated, injury to the wife, such that would render her vulnerable to seduction. The period of such absence or imprisonment must be 6 months, according to Ahmad, and a minimum of one year, according to Malik. Of course, the absence must lack a justa causa. Malik considers such a dissolution an irrevocable divorce, while Ahmad considers it an annulment. There is unanimity in the legislation of Egypt, Syria, Morocco and Algeria in that the period of absence is one year.

Furthermore, the wife maintains the right to apply for judicial divorce (faskh) where the husband fails to abide by any conditions agreed upon in the taqliq (prenuptial agreement). In the Koranic verses concerning divorce the word ma'aruf appears a total of ten times. Ma'aruf may be translated as equity, reasonableness, fairness, honour and harmony. Thus the overall spirit, purport and tenor of Islamic divorce law is one of justice, equity, fairness, reasonableness, harmony, kindness, and, above all, human dignity.

DIVISION OF PROPERTY UPON DISSOLUTION OF MARRIAGE

Another common misconception, particularly amongst western writers, concerning Islamic family law is that the division of property upon the dissolution of a marriage is invariably unfair and unjust in respect of the wife. The approach of the Malaysian Sharia court easily dispels this misunderstanding.

In Malaysia property acquired during a marriage is known as harta sepencarian and is defined in the Islamic Family Law (Federal Territory) Act 1984 as "property jointly acquired by husband and wife during the subsistence of marriage in accordance with the conditions stipulated by hukum syara" (Sharia law). Section 58 of the Act provides:

> (1) The court shall have power, when permitting the pronouncement of talaq or when making an order of divorce, to order the division between the parties of any assets acquired by them during the marriage by their joint efforts or the sale of any such assets and the division between the parties of the proceeds of sale.
> (2) In exercising the power conferred by subs (1), the court shall have regard to:
> (a) the extent of the contributions made by each party in money, property, or labour towards acquiring of the assets;
> (b) any debts owing by either party that were contracted for their joint benefit;
> (c) the needs of the minor children of the marriage, if any;
> and subject to those considerations the court shall incline towards equality of division.

Section 2 of the Administration of Muslim Law Enactment 1952 of the state of Selangor states that "property" includes all estates, interests, easements and rights, whether equitable or legal, in, to, or arising out of, property and things in action. In the past, claims to harta sepencarian were dealt with in both the High Court as well as the Sharia Court. The High Court regarded the matter as one of Malay custom (adat). However, the Sharia Court and the Board of Appeal of the Federal Territory have endeavored to find support for the concept of harta sepencarian in Islamic law. In the case of *Mansjur bin Abdul Rahman v Kamariah bte Noordin*[28] the appellant had been given the right to develop government land. Both the appellant and the respondent worked on the land. The parties had five children. Upon divorce, four of the children lived with the appellant, while the other lived with the respondent. No order was made as regards the division of the property at the time of the divorce, but subsequently the respondent applied to the Land Committee of the Federal Territory for the land to be equally divided between herself and the appellant. Later the Land Committee gave approval to a company to take over the land to be developed with the adjoining lands as a housing estate, and gave permission to the appellant to sign the agreement with the company, on the condition that the compensation payable by the company would be divided equally between the appellant and the respondent. The appellant appealed against this decision of the Land Committee but the appeal was dismissed. No agreement could be reached between the appellant and the respondent and the respondent applied to the Sharia Court for a half share of the compensation and properties given to the appellant by the company that took over the land. The learned Chief Kadi held that the property was harta sepencarian. He ordered the appellant to pay to the respondent a half share of what he had received for the land from the company.

In the case of *Rokiah bte Haji Abdul Jalil v Mohamed Idris bin Shamsudin*[29] the appellant, having been divorced by her husband, claimed a share of the jointly acquired property. The Chief Kadi, in dismissing the claim, held that the property (which comprised a house, a piece of land, investments and some shares) had been acquired by the respondent with his own money and by his sole efforts. The appellant appealed against the dismissal of her claim for harta sepencarian. Ahmad Ibrahim, Chairman of the Sharia Appeal Committee, stated that the Chief Kadi had ignored the indirect contribution of the wife to the acquisition of the property during the marriage by her looking after the house and the family. He relied on a number of earlier Malaysian decisions in which similar reasoning prevailed. In the case of *Noorbee v Ahmed Sanusi*[30] the Chief Kadi of Penang stated that harta sepencarian is approved by Islamic law on the basis of the work and the life partnership of the parties. The wife administers and looks after the house and the husband goes out to seek a livelihood. The wife, according to the law, is entitled to have a servant to help in administering the household and, if she does not, then her contribution of cooking, washing and looking after the house should be regarded as part of the effort to reduce the burden of the husband.

In another *Penang* case, that of *Haminah v Samsudin*,[31] the Chief Kadi said that where a wife performs certain duties without any assistance from servants it can be inferred that the assets acquired during the marriage were acquired by their joint efforts. The work that is done by such an unassisted wife relieves the burden of the husband to the extent of at least one-third. In the Selangor case of *Tengku Anun Zaharah v Dato Dr. Hussein*[32] the divorced wife had claimed a share of the jointly acquired property. The defendant husband claimed that all the properties acquired by him during the marriage were the result of his own efforts and initiative, and the wife had not contributed with her money or efforts. The learned Chief Kadi, however, held that even if that was true and the wife had not contributed in the form of money, she had contributed morally, as it was his marriage with her, a member of the royal family, that had brought people to trust him and had helped him to get the award of Dato. The court, therefore, allowed her claim for a share of the jointly acquired property.

The Cape High Court, in the 1997 decision of Ryland v Edros,[33] did have an ideal opportunity of adopting the concept of harta sepencarian in adjudicating the dissolution of Muslim marriages. It is, in my view, unfortunate that the parties' expert witnesses expressed diametrically opposed views on the matter. This led Judge Farlam to declare:

> In view of the fact that no other Islamic country adopts this approach, I cannot see on what basis I can regard the Malaysian rules as being part of the provisions of Islamic personal law incorporated by the parties into their contract unless a custom similar to the Malay adat relating to harta sepencarian prevails among the Islamic community, to which the parties belong, in the Western Cape.[34]

It is submitted that if a future Islamic family law court in South Africa adopts the line of reasoning of the Malaysian Sharia courts, and if legislation vis-à-vis property division upon marriage dissolution follows the tenor and spirit of s 58 of the Islamic Family Law (Federal Territory) Act, no question of the lack of gender equality need arise.

CUSTODY

Although the question of custody is not directly addressed in the Koran, there are a number of Prophetic sayings (ahadith) on this issue. Two illustrations are given here. First, a woman once complained to the Prophet that, upon divorce, her husband wished to remove her young child from her custody. The Prophet commented: "You have the first right to the child as long as you do not marry." Secondly, on a different occasion a woman again complained that her husband wanted to take her son away from her, although her son was a source of great comfort and warmth to her. Her husband simultaneously denied her claim over the child. The Prophet said: "Child, here is your father and here is your mother; make a choice between the two as to whom you prefer."[35] The son took hold of his mother's hand and they dispersed.

Following upon the direction and spirit of the first hadith, all four Sunni schools of thought—the Hanafi, Maliki, Shafi and Hanbali—as well as the Shia school, hold that the mother, whether she is separated or living with her husband, has the prior claim to the custody of the child. In terms of Islamic law, both males and females must comply with two important conditions to be eligible for custody. First, they must be sane and of the age of majority, and secondly, they must have the ability to raise the child. This second condition entails, inter alia, protecting the child both physically and morally, as well as looking after the interests of the child.[36] In addition to these conditions, the wife loses custody if she marries a man whom the child is not prohibited from marrying.[37] This condition is based on the saying of the Prophet: "You have the first right to the child as long as you do not marry."[38] Nasir[39] explains that, although the tradition would imply that the mother, and, a fortiori, any other female custodian, would lose the right to custody of the child once she has remarried, regardless of her husband's relation to the child, it is not interpreted so sweepingly. The Hanafis and Malikis restrict the marriage that deprives the mother of her right to custody to that with a relative who is not prohibited from marrying the child.[40] For example, if the mother marries a cousin of the child, she forfeits her prior right of custody, whereas if she marries the child's uncle, she retains that right.

As stated earlier, there is no express direction in the Koran on the question of custody. Arab and Islamic countries, in their modern legislation on the issue, have, however, upheld the spirit of the Prophetic sayings and the approaches of the Sunni and Shia schools of thought. Inherent in the spirit of the Prophetic traditions and the various schools of law is the principle of the "best interests" of the child. A few illustrations suffice.

Article 20 of the Egyptian Personal Status Law of 1929[41] provides that the right of a woman to custody of her children shall cease on the attainment of the age of ten years in the case of a male child, and twelve years in the case of a female child. After the child has reached that age the qadi can order that the child continue in such custody until the male child reaches fifteen and the female child gets married, if he is satisfied that the welfare of the child so demands. The Article grants the mother the prior right to custody—in terms of the hadith of the Prophet—and then awards custody in accordance with the Hanafi school of thought.

The Malaysian Islamic Family Law (Federal Territory) Act 1984 provides, in Article 84, as follows:

> (1) The right of the hadinah (female custodian) to the custody of a child terminates upon the child attaining the age of seven years in the case of a male and the age of nine years in the case of a female—but the court may, upon application by the hadinah, allow her to retain custody of the child until the attainment of the age of nine years in the case of a male and eleven years in the case of a female.

(2) After termination of the right of the hadinah the custody devolves upon the father, and if the child has reached the age of discernment (mumaiyiz), he or she shall have the choice of living with either of the parents, unless the court otherwise orders.

How have the courts in Islamic countries approached the issue? In Pakistan the courts have developed the presumption that the minor's welfare lies in granting custody in accordance with the personal laws of the minor. In the case of *Atia Waris v Sultan Ahmad Khan*,[42] Mahmud J stated:

> In considering the welfare the court must presume initially that the minor's welfare lies in giving custody according to the dictates of the rules of personal law, but if circumstances clearly point that his or her welfare lies elsewhere or that it would be against his or her interest, the court must act according to the demand of the welfare of the minor, keeping in mind any positive prohibitions of the personal law.[43]

In this case custody was given to the paternal grandparents, so as to ensure that the minor was raised as a Muslim, despite the positive rule of Muslim law—all four Sunni schools of thought are ad idem on this rule—which states that, if the mother is found unsuitable to have custody of her female child, the custodial right devolves on the maternal grandmother.[44] However, the same court, some six years later, in the case of Zohra Begum v Latif Ahmad Manawwar[45] stated that it is permissible for the courts to differ from the rules of custody as stated in textbooks on Muslim law, because there is no Koranic injunction on the point and courts, which have taken the place of qazis, can, therefore, reach their own decisions by the process of ijtihad (individual reasoning).[46] It would thus be permissible to depart from the rules if, on the facts of a particular case, its application would prejudice the welfare of the minor.

There have been a number of cases decided in the Sharia courts of Malaysia on the issue of the custody of children. In one of the leading cases, Nooranita bte Kamaruddin v Faeiz bin Yeop Ahmad,[47] the Sharia Appeal Committee, after referring to the Prophetic sayings on the right to custody,[48] as well as leading authorities such as Imam Shafi and Syed Sabiq, concluded that:

> (1) The primary consideration in all cases of custody under the Islamic law is that the right of the child over whom custody is claimed must be given preference to the right of the persons claiming custody, as the purpose of custody is for the interest and welfare of the child and not for the interest and welfare of the parties contending for custody.
> (2) Based on this legal principle of the Shariah and having considered all the facts of the case, including the reluctance of the child herself to choose between the father and her mother, the Appeal Committee is of the opinion that it is to

the welfare and interest of the child that she should continue to stay with her father, a situation which has existed for over four years, even though the mother appellant could not be blamed for the delay in the hearing of the appeal.[49]

INHERITANCE

The Koran states:

> God directs you
> As regards your children's inheritance
> To the male a portion equal to
> That of two females.[50]

Clearly the 2:1 apportionment favoring males in the Islamic law of inheritance is mathematically unequal. However, the empirical equity inherent in such distribution becomes clear when, as Coulson[51] argues, the structure of family ties and accepted social values and responsibilities within the Islamic community is understood. What, then, is the reason of the 2:1 ratio vis-à-vis inheritance law? The Islamic law of inheritance does not stand in vacuo, but it is complementary to other branches of a comprehensive system of family law, which must be viewed as an integral whole and understood in its entirety. Thus the portion inherited by the widow, daughter(s), mother and other female relatives of the deceased should be evaluated in the light of and in relation to the female's right of dower—in the case of a widow—and her right to maintenance—in the case of a daughter or mother. The duty of payment of dower, as well as the duty of maintenance, rests squarely on the shoulders of the husband or other male relative.

Notwithstanding the rationale for the 2:1 male-female apportionment, gender is not the basis of the mathematical inequality of the predetermined shares. The scheme of equal shares to mother and father (one-sixth to each) and to uterine brothers and sisters (equal shares irrespective of their gender) clearly illustrates the fact that gender is not the basis of the inequality of shares. Where they do not coexist with their male counterparts and thus where no financial support is forthcoming, females have, in their own right, been apportioned adequate shares. For example, a sister gets one half if alone and two-thirds if there are two or more sisters. The same applies to a daughter. These and other females are not discriminated against; rather their shares are reduced, as it were, only where a larger share needs to be given to a male counterpart, in view of the latter's heavier obligations as regards family maintenance, which includes, inter alia, marriage expenses on children as well as education expenses.

Legally, strictly and mathematically speaking, males and females are not accorded equal shares, but when the Koranic rule of inheritance, that a male is entitled to a portion equivalent to that of two females, is looked at from the point of view that the total responsibility of maintaining the female throughout her life is borne by her male counterpart, the wisdom of the law-giver—which, says Tahir Mahmood, prefers an empirical equity to a mathematical equality,[52] is crystal clear, and the inherent and substantive wisdom of the legislation replaces its apparent, but deceptive, inequality. Critics who wish to give men and women equal shares forget that the equality of unequals—economically speaking—amounts, de facto, to inequality. Commenting on the philosophy of the Islamic approach to the law of inheritance, Muhammad Iqbal writes:[53]

> From the inequality of their legal shares it must not be supposed that the rule assumes the superiority of males over females. Such an assumption would be contrary to the spirit of Islam. . . . The share of the daughter is determined not by any inferiority inherent in her, but in view of her economic opportunities, and the place she occupies in the social structure of which she is part and parcel. . . . [T]he rule of inheritance must be regarded not as an isolated factor in the distribution of wealth, but as one factor among others working together for the same end. . . . If you judge the working of the rule of inheritance from this point of view, you will find that there is no material difference between the economic position of sons and daughters. . . . The truth is that the principles underlying the Koranic law of inheritance—this supremely original branch of [Islamic] Law as Von Kremer describes it—have not yet received from Muslim lawyers the attention they deserve.[54]

CONCLUSION

Critics—and critiques—of aspects of the Islamic system of family law, almost without exception, fail to understand when the Koran was revealed to the Prophet Muhammad (peace be upon him) and, more importantly, fail to compare the provisions regarding women, and females in general, in other legal systems at the same time, i.e., around 1,400 years ago, and preceding it. A brief comparative survey of similar legislation in such legal systems would serve to abundantly show the gender equality inherent in the Islamic family law system. The laws of inheritance are here the focus of this brief comparative survey.

Under the ancient Hindu legal system the right to inherit was confined to male agnates. The rule of primogeniture, in terms of which the eldest son of the deceased inherits the entire estate to the exclusion not only of daughters, but also of other sons applied.[55] It was only in 1937, under the Hindu Women's Right to Property Act in India, that widows were allowed to enjoy a limited interest in their deceased husband's property.[56] In terms of the

Hindu Succession Act 1956 Hindu mothers, daughters, widows and sisters finally merited inclusion in the category of persons called heirs.

In Roman law, the great legal system which preceded the advent of Islam, the doctrine of patriapotestas was all-pervasive. Through the application of this doctrine women remained under their husband's power for the duration of their married life. On the husband's death, widows—being alieni iuris—were subject to control by their sons. To add insult to injury, females, regarded in Roman society as being of unfirm mind, were subject to perpetual (male) tutelage (tutela perpetua). It was only in the post-classical era of the Roman Empire that the Emperor Justinian, through substantial law reform, enhanced the position of women in general. For example, believing that close relatives and primary dependants should be provided for by the deceased's estate, he imposed restrictions on freedom of testation. In his great work, the Novellae, Justinian provides that a testator should set aside at least one-third or one-half of the estate if he has four or more children (male or female).[57] This strikingly resembles the Prophet Muhammad's (peace be upon him) one-third restriction on bequests. The rationale in both cases is that the close dependants should be adequately provided for. Perhaps Justinian's legislation was a sign of what was to come half a century later, for Justinian died 4 years before God's final Prophet was born.

As far as the English law of succession is concerned,[58] in the thirteenth century the general rule was that a man could leave by will only one-third of his property if his wife and children survived him. What a striking meetings of the minds at a particular historical juncture of Roman law, Islamic law and the English legal system. If either his wife or children, but not both, survived him, he was restricted to leaving half by testate succession, while, if he was survived by neither, he was free to dispose of his entire estate.

The characteristic features of the Inheritance Act 1938, the Intestate Estates Act 1952 and the Family Provision Act 1966 were that they empowered the courts with a discretion to award maintenance for certain dependants out of income. The latest legislation, the Inheritance (Provision for Family Dependants) Act 1975 maintains the basic notion of the court's discretion, but in the important case of husband and wife, it has moved away from the idea of providing maintenance for a dependant to one of giving to the surviving spouse reasonable financial provision, either from income or capital, whether or not that amount is required for the surviving spouse's maintenance.[59] Whereas English succession law put forward the concept of "reasonable financial provision" in 1975, Islamic law provided for this 14 centuries ago.[60] It is no wonder, then, that David Powers states:

> Now I find it striking that a woman in seventh-century Arabia—whether living in a town or among the nomads, either before Islam or after—should inherit in

her capacity as a wife. Of all the legal systems of the Near East, only Islamic law treats a wife as a legal heir upon intestacy.[61]

Finally, as far as African customary law is concerned, there exists a bar on female inheritance.

The Islamic approach to scriptural interpretation should be constantly borne in mind in the interpretation of any aspect of the Sharia. According to Kamali, Islamic jurisprudence is concerned with the way in which laws are derived from the Koran and Sunnah. Revelation, given to the human being in order to restore unity and assist him to achieve a just and devout order in society, as well as in the soul, must be interpreted so as to render it practicable in every culture, "while not betraying its spirit and immutable provisions" (emphasis added).[62]

NOTES

1. Project 59, Issue Paper 15, May 2000.

2. *Id*. at 7.

3. Chapter 2, verse 187.

4. Chapter 2, verse 228.

5. Mahmood "The Grandeur of Womanhood in Islam" (1986) Islamic and Comparative Law Quarterly 1, at 8.

6. *Id*.

7. Principles of Islamic Jurisprudence (1991).

8. *Id*.

9. *See* Kamali "Source, Nature and Objectives of Sharia," a paper presented at Sharia symposium, Malaysia 1989; *see* also Kamali "Maqasid Al-Sharia: The Objectives of Islamic law" (1998) 3(1) Newsletter of the Association of Muslim Lawyers and the Islamic Foundation's Legal Studies Unit 13.

10. *Id*. at 17.

11. Mahmood Personal Law in Islamic Countries (1987) at 80.

12. Chapter 5, verse 1.

13. Chapter 2, verse 229.

14. Chapter 2, verse 231.

15. Tan Sri Datuk Professor Emeritus, former Dean/Shaikh of the Faculty/Kulliyyah of Laws, International Islamic University Malaysia and Chairman of the Sharia Appeal Board, Kuala Lumpur.

16. *See* Rojmah bte Abdul Kadir v Mohsin bin Ahmad (1991) 3 MLJ xxx. *See* further, for a detailed analysis of the philosophy of divorce law in Islam Re Mohd Hussin bin Abdul Ghani and Anor (1990) 2 MLJ lxxv.

17. *See* Supra note 4.

18. PLD 1967 SC 97.

19. *Id*. at 102.

20. *Id*. at 112.

21. Koran, chapter 2, verse 237.

22. See Nasir The Islamic Law of Personal Status (Graham and Trotman, 1986), at 96.

23. Leaders of two Sunni schools of thought, Maliki and Hanbali respectively—the other two schools being the Hanafi and Shafi.

24. Chapter 4, verse 35.

25. Chapter 2, verse 24.

26. Followers of Imam Abu Hanifa. *See* Supra note 23.

27. *See* Supra note 23.

28. (1988) 3 Malayan Law Journal xlix.

29. (1989) 3 Malayan Law Journal ix.

30. (1978) 1 Journal Hukum 63.

31. (1979) 1 Journal Hukum 71.

32. (1980) 3 Journal Hukum 125.

33. (1997) 1 BCLR 77 (C).

34. *Id.* at 100.

35. Sunan Abu Dawud, Kitab at Talaq (2) 616–617.

36. *See* Supra note 22, at 178.

37. *See* further Moosa "Muslim Personal Laws Affecting Children: Diversity, Practice and Implications for a New Children's Code for South Africa" (1998) South African Law Journal 479.

38. *See* Supra note 35.

39. *See* Supra note 22.

40. *See* Supra note 22, at 179.

41. As amended by Law 100 of 1985; *see* also Mahmood, *see* Supra note 11.

42. (1959) PLD (WP) Lah 205.

43. *Id.* at 214.

44. Pearl A Textboook on Muslim Personal Law (Croom Helm, 1987), at p. 93.

45. (1965) PLD (WP) Lah 695. *See* also Fahmida Begum v Habib Ahmad (1968) PLD Lah 1112.

46. For a comprehensive analysis of the concept of ijtihad, which he refers to as the "principle of movement," *see* Iqbal The Reconstruction of Religious Thought in Islam (Khitab Bhavan, 1981). *See* Further Kamali, *see* Supra note 7, at pp. 366–394.

47. (1989) 2 Malayan Law Journal cxxiv.

48. *See* Supra note 35.

49. For a more detailed analysis *see* my article "Constitutional interpretation of the 'best interests' principle in South Africa in relation to custody" in Eekelaar and Nhlapo (eds.). The Changing Family: Family Forms and Family Law (Hart Publishing, 1998), at 369–378; *see* further Moosa, *see* Supra note 37, at 488–490.

50. Chapter 4, verse 11.

51. Coulson Succession in the Muslim Family (Cambridge University Press, 1971), at 1.

52. *See* Supra note 5, at 12.

53. *See* Supra note 46.

54. *See* Supra note 46, at 169–179.

55. *See* Markby Hindu and Mohammedan Law (Inter-India Publications, 1977), at 50.

56. *See* Khan Islamic Law of Inheritance (Khitab Bhavan, 1989), at p. 7 and Derrett Essays in Classical and Modern Hindu Law (E. G. Brill, 1977), at p. 51.

57. *See* Khan, *Id.* at 3.

58. *See* Mellows The Law of Succession (Butterworths, 1983), at p. 176.

59. *Id.* at 177.

60. *See* Supra note 25.

61. Powers Studies in Qur'an and Hadith: The Formation of the Islamic Law of Inheritance (University of California Press, 1986), at p. 55.

62. *See* Supra note 7.

7

Islam as Intellectual Property: "My Lord! Increase me in knowledge."

Ali Khan

INTRODUCTION

This chapter presents Islam as protected knowledge, a form of intellectual property. The Quran, the Sunna,[1] and the unique marks and symbols of faith, together constitute the protected knowledge of Islam.[2] These timeless assets establish a way of life devoted to none but One God. As a favor, God has placed these knowledge-based assets in an irrevocable Trust for an indefinite period of time. He established the Trust for the benefit of all human beings.[3] However, Muslims have entered into an irrevocable Covenant with God to be the good faith trustees of these timeless assets. As beneficiaries, Muslims draw upon these assets to lead morally intelligent lives. As trustees, they preserve these assets from the irreverence of misinformed critics, from the assault of misguided assailants, and from the mockery of fools.[4] As trustees, they also transfer these assets to the next generation of Muslims without changing the nature of the Trust and without depreciating the value of its assets. For the preservation of these assets, any property can be expended, and every life can be sacrificed; to Muslims, nothing is more precious than the integrity and honor of these timeless assets.

The distinction between assets and ideas lies at the core of the misunderstanding between Islam and secularism, the strongest version of which is unfolding in the United States. Muslims view Islam as knowledge-based (intellectual) property, not an idea. Secularists reduce Islam to a mere idea, reserving the notion of intellectual property for literary and artistic works,

135

inventions, patents, films, computer programs, designs, trademarks, and trade secrets.[5] Muslims elevate the knowledge-based assets of Islam to the highest level of protection, more than the intellectual work of any scientist, artist, or corporation. Even in the face of a rising tide of secularism throughout the world, they refuse to consign their religion to the marketplace of ideas, a place where ideas are depreciated and trashed. This clash of understanding between Islam as an idea and Islam as intellectual property breeds mutual mistrust between secularists and Muslims.

This article is written from an internal viewpoint.[6] It will be useful for the readers of this article to bear in mind a fundamental distinction between the internal viewpoint of Muslims and the external viewpoint of non-Muslims who may or may not be secularists. The internal viewpoint is tied to the Trust; it treats the timeless assets of Islam as protected knowledge that no one may alter or dishonor. The external viewpoint flourishes on freedoms; it defends the freedom of belief,[7] granting individuals the right to make any changes in the protected knowledge of Islam. The external viewpoint protects freedom of speech, granting individuals the right to denigrate God, the Quran, and the Prophet.

The gap between the two viewpoints can be enormous. Take the example of Salman Rushdie's novel, *The Satanic Verses*. From an internal viewpoint, the publication of the novel was an act of extreme disrespect toward the Quran and the Sunna, an assault designed to depreciate the assets of Islam. The novel was banned in all Islamic countries, worldwide angry protests were staged, and Imam Khomeni, the spiritual leader of Iran, issued a fatwa (decree) for the execution of the author. The external viewpoint, however, was one of bewilderment and disgust toward the fatwa. Even though Jewish, Catholic, and Protestant leaders condemned the novel,[8] the predominant external viewpoint, particularly among secularists, defended the author's right to freedoms of speech and belief. This and many other episodes highlight the clash of the two viewpoints.[9] Muslims view secularists as spiritually barren.[10] Secularists view Muslims as intolerant, self-righteous, behind the times, and having little or no respect for universal human rights that guarantee individuals the freedom of literary and artistic expression.[11]

One purpose of this chapter is to present and describe the knowledge-based assets that Muslims have vowed to protect. The other is to examine these assets in light of secular freedoms of belief and speech. As a broad thesis, I will argue that the internal viewpoint sees Islamic assets as analogous to intellectual property, whereas the external viewpoint sees the same assets through the bifocal freedoms of belief and speech. While these freedoms may be appropriate for positioning religion in the frame of a secular society, they distort the image and reality of Islamic assets. It is hoped that secularists will gain a new understanding of the internal viewpoint, respecting Muslims as spiritual people who want to protect their knowledge-based property. It is also hoped that Muslims will see the external viewpoint more forgivingly, without branding all critics as sworn enemies of Islam.

I. PROTECTED KNOWLEDGE OF ISLAM

Indeed God bestowed a great favor by furnishing the knowledge of Al-Kitab (the Quran) and Al-Hikma (the Sunna)[12]

Islam is based on assets (mulkyyah) founded on knowledge (al-elm). The concept of mulkyyaht al-elm, that is, the knowledge-based assets or the protected knowledge, establishes Islam as a form of intellectual property.[13] The protected knowledge of Islam is known and unknown,[14] rational and mystical,[15] revealed and hidden.[16] God alone has "the keys of the Ghaib"[17] because "not a leaf falls, but He knows it"[18] and because "there is not a grain in the darkness of the earth . . . but is written in a Clear Record."[19] Out of His vast knowledge, God has imparted a little to human beings, some through divine revelation and some through human reason.[20] The protected knowledge that Muslims have received through the Quran and the Sunna constitutes the precious property of Islam. This knowledge is accessible to those who study[21] and understand.[22] Islam, however, as noted above, is not confined to rational or understandable knowledge. It also embodies a secret source code, the hidden knowledge (Al-Ghaib), which only God knows.[23] And to God belongs the knowledge of the day and the knowledge of the night for "He is the All-Hearing, the All-Knowing."[24] Muslims adore the protected knowledge they can study and understand. But, out of humility and submission to God, they honor and fear the hidden knowledge they cannot fathom and ascertain.[25]

The concept of intellectual property provides a vehicle, though defective and inadequate, for understanding the protected knowledge of Islam. It opens up a window, particularly for non-Muslims, for looking into the uniqueness of Islamic knowledge. The analogy between intellectual property and the protected knowledge is by no means perfect. In fact, it breaks down in many ways. Intellectual property, for example, which includes copyrights, patents, trademarks, and other proprietary knowledge, is the product of human intellect, innovation, and effort. In contrast, Islamic assets are the Quran and the Sunna, which no ordinary human being can create. The Quran is God's own knowledge, beyond the creative reach of man. The Sunna is the knowledge attributable to the Prophet's inspired reason, always submissive to the will of God. Thus, the protected knowledge of Islam—the Quran and the Sunna—is the combined treasure of revelation and reason. It is God's knowledge (Al-Kitab) enmeshed with the Prophet's wisdom (Al-Hikma).

Another important attribute distinguishes intellectual property from the protected knowledge of Islam. Intellectual property is often commercial in nature, protected only for a short duration. Furthermore, the knowledge underlying intellectual property may be faulty, frivolous, or even harmful. Unlike intellectual property, the protected knowledge of Islam is not for sale or commercial exploitation. Islamic knowledge is based on assured certainty, which the Quran describes as elm-al-yaqqin.[26] As such, the protected knowledge of Islam is timeless and imperishable. It is handed down from one generation of Muslims to the next without innovations, alterations, or diminishment in value. Each generation uses this knowledge to protect and nurture a morally intelligent life.

A. Protected Knowledge of The Quran

Of all the assets of Islam, the Quran is the foremost and the most precious asset that God has created for the benefit of all human beings.[27] The Quran is God's gift of knowledge, donated to human beings through the medium of the apostle. Critics and secularists may question the gift, arguing that the Quran offers a set of intangible beliefs, not intellectual or tangible property. This critique is quite familiar to Muslims. In fact, the Quran highlights the disbelief of the external viewpoint, saying: "And even if We had sent down unto you (O Muhammad) a Message written on paper so that they could touch it with their hands, the disbelievers would have said: 'This is nothing but obvious magic!'"[28] In the Prophet's own life and since, the external viewpoint has ridiculed the protected knowledge of the Quran as forgery[29] poetry,[30] and the work of the Devil.[31]

1. Divinity

For Muslims, however, the Quran is a divine asset, inscribed in the Preserved Tablet.[32] "And this Quran is not such as could ever be produced by other than Allah (Lord of the heavens and the earth), but it is a confirmation of (the revelations) which was before it (i.e., the Torah, and the Gospel, etc)."[33] Over the past fourteen centuries, the external viewpoint has challenged the Quran's divine origin, alleging that the Quran is not God's work, but that the Prophet forged it.[34] However, the internal viewpoint has remained unshakeable, as each generation of Muslims preserves the divine knowledge of the Quran, believing that "This is the Book (the Quran), whereof there is no doubt."[35] The Quran itself refutes the charges of forgery, daring the critics and secularists to produce a single verse of comparable quality.[36]

The Quran's protected knowledge is woven in layers. It is light upon light. Its study and understanding requires time, patience, faith, and knowledge. Its meaning can escape the most learned. Those who mock the knowledge of the Quran and challenge its divinity find it "a wearisome, confused jumble, crude, incondite. Nothing but a sense of duty could carry [for example] any European through the Koran."[37] To critics and secularists, the knowledge of the Quran is inaccessible and unsuitable,[38] as the Quran itself cautions, because "they have been removed far from hearing it."[39] "Nay, they deny that; the knowledge whereof they could not compass."[40] Yet those who have time, patience, faith, and knowledge may access the Quran, enjoying its grammar and literary beauty, and benefiting from its manifest laws and the layers of secrets that gradually unfold themselves.

2. Authenticity

The Quran's authenticity was preserved at the time of its revelation so that falsehood cannot come to it from before it or behind it.[41] "The Quran is a clear Arabic tongue"[42] "revealed . . . by stages,"[43] that is, a few verses at a time, over a period of twenty-three years.[44] As soon as the verses were revealed, they were carefully written by "the hands of scribes, honorable and obedient."[45] They were also orally memorized. This combination of written and oral records assured the Quran's accuracy.[46] The critics questioned the slow revelation of the Quran, asking "why is not the Quran revealed to him all at once?"[47] God informs the critics that the Quran was revealed in small portions so that "We may strengthen your heart thereby. And we have revealed it to you gradually, in stages."[48] Gradual revelation of the Quran maximized its instructional effect, as each verse came down to respond to a concrete factual circumstance.[49] Each verse calls for, and communicates, special awareness.[50]

This "divine pedagogy"[51] was essential for the gradual transformation of the human Prophet. It also safeguarded the Quran's authenticity because human beings were much more able to accurately write and memorize only a few verses at a time. As new verses were revealed, the Prophet himself selected their proper sequence and placement within the Book, thus organizing the final form of the completed Quran.[52] Fully guarded on all sides, and protected in both substance and form, the Quran's authenticity was preserved during the Prophet's life.

3. Unalterability

The Quran was not only preserved at the time of its revelation. It has also been carefully safeguarded from any alterations, in either form or substance, ever since it was revealed to the Prophet, some fourteen-hundred years ago.[53] In fact, as a matter of principle, the Quran is an unalterable text. No one, neither a Muslim nor a non-Muslim, may lawfully amend, delete, or repeal even a single verse or word of the Quran. Furthermore, not a single verse or word of the Quran can be shifted from its appointed place within the Book. Precisely defined, the Quran is the protected knowledge—a unique form of intellectual property—in that no user is authorized to tinker with its form, substance, integrity, and wholesomeness.[54]

4. Flexibility

The textual constancy of the Quran, however, does not mean that the knowledge of the Quran is inherently rigid. The Quran contains numerous flexible principles, enunciated for the guidance of the Islamic community and individual behavior. These principles are general in nature and broad in application. They cover numerous aspects of communal life, ranging from the law of war and peace to the freedom of religion. Although some principles guide individuals, others direct individuals and social institutions. Moreover, even a single principle may guide in multiple ways.

It is beyond the scope of this article to fully discuss the protected knowledge of the Quran that shapes the contours and character of the Islamic society. Here, however, I will discuss one principle, the principle of consultation, to demonstrate how the protected knowledge of the Quran is inherently flexible and, therefore, evolutionary in its guidance and application.

The Quran's consultation principle mandates that Muslims engage in mutual consultation before making decisions on worldly affairs.[55] The principle disapproves of egotistical and dictatorial decisions and requires the sharing of information, experience, and analysis before decisions are made. Furthermore, the principle can have a wide application. As applied to family matters, the principle forbids any one member from imposing his own will on the entire family. When applied to statecraft, it prohibits the ruler from implementing any legislative policy without expert or popular advice.

Furthermore, each generation of Muslims may use the consultation principle in new and creative ways to respond to their unique social and political circumstances. For example, the consultation principle was fully compatible with the caliphate form of government, established soon after the Prophet's death,[56] under which the caliph ruled with the assistance of a council of wise men and women. Despite the golden period of Islamic statecraft under the first four caliphs,[57] the consultation principle imposes no requirement that the caliphate be the only form of government that Muslims may lawfully have. The consultation principle is equally compatible with modern democracy under which decision-making officials are accountable to the people. In addition, a parliament of elected officials, who make social policy after debate and exchange of views, is a sound political institution founded on the consultation principle. Due to the inherent flexibility of the consultation principle, Islamic statecraft is not rigid but evolutionary. Thus, Muslims may lawfully demand a democratic form of government, particularly in times when the rest of the world has embraced democracy on a universal basis.[58]

5. Specificity

While the Quran's principles are general and flexible, its rules, however, are specific and firm. Some rules are more specific than others.[59] With varying degrees of firmness, the Quran's specific rules cover a wide range of legal matters, including family law, wills, trusts, contracts, evidence, and property. Whereas flexible principles allow Muslims to adapt social institutions to the needs of the times, the Quran's firm rules anchor the Islamic community in an otherwise changing world. Flexible principles promote harmony between Muslims and non-Muslims, allowing Muslims to follow universal trends that other nations have established. On the other hand, firm rules may cast Muslims in a head-on collision with the rest of the world. In all situations, however, Muslims are committed to preserve the Quran's authentic and wholesome knowledge, without accepting any changes to its rules or principles.

Consider the Quran's specific rule of written contracts. To avoid confusion, fraud, and injustice, the Quran favors written contracts.[60] The rule of written contracts has triumphed in all legal systems, thus affirming the Quran's inherent wisdom and pragmatism. However, the Quran further states that two male witnesses must sign a written contract of debt. If a male witness is unavailable, two female witnesses may be substituted for one male.[61] The Quran justifies this inequality on the presumption that if one woman errs, the other can correct her.[62] This gender inequality in witnessing contracts may harden the popular stereotype that Islam treats men more favorably than women. The specific evidentiary rule seems to oppose the modern movement of gender equality, which advocates nondiscrimination in matters of law.[63]

Muslim women enjoy broad-based respect and general equality.[64] The Quran establishes principles of equity and fairness between males and females. "Never will I allow to be lost the work of any of you, be he male or female. You are (members) one of another."[65] While recognizing equal interdependence between males and females, the Quran rejects the doctrine of sameness under which men and women have no distinguishing characteristics. The Quran also rejects the phantom of strict equality, advising Muslim men and women: "And wish not for the things in which Allah has made some of you to excel others. For men there is reward for what they have earned, (and likewise) for women there is reward for what they have earned."[66] Thus, the Quran finds it perfectly normal that men may excel in some aspects of life and women in others. In some areas, they may both excel.[67] In all cases, however, men and women are the offspring of another. They share a collaborative enterprise. They are not set against each other. Even though they are not the same, men and women are entitled to receive equal reward for what they have earned.[68]

Despite this pragmatic equality between Muslim men and women, the specificity of the Quran's evidentiary rule in debt contracts poses a direct conflict between the external and internal viewpoints. The external viewpoint demands that Muslims ignore the Quran's gender inequality in matters of contract evidence. However, from the internal viewpoint, the Quran cannot be ignored or altered. Despite the emergence of a universal rule that allows no gender discrimination in matters of witnessing contracts, Muslims have no other option but to adhere to the Quran's specific exceptions. The internal viewpoint cannot change; it cannot question God's wisdom; it cannot provide gender equality where the Quran has clearly withheld it.[69] When the external viewpoint cannot be reconciled with the internal viewpoint, Muslim men and women submit to the will of God and not to shifting paradigms of the external viewpoint. Unlike the followers of other religions, Muslim men and women refuse to compromise the integrity of the protected knowledge. "And those who are firmly grounded in knowledge say: 'We believe in it; the whole of it (clear and unclear verses) are from our Lord.'"[70] And once the law has been laid, Muslim men and women do not question its authority.[71] No reason may alter what a clear revelation of the Quran has established.[72]

Thus, the protected knowledge of the Quran reigns supreme in Islamic communities. Guided by their reason, secularists may criticize the Quran's principles and rules as anachronistic and reactionary. Even misguided Muslims may pick and choose the rules and principles they would obey and respect. They may "distort the Book with their tongues"[73] to "purchase a small gain."[74] It serves no purpose to expect secularists and critics to respect the protected knowledge of the Quran in its entirety, because they would say: "Shall we believe as the fools have believed?"[75] Muslims fully realize that the external viewpoint may or may not coincide with the Quran's protected knowledge. Muslims are willing to evolve with the rest of the world but only if the evolution is consistent with the flexible, as well as firm, knowledge of the Quran. If not, Muslims choose the Quran. In all cases, they submit to the will of God, honoring what has been revealed and fearing what has been hidden.[76]

B. Protected Knowledge of the Sunna

In addition to the Quran, the Sunna is the protected asset that constitutes Islamic intellectual property. While the Quran provides the written law, the Sunna supplies the case law, consistent with the Quran's text. The Sunna embodies the application of the Quran's written law to concrete disputes and hypothetical questions that arose during the Prophet's life. Some Sunna cases simply explain the Quran's principles and rules. Some cases interpret the Quran's text, providing new insights into the written law. Some provide new principles and rules, supplementing the Quran's protected knowledge.

The Quran itself validates the Sunna's authority, commanding Muslims that "whatsoever the Messenger (Muhammad) gives you, take it, and whatsoever he forbids you, abstain (from it)."[77] The Quran reposes this confidence in the Prophet because he had no inclination but to follow and disseminate the law of God. In yet another verse, the Quran brings together the two sources of the protected knowledge of Islam: "Indeed, Allah conferred a great favor on the believers when He sent among them a Messenger (Muhammad) from among themselves, reciting unto them His Verses (the Quran) and purifying them (from sins by their following him), and instructing them (in) the Book (the Quran) and Al-Hikma, . . . while before that they had been in manifest error."[78] Here, Al-Hikma refers to the Sunna. The Quran is Al-Kitab

It is important to note that the Prophet was a mortal human being. Accordingly, he made no claims to possess the unlimited knowledge that God commands. In fact, the Quran advised the Prophet to publicly announce his limited knowledge in the following words: "Say (O Muhammad) . . . [I do not] know what will be done with me or with you. I only follow that which is revealed to me, and I am but a plain warner."[79] Thus, what the Prophet said or did was in harmony with the protected knowledge of the Quran.

The synergy between the Quran and the Sunna is seamless. The Quran is the word of God; the Sunna is the conduct of the Prophet. Each word of the Quran is protected; each authentic case of the Sunna is protected.[80] The Quran is the protected knowledge of God; the Sunna is the protected knowledge of the Prophet. The Quran and the Sunna together constitute the Shari'ah, that is, the protected knowledge of Islam.[81] Both the Quran and the Sunna are equally binding sources of law. However, the Quran is superior to the Sunna. No Sunna case, therefore, may be read or understood in a way that it ignores, refutes, or supersedes the Quran's protected knowledge.

1. Preservation of the Sunna

Great care was taken to collect the Sunna cases, known as the ahadith.[82] Because these cases were compiled decades after the Prophet's death, the accuracy of their content and source needed verification. Great scholars of Islam authenticated each Sunna case after a careful examination of its chain of transmission, as each case must be traced back to the Prophet. Thus "authentic cases (sahih)"[83] were separated from "weak cases (da'if)."[84] Authentic cases were transmitted through a chain of credible narrators, men and women,[85] whose characters were unimpeachable and whose memory was reliable. Many authentic cases were traced back to the Prophet through distinct and separate chains of transmission, thus adding to their veracity. In contrast, weak cases lack a credible chain of transmission. Some of these cases were falsely attributed to the Prophet. Some failed the rigorous test of scholarly authentication.[86] Weak cases are not included in the most reliable compilations of the Sunna. Accordingly, they carry little or no weight in the realm of protected knowledge. Authentic cases, however, serve as binding precedents.

2. Substance of the Sunna

Authentic cases of the Sunna may or may not report the Prophet's precise words. Different narrators in the chain of transmission do not use the same words to describe what they heard from the Prophet or what they saw him doing.[87] In the case of the Sunna, therefore, the focus is more on the content (matn) of each reported hadith rather than the words in which the content was reported. This is an important distinction, because in the case of the Quran, each word in itself is protected.

The substance of the Sunna, reported in thousands of authentic cases, covers a wide range of spiritual, ethical, social, economic, and legal topics. These cases, in their cumulative effect, provide detailed instructions on religious matters, including prayer, fasting, zakat (obligatory charity), jihad, and hajj (pilgrimage). They also examine legal questions and provide rules and guidelines regarding sales, contracts, marriage, divorce, wills and testaments, inheritance, gifts, mortgage, partnership, distribution of water, gifts, renting, interest, and rules of evidence.

The protected knowledge of the Sunna contains contentious and advisory cases. In contentious cases, the Prophet resolved actual controversies. For example, once a Bedouin urinated in the mosque. The Muslims got angry and started shouting at him. To resolve this conflict between the Bedouin and the Muslims, the Prophet told the Muslims not to disturb the Bedouin. When the Bedouin finished, the Prophet had the spot cleaned with a bucket of water, and then instructed the Muslims at the congregation: "You have been sent to make things easy and not to make them difficult."[88] This treatment of the Bedouin set a precedent that Muslims must treat the uninformed non-Muslims with kindness, even when they engage in ignorant or (unintentional) offensive conduct.[89]

Most cases reported in the Sunna are of advisory nature. Advisory cases contain the Prophet's statements, acts, and gestures, all of which are informative and instructive. Advisory cases also include questions and hypothetical situations on which the Prophet commented. For example, a man asked the Prophet about the lawfulness of finding and keeping a lost object. The Prophet advised the man to make a public announcement and, in the meantime, preserve the lost object in the manner of a trust. If, however, no owner claimed the lost property within a year, the finder may lawfully keep it or dispose of it. The man then asked about the lawfulness of keeping a lost goat.

The Prophet advised the man: It is yours or for your brother, or for the wolf. In other words, if a lost object is likely to perish, the finder has a superior right to consume it. However, when the man asked about appropriating a lost camel, the Prophet distinguished the case, saying: You have nothing to do about that; (the camel) has feet and a leather bag (to quench its thirst) until its owner finds it.[90] On these and other reported cases, the Sunna law of lost and found property offers sophisticated insights into the finder's rights and obligations.

The protected knowledge of the Sunna is a core Islamic asset. It supplements the protected knowledge of the Quran. Mere transmission of God's knowledge to the people does not exhaust the Prophet's duties. The human Prophet must also explain the purposes of divine revelations, not only through speech but also conduct. This enables the followers to apply God's injunctions to their real lives. Words alone, powerful and pointed, cannot be fully comprehended unless they are translated into definite forms and shapes of behavior. Even divine knowledge begins to become inaccessible unless illustrated by living examples.[91] Deeds, not mere words, are the final message of Islam. The Sunna provides the experiential dimension to the spiritual. It humanizes the divine.

C. Protected Marks and Symbols of Faith

Derived from the Quran and the Sunna, Islamic assets contain protected marks and symbols that define, identify, and preserve Islamic practices and rituals.[92] For example, the masjid is the house of worship, which is not simply a building but a protected symbol of Islam. The very word "masjid" in Arabic or "mosque" in English represents and identifies the masjid as a house of prayer for Muslims and for no one else.[93] Along with its universally recognized association with Islam, the masjid possesses unique characteristics throughout the world, which have lasted for centuries. Though flexible and variant in its architecture, the masjid is nonetheless a pure house of worship, which contains no idols, musical instruments, pews, or chairs. Also, no shoes, food, or drinks are admitted into the masjid. Thus the masjid, both as a symbol and as a design, is a protected part of Islamic intellectual property.[94]

Accordingly, Muslims of the world have a right to protect the symbol and the design of the masjid from any unlawful use or misuse. For example, Muslims will strongly disapprove if someone intentionally appropriates the word masjid to designate a non-Muslim house of worship[95] or, worse, to name a governmental structure, private residence, casino, bar, or any other building. Any such infringement of Islamic intellectual property will authorize Muslims to demand that the word "masjid" not be associated with any such building. If no such relief is forthcoming, Muslims will have a lawful basis to forcibly remove the word "masjid" from the name of the building, particularly when the building is located within an Islamic state. When the building is located in a non-Muslim state, the right to protest through international forums will continue to exist until the infringement is remedied.

Islamic intellectual property has numerous other protected symbols and marks. The adhan is the call to prayer, which is a unique symbol of Islam. No one may use the adhan to call the people to any other gathering or for any other purpose. Likewise, the five daily prayers with prescribed physical movements identify Muslims worshiping One God. Other permanent features of Islam include the ramadhan, the month of fasting, the zakat, the paying of a fixed share of one's income to the poor and the needy, and the hajj, the annual pilgrimage when Muslims of the world congregate in the holy cities of Mecca and Medina. Furthermore, the Islamic greeting of "assalam-u-alaikam" (peace be upon you) is part of Islamic assets.[96] Since the inception of Islam, each practice has been carefully defined to eradicate confusion, speculation, or alteration. These symbols and practices identify the religion as Islam and its follower as Muslims.[97] Muslims of all nations and of all times are obligated to preserve the integrity of these marks and symbols from confusion, misappropriation, and subversion.[98]

II. AL-AMANAH: THE TRUST OF PROTECTED KNOWLEDGE

For the protection of their integrity and dignity in this world, the core assets of Islam—the Quran and the Sunna—have been placed in a Trust (Al-Amanah). The Trust is universal, timeless and irrevocable. The Trust is established for the benefit of all, as every human being, Muslim or non-Muslim, is free to benefit from the protected knowledge. However, not everyone has accepted the obligations of the Trust. Nor can anyone be forced to do so. All Muslims, born and naturalized,[99] are trustees of the protected knowledge, because their faith is inseparable from the Trust. They understand the obligation of the Trust. They know that the protected knowledge placed in the Trust cannot be altered; it cannot be assaulted; it cannot be disrespected. They accept the Trust in its entirety as it is. They also understand that they cannot accept the Trust on conditions or accept part of the Trust property and reject the remainder.[100] They preserve all assets of the Trust at all costs and from all assailants. More than the rest of the world, they, as trustees, are under a higher obligation not to dishonor the Trust or diminish the value of its assets.[101]

A. No Ownership

It is important to understand that Muslims are the trustees, not the owners of protected knowledge. No individual, no family, no nation, and no one generation of Muslims can claim proprietorship of these assets, simply because no one owns these assets. Even Muslims, in their totality, do not own these assets. In fact, no concept of ownership applies to the knowledge based assets of Islam, as it does to intellectual property. This difference cannot be overemphasized. To prevent any competing claims of exclusive ownership, God has wisely placed the protected knowledge in a Trust. All human beings, including Muslims, are its beneficiaries,[102] although the obligation to protect these assets has been assigned to Muslims.[103]

B. Trust Obligations

The Quran highlights obligations of the Trust in a historical context. When God first proposed the idea of the Trust, the heavens, the earth, and the mountains declined to be the trustees because they knew they would be unable to execute its responsibilities in a fair and faithful manner.[104] Despite onerous burdens of the Trust, man unwittingly accepted to be the trustee, partly because he was prone to injustice and partly because he was ignorant.[105] Mired in ignorance and injustice, man failed to carry out the responsibilities of the Trust. Nor did he fully benefit from the revealed knowledge. Instead of holding firmly to the Trust,[106] he protected only selective assets of the protected knowledge and threw away the rest.[107]

This state of ignorance, however, changed when the protected knowledge of the Quran and the Sunna was conferred upon humanity. Benefiting from this new knowledge, human beings acquired a better understanding of benefits and burdens of the Trust. Just like previous peoples of the book, Muslims have also entered into a Covenant with God to honor and fear His sovereignty. However, Muslims are determined to succeed in their Covenant with God and honor the Trust. They want to make no mistakes. They want to honor the Trust and they are willing to protect the received knowledge from alterations and indignities. In this effort, they are fully aware of the fact that "those who break Allah's Covenant after ratifying it, . . . it is they who are losers."[108]

C. Keys of the Trust

If God possesses the keys to all the hidden knowledge, He has donated the keys of the Trust to Muslims. The Islamic faith, called iman, is composed of two keys that safeguard the knowledge placed in the Trust. One key safeguards the protected knowledge of tauhid, that is, monotheism—a realm of knowledge in which one understands and experiences the Oneness of God, believing without doubt that there is only One God, the Creator of all the worlds, and none but He has the right to be worshiped. This key has previously been given to other religions, including Judaism and Christianity, so that they could access the protected knowledge of One God.[109] Nonetheless, the Islamic knowledge of tauhid is the most protected as it carries not even a shadow of any god but One God.[110] This key becomes uniquely Islamic when the knowledge of One God is received through the verses of the Quran.[111]

The second key of iman is the exclusive property of Islam. It accesses the protected knowledge of the Sunna. In the realm of the Sunna, Muslims find a detailed manual for living an authentic Islamic life. This practical manual also provides great insights into understanding the protected knowledge of the Quran. The Sunna illuminates a simple fact that a morally intelligent and materially prosperous life can be lived in accordance with dictates of the protected knowledge. It offers Islam as a natural and easy religion, imposing no obligation that an individual cannot bear in his natural state of being.[112]

Whereas the first key unlocks the knowledge of One God through the medium of the Quran, the second key unlocks the knowledge of the Prophet's life, the Sunna, devoted to practical demonstration and direct application of the protected knowledge of the Quran. The two keys together are indispensable for understanding, protecting and preserving Islamic assets placed in the Trust—for one key without the other does not work. That is why the complete Islamic faith is comprised of the shahada: There is no god but Allah and Muhammad is His messenger. The Quran and the Sunna, the two keys are freely available, and, therefore, no key can be hidden, damaged or forged. Free availability of the two keys also makes it impossible for any single nation, individual, scholar, or sect to appropriate or misappropriate the intellectual property of Islam.[113]

III. MORAL RIGHTS OF ISLAM

Secular intellectual property is most often associated with economic rights. However, another important set of rights related to secular intellectual property is recognized at both national and international levels. Originating in France, the set is known as droit moral or "moral rights."[114] The term captures "rights of a spiritual, noneconomic and personal nature. The rights spring from a belief that an artist in the process of creation injects his spirit into the work and that the artist's personality, as well as the integrity of the work, should therefore be protected and preserved."[115] DaSilva states the concept more simply and succinctly: "the author has, in a sense, made a gift of his creative genius to the world; in return, he has a right—a moral right—to expect that society respect his creative genius."[116]

Though related to economic rights, moral rights are founded on a separate raison d'etre.[117] Whereas economic rights protect the author's financial interests in his creative work, moral rights recognize the unique relationship between the author and his work.[118] Economic rights may be assigned or sold, but moral rights cannot be traded away as they are tied to the person or the author. Moral rights remain with the author even when he has alienated pecuniary and contractual rights of his work.[119] There may even be a public interest in preserving the integrity of cultural and artistic creations.[120]

Among important moral rights, the right to attribution and the right to integrity are the most relevant rights.[121] The right to attribution demands that the author's name always be associated with his work. This right also prohibits any false attribution of the author's name to a work he has not created. Of all the moral rights, the right to attribution is the least controversial. While economic rights involving intellectual property expire after a designated period, the right to attribution may be granted in perpetuity.[122]

The right to integrity protects the author's work from "any distortion, mutilation or other modification of the said work which would be prejudicial to his honor or reputation."[123] Even excessive criticism may be prejudicial to the work's integrity. In one case, a United States court prevented American Broadcasting Companies from airing distorted versions of a program produced by British writers and performers known as "Monty Python."[124] The court stated:

> This cause of action, which seeks redress for deformation of an artist's work, finds its roots in the continental concept of droit moral, or moral right, which may generally be summarized as including the right of the artist to have his work attributed to him in the form in which he created it.[125]

Ironically, however, Monty Python made a series of movies that lampooned Jesus Christ, parables of the New Testament, and the Catholic Church.

The moral rights, despite the misleading word "moral," safeguard the name and the work of artists, authors, and sculptors, not prophets. They are nonetheless insightful for understanding the protected knowledge of Islam. Islamic moral rights mandate that the Quran's integrity and honor be upheld against any physical or verbal attack. Islamic law prohibits any intentional and hateful burning or mutilating the pages of any copy of the Quran.[126] Furthermore, any proposal to amend the Quran is offensive to the Book's inherent dignity. Likewise, any attack on the person of the Prophet infuriates the entire Islamic community. In fact, any derogatory remarks about Allah or the Quran or the Messenger are occasions for Muslim revenge and punishment. When authors face death threats for their novels and comments, the outside world, particularly the secular west, accuses Muslims of intolerance and extremism. An examination of the Islamic rights of attribution and integrity may explain some of the misunderstanding.

A. Islamic Right to Attribution

"No change can there be in the Words of Allah. This is indeed the supreme success."[127]

The Islamic right to attribution, which safeguards the purity of protected knowledge of Islam—the Quran and the Sunna—has now been firmly established in Islam. In the case of the Quran, the right to attribution preserves the authentic text in its original form, without any alterations, additions, and deletions. Though revealed through the medium of the Prophet, no one but God is the Quran's sole creator. Each and every verse of the Quran is the word of God. Accordingly, the Islamic right to attribution demands that no man-made verse be attributed to God, nor any verse of the Quran be attributed to man. In the case of the Sunna, the right to attribution preserves the authenticity of the Prophet's decisions, statements, and comments. Thus, any false attribution of a decision, statement, or comment to the Prophet violates the right to attribution.[128] Moreover, the right to attribution also prohibits the Prophet's decisions, statements, and comments from being attributed to any one but the Prophet. In sum, the right to attribution preserves the authenticity of the Quran and the Sunna.

The right to attribution was much more critical in the early decades of Islam when the Quran and the Sunna were in the process of compilation. Then, it was not uncommon for non-Muslims to attribute false verses to the Quran and false ahadith to the Prophet. Once the authentic text of the Quran was ascertained, false attributions began to disappear.[129] It is no less than a miracle that, for more than fourteen centuries since the revelation of the Quran, there has been, and is, only one authentic text of the Quran throughout the world. The Quran's own claim that "this is a Book about which there is no doubt" has now been firmly established.

In the early years of Islam, false attribution of ahadith to the Prophet was more common than false attribution of verses to the Quran. Known as maudu ahadith, these were fabricated words and deeds attributed to the Prophet. The ahadith were forged to please rulers and to corrupt the religion of Islam. Among countless ahadith attributed to the Prophet, scholars[130] of immense knowledge and immaculate character spent decades carefully researching and authenticating the chain of transmission (isnad) and the content (matn) for each hadith.[131] Imam Bukhari, the most respected scholar of ahadith, collected over 300,000 ahadith, but selected in his compilation only about 7,000 ahadith whose authenticity was irrefutable.[132]

In order to establish authenticity, the content (matn) of a hadith was evaluated for its substantive harmony with the Quran. If any contradiction arose between the Quran and the reported hadith, the hadith was disregarded. Furthermore, the content of a hadith was also scrutinized for its compatibility with other authentic ahadith. Even when the content of a reported hadith was in harmony with the Quran and other authentic ahadith, great care was taken to carefully assess the reliability of each narrator in the hadith's chain of transmission. A hadith, unimpeachable both in content (matn) and transmission (isnad), was granted the status of a sahih hadith. These two scholarly verifications—content (matn) and transmission (isnad)—defined the right of attribution. The treasured collection of the sahih ahadith constituted the protected knowledge of the Sunna.[133] Thus, from an internal viewpoint, the right to attribution has been finally resolved and firmly established. The umma, that is, the community of believers, are no longer equivocal or confused about the authenticity of the protected knowledge. From an external viewpoint, however, the challenges to the authenticity of the protected knowledge may continue to be presented.

B. Islamic Right to Integrity

"Say: 'Are those who know equal to those who know not?' It is only men of understanding who will remember."[134]

In addition to the right to attribution, the integrity of protected knowledge is the most significant right that distinguishes Islam from other religions. This right safeguards the protected knowledge from innovations, repudiation, internal disrespect, and external assaults. It also protects the honor of the Prophet who served as the sole medium to transmit the protected knowledge to the world. The integrity of protected knowledge and the Prophet's honor are vested in Islam, but their enforcement has been trusted to Muslims. As trustees, Muslims of all nations and all times are under an irrevocable obligation to carry out this fiduciary duty in good faith and to the best of their ability.

To fully appreciate the integrity of protected knowledge, three important points may be noted. First, Islam encourages the study and understanding of the protected knowledge. Second, it discourages innovations that compromise the integrity of protected knowledge—any such innovations are known as bid'a. Third, it abhors situations in which trustees of the protected knowledge themselves repudiate its integrity—an activity known as ridd'a. To safeguard the integrity of protected knowledge from innovations and repudiations, Islam punishes both bid'a and ridd'a. Furthermore, it punishes severely every malicious and public act of ridd'a.

1. Understanding the Protected Knowledge

Islam is a religion of knowledge; it encourages the study and understanding of the protected knowledge.[135] Islamic quest for knowledge, however, is not confined to the study of the Quran and the Sunna. Ever since the advent of Islam, Muslims of successive generations and diverse regions have engaged in the study and research of science, architecture, philosophy, and literature. "Muslim contributions to astronomy, mathematics, medicine, chemistry, zoology, mineralogy, and meteorology often surpassed the received heritage of Greek, Persian, and Indian ideas."[136] The Prophet himself encouraged the tradition of learning, advising his followers "to pursue knowledge, even if you have to go to China."[137] This proposed journey to China approved learning of not only what is sacred and familiar, but also of what is material and remote.

Even with respect to protected knowledge of the Quran and the Sunna, the right to integrity allows multiple understandings of the same sources. This understanding depends upon the person's background, preparation, state of mind, intention, and the quality and quantity of knowledge he already possesses. "As he reaches higher stations, new doors are open to him through which he looks upon new and subtle meanings."[138] The grasp of protected knowledge, therefore, varies from person to person and stage to stage. It also varies from age to age, as the protected knowledge contains secrets that may be disclosed to one generation, but not another.[139]

Multiple understandings of the protected knowledge are most pronounced in the realm of Islamic law. Muslim jurists of high learning and sincere intentions understood the protected knowledge of the Quran and the Sunna at different levels of sophistication, and sometimes, disagreed with each other on key issues. No one school of jurisprudence has claimed a monopoly on interpretation of the protected knowledge. In the last fourteen centuries, Muslim scholars have continued to provide new insights and nuances. Even non-Muslims of high learning and sympathetic intentions have contributed to expanding the understanding of the protected knowledge of Islam. Such interpretive expansions, and even disagreements, do not violate the right of integrity. The Prophet has declared, "difference of opinion among my community is a sign of the bounty of God."[140] By all means and in all times, therefore, the flourishing of the internal viewpoint has been, and continues to be, an integral part of the Islamic evolution.[141]

The right to integrity respects doctrinal decisions of past scholars, not merely as historical literature, but as a source of guidance for present and future generations; it refuses to declare scholarly literature of the past as time-specific or culture-specific. Islamic scholars of all times and all cultures must be respected, their works must be studied, and their interpretations must be seriously honored. Despite this deference to historical scholarship, however, the right to integrity discards the doctrine of taqlid, which forces Muslims to follow interpretations of the early scholars of Islam. Accordingly, Muslim scholars of each generation are free to study and understand the protected knowledge of the Quran and the Sunna in the context of a broader evolution of human civilization. The gate of ijtihad—that is, research and reasoning, serious, sincere, but always submissive to the will of

God and always deferential to the protected knowledge of the Quran and the Sunna—must never be closed.[142]

2. Bida: Innovating the Protected Knowledge

While understanding the protected knowledge is mandatory for the constant revival of Islam, bida or innovations are prohibited. Bid'a[143] is a mischievous assault on the integrity of the protected knowledge of Islam.[144] Two distinct elements define the act of bid'a. First, most often, the intention of the innovator is to reform Islamic law or beliefs. Sometimes, the innovator intends to create public mischief. "And when it is said to them: 'Make not mischief on the earth,' they say: 'we are only peace-makers.'"[145] Even when the innovator is well intentioned and religiously inspired, the innovation sullies the integrity of protected knowledge though the innovator fails to perceive his mischief.[146] Second, almost always, the innovation is a dramatic departure from the existing understanding of the protected knowledge. Often, the two elements are simultaneously present. Sometimes, the dramatic departure itself is a sufficient basis to characterize an innovation as bid'a.

Thus, bid'a is a precept that modifies the established meaning of protected knowledge. Its purpose may be reformative or mischievous. The person who commits bid'a is a Muslim. The innovator does not renounce the faith in its entirety, and he may even wish to lead a new sect within the fold of Islam or remain loyal to an established school of law.[147]

All bid'a are prohibited because the core identity of Islam cannot change. The protected knowledge of Islam needs no reformation; it needs understanding, not renovation. Islam allows no intellectual revolution that would dramatically reformulate the meaning of protected knowledge. Science, law, literature, philosophy, or any other discipline may illuminate the meaning of protected knowledge, but nothing can weaken its integrity. That is why, over the centuries, all Islamic revolutions and movements have been toward eradicating innovations that accrue over time.[148] Almost always, they strive toward reinstating the integrity of protected knowledge.

It is important to distinguish between kufr (disbelief) and bid'a (innovation). Kufr is the rejection of a basic element of the protected knowledge, whereas bid'a is an innovation in the basic element. To completely deny, for example, that Prophet Muhammad (peace be upon him) was God's Messenger is kufr. To assert that Muhammad (peace be upon him) is indeed God's Messenger but not the last Prophet is bid'a, an innovation that dramatically departs from the established meaning of the protected knowledge of Islam. In proposing his innovations, the innovator does not reject the protected knowledge of Islam.[149] He may not question the textual integrity of the Quran, he may even adhere to the substantive integrity of the Sunna, and his bid'a simply attaches innovative meaning to the Quran's text or the Sunna's substance. Thus, bid'a may not be a false attribution; it may simply breach the Islamic right to integrity.

A recent example of Islam's treatment of innovations is its response to Mirza Ghulam Ahmed (1835–1908) of India who claimed prophethood within the fold of Islam. It is disputed whether he was motivated to reform Islam or to create mischief by dividing the Muslims of British India. In claiming prophethood, however, Ahmed proposed no changes in prayers, fasting or the sacred text of the Quran. However, he introduced dramatic new meaning in the firmly established understanding of the Quran. Mirza Sahib[150] claimed to be the "Ahmed," an apostle that Jesus had predicted would come after him.[151] Under the established meaning of the Quran and the Sunna, "Ahmed" was a reference to Prophet Muhammad (peace be upon him), not to Mirza Sahib.[152] Ahmed's claim to prophethood also dramatically altered the meaning of another verse of the Quran, which declares that Muhammad (peace be upon him) is the last Prophet. "Muhammad is not the father of any of your men, but he is the Messenger of God and the last (end) of the prophets."[153] Thus, Ahmed's innovative reading of the Quran disturbed the fundamental meaning of key verses that have remained uncontroversial throughout the ages.

Ahmadis, the followers of Mirza Sahib, have not been well received in Muslim communities of the world.[154] They have been banned from pilgrimage to Mecca. They have been declared non-Muslims under the Pakistan Constitution.[155] Furthermore, they have been forced by Pakistani laws not to use any Islamic symbols and practices. When they challenged these laws under the freedom of religion, the Pakistan Supreme Court held that laws restricting religious practices of Ahmadis are constitutional.[156] Thus, the Islamic right to integrity preempted the right of Ahmadis to freely practice their innovative version of Islam.[157]

The case embodies the principle that every Muslim, as a trustee, is under a fiduciary obligation to protect the integrity of protected knowledge. Islam prohibits its followers from making or proposing any innovations in the fundamental structure, design, and ingredients of the protected knowledge. In contemporary society, this prohibition is perhaps best understood by an analogy to the computer world. For example, no secular state will protect a person who makes unauthorized alterations in proprietary software,[158] and it may even criminally punish or impose punitive damages if a hacker introduces a computer virus that infects the system.[159] This offense will be even more punishable if the person subverting the source code of a software program is a trusted insider. The prohibition in Islam is similar, but much stricter.[160] Islam forbids Muslims from making any innovations in the essentials of protected knowledge.

3. Ridda: Repudiating the Protected Knowledge

Ridda, that is, the repudiation of protected knowledge, is a more serious offense than bid'a.[161] Whereas bid'a aspires to reform the protected knowledge, ridda aims at its total rejection. Ridda is the highest breach of Trust under which Muslims have vowed to uphold and preserve the dignity and integrity of protected knowledge. The concept of ridda applies to Muslims only—"those who have turned back (have apostated) as disbelievers after the guidance has been manifested to them."[162] No non-Muslim may be charged with the offense of ridda, because he has undertaken no fiduciary duty of honoring the integrity and dignity of protected knowledge. When non-Muslims mocked the verses of the Quran, the Prophet was advised to leave their company and stay away from them until they changed the conversation,[163] but they were not guilty of ridda.

To fully understand the concept of ridda, the privacy of belief must be distinguished from public pronouncements. Islam protects the privacy of belief. The Quran prohibits Muslims from spying on each other.[164] The Sunna also affirms the privacy of belief.[165] No ruler, therefore, has any lawful authority to question Muslims about the authenticity of their private faith. As a general rule, it is forbidden to investigate whether Muslims observe the Shari'a, and whether their beliefs are correct from all points of view.[166] Each Muslim, in the privacy of his heart or home,[167] is accountable to none but God. In matters of faith, the Quran forbids Muslims from defaming one another or calling each other with insulting names.[168] In short, no one is authorized to scrutinize, much less punish, the private faith of a Muslim who shows no outward disrespect for the protected knowledge of Islam.

Ridda is an offense involving public repudiation of the protected knowledge of Islam. This repudiation does not take place in the privacy of one's heart or home; it is openly advocated. According to the Quran, the murtaddun (apostates), persons who commit ridda, are "those who purchase a small gain at the cost of Allah's Covenant and their oaths."[169] Ridda is an offense committed by a trusted insider. Most often, the murtaddun live in Muslim nations. But even when they live elsewhere, their ridda is aimed at dishonoring the protected knowledge of Islam.[170] The murtad (apostate)[171] is akin to a corporate insider who discloses the secrets he has undertaken to protect; he is akin to a state official who turns traitor and joins the ranks of the enemy; he is akin to a custodian who destroys the very monument he was safeguarding on behalf of the community. All legal systems punish insiders who breach their trusts; Islam punishes murtaddun too, sometimes severely.[172]

The punishment for ridda varies under different Islamic schools of jurisprudence. It could be death in serious cases.[173] Aggravating facts surrounding ridda and the social status of the murtad may affect the severity of the punishment. If the attack on protected knowledge is open, hostile, and voiced contemptuously, the punishment is likely to be stiff. Furthermore, if the murtad is a notable person in the community or famous in the world, the offense of ridda is considered more serious.[174] Again, this treatment of the murtad is no different from the one meted out to a malicious and non-repentant traitor or a prestigious official who compromises the security and honor of a secular state. In Islam, however, public repudiation of the protected knowledge is the most serious crime, even more serious than giving away nuclear secrets.

The severe punishment prescribed for ridda is designed to deter imposters who embrace Islam in complete bad faith; they accept Islam as a means of subversion either to dishonor the protected knowledge or to physically harm the Islamic community. A key case illuminates the concept of ridda. Some members of the tribe of Ukl embraced Islam and swore allegiance to the Prophet. Afterwards, they complained to the Prophet that they were ill. The Prophet sent them to the fold of his camels so that they could rest, drink milk, and treat their pleurisy. After regaining health, however, they denounced Islam, killed the shepherds, and ran away with the Prophet's camels. This is a classic case of ridda. On the Prophet's orders, therefore, the apostates were captured and killed.[175]

The Ukl case clarifies several elements of ridda. First, the members of the tribe embraced Islam without any coercion. Second, they repudiated the faith after receiving a substantial benefit. Third, they violated the trust that the Prophet and other Muslims had reposed in them. Fourth, they inflicted serious harm on Muslim life and property. Under these circumstances, their punishment was appropriate both for retributive and deterrence purposes.

From an internal viewpoint, therefore, ridda is enforced to prevent and punish mischief against the protected knowledge of Islam and to safeguard Muslims from traitors and imposters. Ridda is not brute force to discourage Muslims from changing their religion, nor is it a license in the hands of a government to investigate Muslims' private beliefs and in no case does it apply to non-Muslims. The meaning of ridda becomes even more lucid when one learns that Islam prohibits any and all forcible conversions. No one is required to assume the trustee obligations of the protected knowledge, but when they do, they cannot abandon the trust. These rules preserve the dignity of protected knowledge, discouraging an "easy in, easy out" attitude toward Islam. Therefore, as the section below explains, the dissemination of protected knowledge is based on informed consent, not deception or coercion.

IV. DISSEMINATION OF PROTECTED KNOWLEDGE

"Verily! You (O Muhammad) guide not whom you like, but Allah guides whom He wills. And he knows best those who are guided."[176]

Although Islam is a religion of protected knowledge, a common misperception festers that Islam was forcibly spread with the sword. Part of this misperception might have arisen from specific enforcement of ridda. Part of it arose from the war-prone state of human civilization in general. In the early centuries of Islam, when international law recognized war as a lawful means of conquering territories, Muslim rulers, like non-Muslim kings and monarchs, used force to conquer and subdue foreign nations and peoples.[177] This conquest of land, however, should not be confused with forcible conversion to Islam. Even during the period when international law allowed the use of force to conquer foreign lands, Muslim rulers remained under a clear obligation not to forcibly convert the conquered people to Islam; most observed the commandment. If any ruler used the sword to spread Islam, his act violated the principles of the protected knowledge. Indonesia, the largest Islamic country in the world, was never invaded or conquered by a Muslim ruler.

Islam is the truth beyond doubt.[178] Yet, it cannot be imposed on any non-Muslim. Even the Prophet himself was unable to guide his beloved uncle Abu Talib,[179] about which Allah said: "Verily! You (O Muhammad) guide not whom you like, but Allah guides whom He wills. And he knows best those who are guided."[180] Muslims are required to convey the message of Islam. However, they are under no obligation to convert.

Two great principles of the Quran guide the dissemination of protected knowledge. First, the Quran mandates the principle of non-compulsion. Second, it enunciates the principle of invitation. These two principles reaffirm the inherent dignity of the protected knowledge, which cannot be innovated, repudiated, or imposed. They also underscore the importance of the Al Amanah (Trust) in that no one can be forcibly recruited as a trustee of the protected knowledge.

A. Principle of Non-Compulsion

"There is no compulsion in religion."[181]

Islam is submission to the will of God. Force or deception must not enter the equation, if the acceptance of protected knowledge is to be genuine, voluntary, and informed.[182] The Quran, therefore, declares the principle of non-compulsion, known as al-ikrah, which outlaws coercive and manipulative methods for the conversion of non-Muslims. Submission to Islam is a contract that a non-Muslim freely makes with God—and with no one else—to accept the benefits and obligations of the Trust. Submission is essentially a private matter. It is also a public declaration that one makes to join the community of believers. In the realm of protected knowledge, submission begins a lifelong process of beneficial learning. "So whosoever receives guidance, he does so for the good of his own self."[183] But even the most beneficial knowledge requires effort and rarely can the attainment of knowledge be coerced or imposed, for, most often, it demands a voluntary opening of the mind and the soul.

Thus the principle of al-ikrah[184] mandates that the protected knowledge of Islam be clearly presented to non-Muslims sincerely and without the use of force, tricks, or strings. For example, converting the hungry, the sick, the disabled, the homeless, or any other non-Muslim suffering under a disability will be unlawful if conversion is obtained as an exchange for food, medicine, or shelter. Any overt precondition or covert manipulation underlying conversion violates the principle of alikrah. This is not lawful evangelism, but an unkind betrayal. The Prophet said: "For every betrayer there will be a flag by which he will be recognized on the Day of Resurrection."[185]

The principle of al-ikrah also promotes interfaith respect.[186] As there is no compulsion in religion, Muslims must not put down other creeds. Under Muslim rule, Jews and Christians enjoy special protection, as, according to the Quran, they are the people of the book.[187] Their faith is close to Islam in many essential attributes, such as belief in One God, and the concepts of sin, revelation, prophethood, angels, the Day of Judgment, hell, and heaven.[188] In fact, the Quran states that Adam, Moses, and Abraham were the first Muslims.[189] Thus, the protected knowledge of Islam is inclusive of monotheistic religions. As a general principle, Islam respects religions, prophets, and holy books, except the ones that corrupt the purity of its protected knowledge.[190]

B. Principle of Invitation

"Invite (mankind, O Muhammad) to the Way of your Lord (i.e., Islam) with wisdom (i.e., with the Divine Inspiration and the Quran) and fair preaching, and argue with them in a way that is better."[191]

The principle of invitation further explains the principle of non-compulsion. Known as da'wah, the invitation principle invites non-Muslims to accept the protected knowledge of Islam, as trustees and beneficiaries. Although da'wah may be roughly translated into proselytization or evangelism, it literally means invitation. Proselytization is a more generic term that means religious activism aimed at others for the purpose of changing their religion or belief. Evangelism is a more specific concept that characterizes efforts of missionaries to convert Christians from one church (Catholic) to another (Protestant) or to convert non-Christians to a specific Christian faith (Baptist). Rather than drawing contrasts or parallels between da'wah and evangelism, I will simply explain the manners of da'wah.

The most pertinent injunction of the Quran for da'wah reads: "Invite (mankind, O Muhammad) to the Way of your Lord (i.e., Islam) with wisdom (i.e., with Divine Inspiration and the Quran) and fair preaching, and argue with them in a way that is better. Truly, your Lord knows best who has gone astray from His Path, and He is the Best Aware of those who are guided."[192]

The Quran's invitation principle lays out at least three distinct rules of guidance. First, da'wah is an invitation, not a forced initiation. A non-Muslim invited to accept the protected knowledge of Islam may or may not accept it. Because the protected knowledge of Islam is placed in an irrevocable Trust in perpetuity, no invitee can be lawfully forced to accept the obligations of a trustee against his will. Likewise, even the benefits of the protected knowledge cannot be imposed on anyone, simply because no gift is valid without the donee's acceptance. Thus, an invitee to Islam may refuse the invitation on either account. The invitee may refuse obligations of the trust, which include safeguarding the knowledge-based assets of Islam; or, the invitee may decline its benefits, which include enjoying an authentic spirituality, leading a balanced life of moral intelligence, and sharing a sense of community with other Muslims.

Second, da'wah mandates wisdom and fair preaching. The invitor is prohibited from presenting a distorted or pandering picture of the protected knowledge. For example, highlighting only the benefits of protected knowledge without mentioning the corresponding obligations will be unwise because the invitee would eventually learn that Islam is a complex composite of obligations and benefits and the one cannot be severed from the other. Nor should the invitee be presented only the obligations of Islam. For example, a lower caste Hindu is entitled to know whether he would enjoy complete equality with other Muslims once he accepts the Trust of Islam. The rule of fair preaching requires that the invitee be informed that Islam abhors prejudice on the basis of race, caste, nationality, property, or language. Thus, an invitee belonging to a prejudiced race, nation, social class, or linguistic group must be honestly informed that Islam prohibits any such bigotry. Ignoring or pandering to the invitee's prejudice will violate the rule of wisdom and fair preaching.[193] Similarly, the invitee, if a female, is entitled to know that Islam imposes a distinct regime of rights and duties on women as daughters, mothers, and wives. The rule of fair preaching will be breached if the female invitee is enticed only with the rights available under Islam, such as the right to divorce, to possess property, and to hold separate accounts. Any deliberate attempt to de-emphasize the duties of a woman to the Islamic community in general, including wearing a modest dress,[194] and upholding the family in particular, including respecting the husband and treating children with kindness, care and dedication, will not only be counterproductive but deceptive.[195]

Third, da'wah is founded on a basic rule that the invitee's decision to accept Islam is a matter that resides in the will of God, and not that of man. No human effort, without the will of God, can succeed in matters of faith. Even the Prophet had no power to bring a nonbeliever to the faith. Several Quranic verses explain this element of da'wah: "Say 'It is not in my power to cause you harm or to bring you to the Right Path.'"[196] Thus, a Muslim is obligated only to invite others to Islam in a noncoercive atmosphere of wisdom and fair preaching. The invitor should claim no credit if the invitee accepts Islam, nor should he be disheartened if the invitee rejects Islam after a fair preaching done with good manners. The Quran reinforces this rule of da'wah in saying: "And had your Lord willed, those on earth would have believed, all of them together. So, will you (O Muhammad) then compel mankind, until they become believers."[197] This da'wah is an extension of the al-ikrah principle in that there is no compulsion in religion. For example, the Quran states with no ambiguity that "It is not for any person to believe, except by the Leave of Allah."[198] Related to da'wah are the manners of discourse that the invitor must observe in introducing Islam to the invitee. The Shari'a prohibits excessive argumentation or impolite criticism of others' beliefs.[199] The Quran states rather candidly that when an invitee begins to ridicule God's message, the invitor must leave the company and not engage in a nasty or hurtful conversation.[200] The Sunna also prohibits annoying questions in matters of faith.[201] Thus, da'wah is not a contest for winning an intellectual debate. It is a sincere invitation to Islam, a positive message that does not vilify other religions.

Although Muslims disseminate the protected knowledge of Islam with wisdom and fair preaching, the enterprise of dissemination will fail if invitees have no freedom of religion and invitors have no freedom of speech. Both freedoms of religion and speech are necessary and inseparable for the propagation of any religion, including Islam. Even if Islam is intellectual property, and not an idea, its dissemination still needs both freedoms. It has already been suggested that non-Muslims are not required to assume trustee obligations of the protected knowledge. However, if they do, they cannot innovate or repudiate the knowledge. The next section examines the Islamic conception of free speech that further safeguards the integrity of protected knowledge. It also contrasts the Islamic conception of free speech with secular speech, drawing out their underlying assumptions and values.

V. CONFLICTING CONCEPTIONS OF FREE SPEECH

"And those who annoy believing men and women undeservedly, bear on themselves the crime of slander and plain sin."[202]

If Islam protects free speech, why, the critics ask, do Muslims all over the world want to kill authors and artists who, exercising their right to free speech, criticize Islam.[203] Muslims, on the other hand, get publicly angry when their most precious assets are verbally abused and attacked. In this conflict, secularists uphold the right of the attacker, because the protection of free speech is dearer to them than preserving religion's right to integrity;

they ignore the feelings of Muslims and advocate tolerance. From the internal viewpoint, however, Muslims have no option but to perform in good faith the Covenant they have entered with God, the All-Seer, All-Knower. The Covenant is not to protect the free speech of authors and artists; it is to safeguard the integrity of protected knowledge. Ordinarily, Muslims have no obligation to censor "nonsensical" speech of non-Muslims.[204] Yet, they would accept no version of free speech that openly dishonors Allah, the Quran, or the Messenger.

Western criticism of Islamic intolerance thrives on free speech. Freedom of speech, embodied in the Universal Declaration of Human Rights,[205] is a universal right that most Muslim nations have vowed to protect. However, the Islamic version of free speech is different from the Western version, particularly that of the United States. The First Amendment to the United States Constitution protects two prominent competing freedoms.[206] First, it protects the free exercise of religion, a right without which no spiritual life is possible.[207] Second, it also protects free speech.[208] The American concept of free speech, for the most part, is a precious contribution to global law. Muslims living under repressive and unaccountable regimes can particularly benefit from the jurisprudence of the First Amendment.[209]

A. Secular Speech

In the past few decades, the First Amendment has been overly secularized. The Free Exercise Clause of the First Amendment protects the freedom to religion and belief in teaching, practice, worship, and observance. It does not, however, safeguard the dignity of any religion.[210] The Free Speech Clause allows attack on any and all religions. Although any individual may freely assail religion, authors and artists are at the forefront in dismantling the traditional respect for religion. Most often, the religion they assault is Christianity.[211] When literary and artistic works collide with religion, the First Amendment protects secular speech. This legal development does not demonstrate that Americans are secular. In fact, Americans are religious people and they do not wish to denigrate any religion.[212] Nor do they encourage artists and authors to do so. They may even disapprove of the art that assaults religion. Yet, they are unwilling to allow government to suppress creative expression.[213] Free speech, not the dignity of religion, is the most precious value that most Americans cherish.[214]

The triumph of art[215] over the protection of religion is a compelling story of secular speech. Using public funds obtained through the National Endowment for the Arts (NEA), for example, Andres Serrano produced the so-called artistic work named Piss Christ, a photograph of a crucifix immersed in urine. Several members of Congress, along with many Christians, were outraged at the artist's offensive audacity. In view of this and other artistic intemperance, Congress debated several proposals to reform the NEA's grant-making criteria. One proposal would have prohibited any grants used "to promote, distribute, disseminate or produce matter that has the purpose or effect of denigrating the beliefs, tenets, or objects of a particular religion."[216] Secular forces within Congress defeated this proposal. A more watered-down legal standard, however, was enacted into law. In funding artworks, the NEA is now required to "tak(e) into consideration general standards of decency and respect for the diverse beliefs and values of the American public."[217]

Secular forces were unhappy even with these weak "decency and respect" standards. They challenged the law on constitutional grounds, asserting the artist's right to be obnoxious.[218] However, the issue involved was rather narrow in scope. Serrano was free to produce, promote, distribute, and disseminate his obnoxious work with private funding as no decency and respect standards can be invoked to suppress a privately funded work. The First Amendment protects artists' rights to express themselves as indecently and disrespectfully as they choose.[219] To this extent, the concept of free speech is noncontroversial.

The critical issue was whether the First Amendment compels the government to fund indecent and disrespectful works. The Supreme Court upheld the statute, declaring that the government is under no such compulsion.[220] However, the Court's holding is weak; it provides no guarantee for withholding public funds for indecent and disrespectful works and it imposes no categorical requirement that an application in violation of the enacted decency and respect standards must be denied.[221] In fact, the Court seems to suggest that even in the provision of subsidies, the government may not suppress disfavored viewpoints. Accordingly, the NEA may consider the decency and respect standards in reviewing grant applications, but it cannot disfavor works simply because they are disrespectful to a certain religion.

The Serrano controversy tells the story of how secular speech has placed religion in the open market of ideas where it may be repudiated and discredited. Driven by profits and liberty, the free market has unleashed a pornographic and hateful infrastructure of speech that annoys believing men and women, and thus, disturbs their spiritual tranquility. The free market allows artists and authors to challenge what religion holds beyond doubt; it may disparage what religion considers the most sacred. It maintains, if not encourages, a culture of abusive speech, in which skeptical and cynical individuals may freely denigrate all norms of any established religion. It spawns a realm of creativity in which artists and authors are at liberty to dismantle the dignity of religion.[222] The bedrock principle underlying secular speech is designed to protect the individual's liberty and creativity. In its doctrinal manifestations, however, the principle becomes antisocial. The government, for example, cannot suppress "the expression of an idea simply because society finds the idea itself offensive or disagreeable."[223] In fact, free speech "invite(s) dispute . . . it induces a condition of unrest, creates dissatisfaction with conditions as they are, or even stirs people to anger."[224] Note the long arm of the principle; the principle is not confined to protecting the expression of an idea offensive to ruling elites, the protection is available even if the idea is offensive to an entire religious community. Few would question the virtue of free speech when it allows individuals to criticize or oppose ruling elites. However, when law allows an individual to freely trash the deepest sentiments and religious beliefs of an entire population, the doctrine of secular speech enters the domain of excess.

Ironically, secular speech can be highly protective of scientific inventions, as well as literary and artistic works.[225] No individual may lawfully break into the source codes of a software company, reproduce musical cassettes, destroy paintings, or alter copyrighted manuals. Thus, speech is subordinated to the protection of intellectual property because no secular doctrine will allow individuals to lawfully change the text of a copyrighted novel or misappropriate the patents of a corporation. However, secular speech will protect the same individuals if they change the text of the Bible, dishonor Jesus,[226] or depict "the Virgin Mary covered with elephant dung, and surrounded by photographs of buttocks and female genitalia."[227] Thus, secular speech has successfully degraded the integrity of religion to a mere idea that individuals may trash with impunity. However, it has upgraded the work of artists and authors to intellectual property that the law must vigorously protect.[228]

Few will dispute that the First Amendment enjoys broad based support in the United States. Problems arise, however, when the United States wishes to export the secularized model of free speech,[229] and Muslim countries resist accepting it. When authors and artists disparage the protected knowledge of Islam, the United States wants to protect the liberty of creative expression while Muslims want to protect the dignity of Islam. Muslims refuse to embrace secular speech that empowers authors and artists to make fun of prophets, sacred books, religious rituals, and worship practices. They are labeled intolerant when they protect the honor of Allah, the Quran, and the Prophet from any verbal abuse.[230] It seems unlikely that Muslims would ever concede to the notion that authors and artists may denigrate the protected knowledge of Islam. It is more likely than not that the world would refuse to universalize secular speech under which intellectual property is protected, but the integrity of religion is not.

B. Islamic Speech

The integrity and honor of protected knowledge is a core Islamic value. Any version of free speech, under which artists and authors may assault the rights of attribution and integrity vested in the protected knowledge, is unlikely to take root in Muslim countries.[231] Just as secular speech protects intellectual property, Islamic speech honors and safeguards the protected knowledge of the Quran and the Sunna. In fact, the protected knowledge of Islam is the most precious intellectual property that no version of free speech may alter, mutilate, deform, or defame. Islamic speech, therefore, treats protected knowledge as a form of intellectual property, and not an idea that individuals may freely dishonor, innovate, and repudiate.

The assumptions underlying Islamic speech are fundamentally different from the ones supporting secular speech. The Quran presents a conception of speech that, in the doctrinal language of secular speech, may be considered unnecessary barriers to vigorous discourse. For example, Muslims are required to speak gently and kindly,[232] in a low voice,[233] without arrogance,[234] or egotistical display of one's knowledge or eloquence, for "Allah does not like such as are proud and boastful . . ."[235] In the Sunna, even eloquence is less than a sure virtue. In matters of public speaking, the Prophet was highly skeptical of the use of captivating rhetoric. He is reported to have warned against its use, saying, "part of eloquence is sorcery."[236] These values are critical for orienting Muslims toward a conception of speech that searches for truth without arrogance, moral relativity, verbal abuse, or disrespect toward other religions.

First and foremost, Islamic speech is content-sensitive and protects the knowledge-based assets of Islam. Under secular speech, no principles are universal. Truth is no more than a viewpoint. God's verses and satanic verses receive equal legal protection. Based on this relativism, secular speech embraces content-neutrality. One may, therefore, challenge the core tenets of any and all religions.[237] Such content-free moral relativity is incompatible with Islam. "And if the truth had been in accordance with their desires, verily, the heavens and the earth, and whosoever is therein would have been corrupted!"[238] Accordingly, Muslims cannot cast doubts on the honor and integrity of protected knowledge. They submit to the truth of Islam. They take God's command seriously: "I have perfected your religion for you, . . . and have chosen for you Islam as your religion."[239] Rarely do they engage in egotistical repudiation of Islam. Even when they have sincere questions about moral, legal, or religious matters, they pursue their inquiries with care and humility, without breaching the standards of decency and respect.[240]

Second, constraints of manner, respect, and decency embodied in Islamic speech encourage, not discourage, scientific invention, creative poetry, and literature.[241] By all counts, Islam is a religion founded on knowledge and hence it is suffused with a spirit of inquiry. Quest has been a permanent feature of Islamic knowledge. The flexible principles of the Quran and the Sunna require free speech for their creative understanding in a changing world so that Muslims may constantly improve their social, political, and economic institutions. The firm principles do not conflict with free speech either because their purpose is to safeguard the identity of Islam in a confusing and chaotic world. The combined knowledge of flexible and firm principles provide a framework in which creative minds may concentrate without distraction. The flourishing of jurisprudence, sciences, and literature throughout Islamic history, most often through the medium of individual and collaborative reasoning, demonstrates that Islamic speech promotes creativity and invention.

Third, Islamic speech spawns, not chills, serious and respectful viewpoints;[242] it simply discourages frivolous and slanderous speech against the protected knowledge. The Quran disapproves the culture of Al-laghw,[243] that is, idle chatter.[244] Any slander against religion is bound to hurt the feelings of its followers. The Quran instructs Muslims "not to annoy" men and women of faith, condemning it as sin and slander.[245] In the Sunna, the Prophet prohibited Muslims from verbally abusing the community. He said, "When you hear a man say, 'The people are ruined.' he himself is the most ruined of them all."[246] The Shari'ah, therefore, places little premium on the individual's right to assault the integrity of protected knowledge, thus, outraging an entire community of believers—a right that secular speech is determined to protect. Muslims are advised to exchange their viewpoints after careful study, with humility, in good faith, and without showing disrespect to the Quran or the Sunna and without injuring the deeply held beliefs of the Islamic community. Standards of respect and decency are not confined to the protected knowledge of Islam; they are extended to other religions, except ones that corrupt the integrity of the protected knowledge of Islam.[247]

Finally, Islamic speech protects the "intellectual property" of other religions, according them due respect and dignity.[248] "Allah does not forbid you to deal justly and kindly with those who fought not against you on account of religion and did not drive you from your homes. Verily, Allah loves those who deal with equity."[249] It is inaccurate, therefore, to assert that Islamic speech advocates homogenization; Islam simply rejects secular pluralism under which every belief counts equally[250] but the "intellectual property" of established religions is no longer entitled to the rights of attribution and integrity. Islamic speech protects the intellectual property of artists and authors. Most importantly, it also instructs Muslims not to malign other religions. This protection, however, is unavailable to innovative sects, arising within the fold of Islam, which tinker with the integrity of protected knowledge.[251]

By protecting the intellectual property of other religions, Islamic speech promotes interfaith coexistence and mutual tolerance; believing Muslims do not denigrate other religions, even when they contest their message or doctrines. Nor do they allow others to denigrate Islam. Non-Muslims are free to examine Islamic doctrines and beliefs. No Islamic principle prohibits their free speech. In Islam, however, interfaith conversations and contacts are carried out within the domain of mutual respect. Islam expects these conversations and contacts to be sincere, serious, and respectful. Good manners are part of Islamic speech. Therefore, Islamic speech mandates Muslims to express their viewpoints without being obnoxious, without insulting prophets and sacred books, and without attacking the integrity of any religion.[252]

CONCLUSION

Islam is a religion founded on knowledge of assured certainty. From an internal viewpoint, therefore, the protected knowledge of Islam cannot be innovated and repudiated. Islamic right to attribution prohibits any alteration in the text of the Quran and in the substance of the Sunna. The right to integrity preserves the honor of Allah, the Quran, and the messenger. In view of these Islamic rights, no one is allowed to attack the dignity of the Quran or show public disrespect for the person of the Prophet. In brief, the internal viewpoint sees the protected knowledge of the Quran and the Sunna as a timeless asset that Muslims are under trustee obligation to preserve at all costs. Under all circumstances, easy and difficult, good and bad, Muslims have chosen to honor their Covenant with God.

The external viewpoint relies on secular freedoms of belief and speech to criticize Muslims' intolerance toward authors and artists who wish to pursue their creativity without constraints. Secularists point out that freedom of religion and speech are indispensable for the preservation of spirituality; they prefer that Muslims tolerate authors and artists who attack the Quran, the Sunna, and the Prophet. They also advocate that Muslims should grant the freedom of religion to sects, within the fold of Islam, which have innovated the established meanings of the Quran and the Sunna.

This clash of viewpoints breeds mutual distrust between Muslims and secularists. In this battle, it seems unlikely that Muslims will accept the secularized version of free speech nor would they allow innovations within the framework of protected knowledge. Secularists do not have to win this battle either, because the world can live and prosper without attacking prophets, holy books, and spiritual rituals. However, if they are determined to allow unbridled literary and artistic activity in countries where they have the law on their side, they have little reason to forcibly export their secular vision to Islamic nations.

In any event, Muslims should resist the pressure to accept the secularized version of free speech. They should continue to practice religious tolerance that the Shari'ah teaches them. Religious minorities are entitled to full protection within Islamic states. When Muslims visit or live in non-Muslim states, they must employ the principles of non-compulsion and invitation in conveying the protected knowledge of Islam. In their philosophical disagreement with secularists, however, Muslims should understand that not every critic of the protected knowledge is a sworn enemy of Islam. Secularists are entitled to their liberties while Muslims are entitled to their profound vision of purity and spirituality. "To us our deeds, and to you your deeds. Peace be to you."[253] If no force is added to the mix from either viewpoint, the dialectical contest between secularists and Muslims carries immense educational value for the generations to come. Quran 20:114.

NOTES

This chapter is adopted from 31 Cumberland Law Review 631(2001). Copyright © 2000 *Cumberland Law Review*. Reprinted with permission.

1. The Sunna consists of the words, deeds, approvals, and disapprovals of Prophet Muhammad (peace be upon him). Sahih Al-Bukhari and Sahih Muslim are the two well-known compilations of authentic traditions of the Sunna.

2. In this article, "Islamic intellectual property," "knowledge-based assets of Islam" and "protected knowledge" are synonymous terms.

3. Quran 10:19 (stating all mankind is one community). 2 Sahih Al-Bukhari hadith 467 (Muhammad Mushin Khan trans., Dar Al Arabia) (stating every child is born in the Islamic faith).

4. Quran 2:14–15. "Show forgiveness, enjoin what is good and turn away from the foolish." Quran 7:199.

5. David Bainbridge, Intellectual Property 3 (2d ed. 1994).

6. I write this article from the internal viewpoint of a Sunni Muslim.

7. Freedom of belief is larger than freedom of religion, as belief includes atheistic and ethical models, whereas religion is most often deistic.

8. The Chief Rabbis of Israel and Britain protested against the publication of the book. The Vatican paper called the book as blasphemous and Reverend Billy Graham of the United States, a noted Protestant leader, expressed his sympathy for the protests against the book. See generally Sacrilege Versus Civility: Muslim Perspectives on the Satanic Verses Affair (M. M. Ahsan & A. R. Kidawi eds. 1991).

9. Another such story is the case of Taslima Nasreen of Bangladesh, an accomplished writer, who suggested that the verses of the Bible, Gita, and the Quran are outdated and, therefore, need revision. Hindus and Christians did not protest but the Muslims of Bangaldesh threatened to kill her. She was forced to leave the country and sought asylum first in Belgium, then in France. See John F. Burns, Furor Over Feminist Writer Leaves Bangladesh on Edge, N.Y. Times, July 16, 1994, at A1; Dexter Filkins, Writer Risks threats on Her Return to Bangladesh, L.A. Times, Nov. 13, 1998, at A5.

10. "Indeed, Islamic perceptions of Western culture as 'materialistic, corrupt, decadent, immoral,' and 'godless' seem painfully accurate." David M. Smolin, Church, State and International Human Rights: A Theological Appraisal, 73 Notre Dame L. Rev. 1515, 1523 (1998) (quoting Samuel P. Huntington, The Clash of Civili-

zations and the Remaking of World Order 70 (1996) (indicated by internal quotation marks)).

11. See Anthony Chase, Legal Guardians: Islamic Law, International Law, Human Rights Law, and the Salmon Rushdie Affair, 11 Am. U. J. Int'l. L. Pol'y 375 (1996). The author rightfully comments that the Rushdie affair is much more complex than "strict dichotomies: Islam vs. the West; . . . divine natural law vs. positive law; . . . the traditional vs. the modern." *Id.* at 377.

12. Quran 3:164.

13. A more appropriate Arabic translation of intellectual property is Mulkyyaht-al-fikria. I, however, use the term mulkyyaht al-elm to distinguish human intellect from the protected knowledge of Islam.

14. Two modes of interpretation are used to understand the meaning of the Quran. They are called tafsir and ta'wil. Tafsir places the meaning of the Quran in historical context, using grammar, the ahadith, plain meaning, logic, and reason. Ta'wil is allegorical, intuitive, meditative, and poetic. Both modes have been used to study and understand the Quran. See John Wansborough, Quranic Studies 154–157 (Oxford Univ. Press 1977).

15. The Sufi movement in Islam strives to decode the mystical, the unknown, and the hidden. Sufis have been both loved and criticized for their libertarian practices. The Sufi, however, experiences spirituality and the Quran's hidden meaning, not accessible to the formalist, the textualist, or the scholar. For a background study of the great Sufis of Islam, see Idries Shah, The Sufis (Octagon Press 1964).

16. One difference between Shi'a and Sunni jurisprudence focuses on the hidden knowledge. Whereas the Sunni believe that no one but God possesses the hidden knowledge, the Shia believes that the hidden knowledge is accessible to the Imams descending from the family of the Prophet. Sayyid Mujtaba Musavi Lari, Imamate and Leadership, available at http://alislam.org/leadership/ (this e-book explains the role of the Imam in the Shi'a faith and highlights the difference between Shia and Sunni views with respect to leadership).

17. Quran 6:59. Ghaib is interpreted "hidden knowledge."

18. *Id.*

19. *Id.*

20. Quran 17:85: "And of knowledge, you (human beings) have been given only a little."

21. Quran 3:79.

22. Quran 6:98.

23. The secret source code works without human awareness. To capture a glimpse of the secrets of the source code, the great Sufi poet Rumi wrote: In Winter the bare boughs that seem to sleep Work covertly, preparing for their Spring.

24. Quran 6:13.

25. Quran 2:3.

26. Quran 102:5.

27. Quran 39:41; 80:11–12.

28. Quran 6:7.

29. Quran 10:38.

30. Quran 36:69.

31. Quran 26:210.

32. Quran 85:22.

33. Quran 10:37.

34. See, e.g., Norman Geisler & Abu Saleeb, Answering Islam 178–204 (1993) (the authors challenge the authenticity of the Quran).

35. Quran 2:2.

36. Quran 10:38.

37. Answering Islam, supra note 34, at 189.

38. Quran 26:211.

39. Quran 26:212. The Prophet said that the knowledge that God has bestowed upon him is like abundant rain, some of which falls on fertile soil, some on hard soil, and some on barren soil. The fertile soil produces vegetation, the hard soil holds the rainwater for drinking, but the barren soil just absorbs the rain, returning no benefits. 1 Sahih Al-Bukhari, supra note 3, at hadith 79 (Muhammad Mushin Khan trans., Dar Al Arabia).

40. Quran 10:39.

41. Quran 41:43. "Nothing is said to you (O Muhammad) except what was said to the messengers before you." *Id.*

42. Quran 16:103.

43. Quran 17:106.

44. Quran 25:32.

45. Quran 80:15–16.

46. In the battle of Yamama (A.D. 633), a lot of the Qurra (individuals who knew the Quran by heart) were killed. Fearing that more of the Qurra might be killed in other battlefields, Umar and Abu-Bakr, the first two caliphs, decided to collect the fragmentary scripts of the Quran. Zaid bin Thabit, a pious and noble scribe for the Prophet, was assigned the job of collecting all the pieces of the Quran in one book. Once the complete manuscript (copy) of the Quran was prepared, it remained with Abu Bakr, the first caliph until he died, then with Umar, the second caliph, and then with Hafsa, the daughter of Umar. 6 Sahih Al-Bukhari, supra note 3, at hadith 509 (Muhammad Mushin Khan trans., Dar Al Arabia). Hafsa gave the manuscripts to Uthman, the third caliph, who ordered the official copies made. The original manuscript was then returned to Hafsa. *Id.* at hadith 510.

47. Quran 25:32.

48. Quran 25:32; 76:23. Though the Prophet lived and died as a mortal man and though he could not read or write, his personhood to receive the Quran was most transparent. Even contemporary non-Muslims recognized and witnessed the Prophet to be sadiq (truthful) and amin (trustworthy). See Karen Armstrong, A History of God 238 (1993) (Prophet Muhammad was insan-ikamil (the perfect man) of his generation).

49. Even the Quran warns the Prophet not to hasten the process of the revelation: "Move not your tongue concerning (the Quran, O Muhammad) to make haste therewith. It is for Us to collect it and to give (O Muhammad) the ability to recite it (the Quran), And when We have recited it to you (O Muhammad through Gabriel), then follow you its (the Quran) recital." Quran 75:16–18.

50. Each verse has a historical context, clear or ambiguous meaning, general or

specific application. Some verses modify the meaning of previous revelations. Some verses have been abrogated. Some verses have both hidden and manifest meaning. Some verses have plain meaning, some are sarcastic, and some refer to biblical stories. In other words, the Quran contains multiple levels of meaning.

51. John Renard, Seven Doors to Islam 3 (1996).

52. Ira M. Lapidus, A History of Islamic Societies 21 (1998).

53. The Quran has been "copyrighted" in perpetuity as God's authentic work, which cannot be distorted, mutilated, or modified in any way. This right to the Quran's integrity is not designed for any pecuniary benefit, as copies of the Quran may be freely made and published without any prior permission and without paying royalties to any person, family, or nation. The Quran is a Book of Dignity. No one may intentionally or maliciously dishonor it through verbal, artistic, literary, or physical assaults.

54. This protection is already available to secular, copyrighted books, in most legal systems.

55. Quran 42:38.

56. The Prophet died in 632, at the age of 62 or 63. Lapidus, *supra* note 52, at 33.

57. The golden period of the rightly guided caliphs (Abu Bakr, Umar, Uthman and Ali), however, lasted only for a short period of about 29 years (632–61). Id. at 54–55.

58. Ali Khan, A Theory of Universal Democracy, 16 Wis. Int'l L. J. 61 (1997) (presenting a concept of democracy that would be acceptable to Islamic countries).

59. For example, the Quran prescribes fixed shares of inheritance for a decedent's children, parents, and spouse. Quran 4:11–12.

60. Quran 2:282.

61. Quran, 2:282. This specific gender inequality in matters of witnessing contracts, however, allows no Islamic state to institute broad-based discrimination against women. In most matters, the Quran preserves equality between men and women.

62. Quran 2:282.

63. Convention on the Elimination of All Forms of Discrimination Against Women, Sept. 3, 1981, 1249 U.N.T.S. 13. Article 15(2) states:

Parties shall accord to women, in civil matters, a legal capacity identical to that of men and the same opportunities to exercise that capacity. In particular, they shall give women equal rights to conclude contracts and to administer property and shall treat them equally in all stages of procedure in courts and tribunals.

1249 U.N.T.S. 13 Art. 15(2) (emphasis added).

64. The general principle of equality is laid down in the following verse:

For Muslim men and women, for believing men and women, for devout men and women, for men and women who are patient and constant, for men and women who humble themselves, for men and women who give in charity, for men and women who fast, for men and women who guard their chastity, and for men and women who engage in God's remembrance, for them God has prepared forgiveness and great reward. Quran 33:35.

65. Quran 3:195.

66. Quran 4:32.

67. The Prophet prohibited the people from wishing to be someone else except in spending your wealth in righteous causes and sharing and teaching wisdom of the protected knowledge of the Quran. 1 Sahih Al-Bukhari, supra note 3, at hadith 73.

68. Islam allows spouses to keep separate accounts, own separate property, and engage in separate occupations and businesses. Zainab Chaudhary, The Myth of Misogyny, A Reanalysis of Women's Inheritance in Islamic Law, 61 Alb. L. Rev. 511, 513–516 (1997) (Islam elevated the status of women providing them with independent legal and spiritual identity).

69. Ikhtilaf or disagreement is prohibited when the text of the Quran or the substance of the Sunna is clear and known. See Islamic Jurisprudence: Shafi's Risala 333–34 (Majid Khadduri trans. 1961).

70. Quran 3:7.

71. Quran 33:36.

72. In early centuries of Islam, a great Rational Movement, known as the Mu'tazila, argued that if there was any discrepancy between reason and revelation, the latter must be construed to conform to reason. They did not suggest to discard revelation but to interpret it within the confines of reason. Under Caliph al Ma'mun (d. A.D. 833), their doctrines were recognized as official. The movement, however, was short-lived as it came to an abrupt end during the reign of Caliph al-Mutawakkil (d. A.D. 847). See Majid Khadduri, The Islamic Conception of Justice 40–43 (1984).

73. Quran 3:78.

74. Quran 3:77.

75. Quran 2:13.

76. The Prophet said that a Muslim is like (as stable and self-protective as) a date-palm tree whose leaves do not fall. 1 Sahih Al-Bukhari, supra note 3, at hadith 58, 59.

77. Quran 59:7.

78. Quran 3:164.

79. Quran 46:9.

80. The words of the Sunna may vary from one chain of transmission to the other, as different transmitters remembered or described the same event in different words. Hence, what is important in the Sunna is the substance rather than the exact words in which the event was reported.

81. These two sources provided the basic texts on the basis of which the scholars, through the medium of reasoning, called ijtihad, laid down the law and the creed. See Majid Khadduri, The Islamic Conception of Justice 3 (1984).

82. Ahadith is plural of the word hadith. Hadith means a piece of news, a tale, a story, or a report relating to a present or past event. In Islamic jurisprudence, the word hadith stands for the report of the words, deeds, approval, or disapproval of the Prophet (peace be upon him). See Introduction to 1 Sahih Muslim, at ix (Abdul Hamid Siddiqi trans., Dar Al Arabia).

83. A sahih hadith means a report properly attributed to the Prophet, in which the chain of transmission (isnad) is flawless and the text (matn) of which is fully compatible with the Quran and other established doctrines of Islam. See *id.*

84. A daif hadith is one in which either the chain of transmission is defective or the content of the hadith is not fully compatible with the protected knowledge of the Quran and other established doctrines distilled through sahih ahadith. In fact, a more

complex classification has been used to sift through the knowledge of the ahadith. For example, a hadith reported by one narrator that differs in context with another hadith reported by a reliable group of narrators is called a gharib (unfamiliar) hadith. If there is an unknown person in the chain of narrators, the hadith is known as majhul (unknown). A musnad hadith, though reported by a reliable chain, is not rated as high as a sahih (authentic) hadith. See *id.*

85. It is important to note that many cases were traced back to the Prophet through a chain of transmitters that ended with Aisha, the Prophet's wife, who finally reported the Prophet's acts and statements. See *id.*

86. A hadith that has a flawless chain of transmission, but some of its narrators are found to have a defective memory, is not rated as high as a sahih hadith. See *id.*

87. For example, the following three ahadith were reported in different words, though the substance is the same. (1) Narrated Sufyan: I said to Amr, "O Abu Muhammad! Did you hear Jabir bin Abdullah saying, 'A man carrying arrows passed through the mosque and Allah's Apostle (peace be upon him) said to him, Hold the arrows by then sic heads!' Amr replied, 'Yes.'" 9 Sahih Al-Bukhari, supra note 3, at hadith 194. (2) Narrated Jabir: A man passed through the mosque and he was carrying arrows, the heads of which were exposed (protruding). The man was ordered (by the Prophet) to hold the iron heads so that it might not scratch (injure) any Muslim. *Id.* at hadith 195. (3) Narrated Abu Musa: The Prophet (peace be upon him) said: "If anyone of you passed through our mosque or through our market while carrying arrows, he should hold the iron heads," or said, ". . . he should hold (their heads) firmly with his hand lest he should injure one of the Muslims with it." *Id.* at hadith 196.

88. Sahih Al-Bukhari, supra note 3, at hadith 218–22.

89. This case also informs Muslims to find easier solutions to problems.

90. Sahih Muslim with Al-Bukhari interpretation Book Al-Luqata, Hadith 1722.

91. Introduction to Sahih Muslim, supra note 82, at I.

92. In the United States, religious institutions are entitled to the protection of the trademark and unfair competition laws to the same extent as commercial enterprises. The enforcement of trademark laws does not abridge the religious freedom rights of a group that is infringing the protected symbols and marks. Purcell v. Summers, 145 F.2d 979, 985 (4th Cir. 1944); National Bd. of YWCA v. YWCA of Charleston, 335 F. Supp. 615, 621, 624 (D.S.C. 1971).

93. "It is not for the Mushrikin (polytheists, idolaters, pagans, disbelievers in the Oneness of Allah), to maintain the Mosques of Allah." Quran 9:17.

94. In secular intellectual property law, the power of symbolism is recognized as having great economic power. The value of the Coca-Cola trademark, for example, is immense. The symbolism of Islamic marks carries great spiritual value for Muslims. If capitalists can protect beverages, Muslims can surely safeguard the masjid and other fundamental symbols of faith and worship.

95. In the law of trademarks, a mark may not be registered if it is deceptive, scandalous, or conflicts with earlier marks. A mark is deceptive if it misleads the consumers about the nature or quality of the product it represents. Bainbridge, supra note 5, at 409.

96. A non-Muslim may use the greeting to show respect for the Islamic commu-

nity. The intention of the user and the use itself determine whether they violate Islam's right to attribution and integrity.

97. Zaheeruddin v. State, 26 S.C.M.R. 1718 (1993) (Pak.). In his dissenting opinion, Justice Abdul Qadeer Chaudhry, relying upon a United States case, holds that the Ahamdis, who do not believe in the finality of Muhammad's prophethood, cannot pass off as Muslims. Justice Chaudhry stated:

And, if a religious community insists on deception as its fundamental right and wants assistance of Courts in doing the same, then God help it. It has been held by the United States Supreme Court in Cantwell v. Connecticut (310 U.S. 296 at 306) that "the cloak of religion or religious belief does not protect anybody in committing fraud upon the public."

Id. at 1754.

98. It is the basis of this analysis that the Pakistan Supreme Court upheld the laws that prohibit Ahmadis from using the traditional symbols and marks of Islam. Id. at 1718; see supra text accompanying notes 92–97.

99. The word "naturalized" is used to describe an individual who converts to Islam. This word is more descriptive and accurate, because according to Islam, every child is born with an Islamic nature. Thus, an individual who embraces Islam simply reclaims his natural state of spirituality.

100. Cf. Denny v. Guarantee Title & Trust Co., 234 P. 966, 967–968 (Kan. 1925) (stating that, conditional acceptance of a trust agreement by a trust company is not acceptance of the trust). "The provisions of [the contract between the parties] obviously formed a material part of the trust agreement. Until the trust company should agree to those provisions, it could not be said to have accepted the trust created by the written agreement between the parties." *Id.* at 967.

101. A parallel concept of public trust exists under environmental law. The public trust doctrine asserts that the government has a duty to promote and maintain a healthy natural environment for current and future generations. This obligation is perpetual. It requires both preventative measures to protect the environment and remedial measures to correct past breaches of the trust. See Joseph L. Sax, The Public Trust Doctrine in Natural Resource Law: Effective Judicial Intervention, 68 Mich. L. Rev. 471, 486 (1970); Peter Manus, To a Candidate in Search of an Environmental Theme: Promote the Public Trust, Stan. Envtl. L. J. 315, 318–321 (2000).

102. Quran 2:213; 10:19.

103. Quran 2:143.

104. Quran 33:72.

105. *Id.*

106. Quran 2:93.

107. Quran 2:85. "Then do you believe in a part of the scripture and reject the rest?" *Id.*

108. Quran 2:27.

109. Professor Witte rightfully points out that the "teachings and practices of Judaism, Christianity, and Islam have much to commend themselves to the human rights regime. Each of these traditions is a religion of revelation, founded on the eternal command to love one God, oneself, and all neighbors." John Witte, Jr., Law, Religion, and Human Rights, 28 Colum. Hum. Rts. L. Rev. 1, 13 (1996).

110. Lapidus, supra note 52, at 34–35. The Quran offers a special originality within the framework of monotheistic religions. *Id.*

111. Once the Quran was complete, God sealed for good the source of revelation. Always guided and restrained by the Quran's perfected message, Muslims no longer look for more divine instruction.

112. "Allah intends for you ease, and He does not want to make things difficult for you." Quran 2:185. For example, prayers may be joined and even shortened during traveling. ALMUWATTA of Imam Malik ibn Anas, The First Formulation of Islamic Law 54 (Aisha Abdurrahman Bewley trans., Kegan Paul Int'l). Malik's book, written about a hundred years after the Prophet's death, is a valuable asset of Islam. "No book has been placed on earth closer to the Quran than the book of Malik." *Id.* at trans. intro. xxxiv.

113. Compare this openness with the secretive and confidential nature of the Scientology religion. There are certain secret and confidential documents that are withheld from "unprepared and uninitiated" members. The founder of the church, L. Ron Hubbard, placed primary importance on keeping fundamental documents from general disclosure. See Religious Tech. Ctr. v. Lerma, 908 F. Supp. 1353, 1356 (E.D. Va. 1995).

114. *See* John Henry Merryman, The Refrigerator of Bernard Buffet, 27 Hastings L. J. 1023, 1025–27 (1976); Raymond Sarraute, Current Theory on the Moral Right of Authors and Artists under French Law, 16 Am. J. Comp. L. 465 (1968). For a discussion of the French cases dealing with moral rights, see Bella Karakis, Moral Rights: French, United States and Soviet Compliance with Article 6bis of the Berne Convention, 5 Touro Int'l. L. Rev. 105, 107 (1994).

115. Carter v. Helmsley-Spear, Inc., 71 F.3d. 77, 81 (2d Cir. 1995).

116. R. J. DaSilva, Droit Moral and the Amoral Copyright: A Comparison of Artists' Rights in France and the United States, 28 Bull. Corp. Soc'y 1, 7 (1980).

117. See Roberta Rosenthal Kwall, Copyright and the Moral Right: Is an American Marriage Possible?, 38 Vand. L. Rev. 1, 3 (1985). Professor Kwall suggests that "moral right" is not an adequate rendering of the term droit moral, which connotes "a right that exists in an entity's ultimate being." *Id.* at 3 n.6.

118. The preamble to the California Art Preservation Act ("CAPA") states:

The Legislature hereby finds and declares that the physical alteration or destruction of fine art, which is an expression of the artist's personality, is detrimental to the artist's reputation, and artists therefore have an interest in protecting their works of fine art against such alteration or destruction; and that there is also a public interest in preserving the integrity of cultural and artistic creations.

Cal. Civil Code § 987(a) (West 2000).

119. The United States has also recognized moral rights, though for a limited category of works. The Visual Artists Rights Act extends moral rights to works of visual art. 17 U.S.C. 106A (1990).

120. *Id.*

121. In common law countries, some aspects of the rights of attribution and integrity are protected under the torts concept of libel and slander. See Dane S. Ciolino, Moral Rights and Real Obligations: A Property-Law Framework for the Protection of Authors' Moral Rights, 69 Tul. L. Rev. 935, 950–52 (1995) (tort theories provide limited protection of moral rights).

122. See Edward J. Damich, The Right of Personality: A Common-Law Basis for the Protection of the Moral Rights of Authors, 23 Ga. L. Rev. 1, 32 (1988).

123. Berne Convention, June 2, 1928, art. 6bis, 123 L.N.T.S. 235, 249. In 1948, article 6bis was amended to extend the maintenance of these rights even after the author's death.

124. Gilliam v. Am. Broad. Cos., 538 F.2d 14, 23 (2d Cir. 1976).

125. *Id.* at 24.

126. Each and every copy of the Quran deserves equal respect.

127. Quran 10:64.

128. The Prophet said, "whoever (intentionally) ascribes to me what I have not said then (surely) let him occupy his seat in Hell-fire." 1 Sahih Al-Bukhari, supra note 3, at hadith 109.

129. The official version of the Quran was promulgated by the Caliph Uthman (644–656). "Small points of detail remained in dispute until the tenth century, when Muslim scholars" embraced the seven variant readings as equally valid. Lapidus, supra note 52, at 21. However, these seven variants do not change the meaning of the Quran. It simply asserts that a word, whose meaning is fixed, may be pronounced in seven different dialects. See Abu Jafar Muhammad B. Jarir Al-Tabari, The Commentary on the Quran 21 (1987, original 9th century). Al-Tabari was born in 839 in northern Iran. *Id.* at ix. From an external viewpoint, however, the authenticity of the text of the Quran has never been fully accepted. See Helmut Gatje, The Quran and its Exegesis 23–30 (Alford T. Welch trans., 1976) (1971).

130. The Prophet's companions were keen observers of the Prophet's words and deeds. Some of them put down the Prophet's judgments, verdicts, utterances, and addresses in written records, called sahifas. These sahifas later provided reliable records for the ahadith. Introduction to Sahih Muslim, supra note 90, at iii.

131. Imam Malik ibn Anas is the most eminent Islamic scholar, "celebrated for his taqwa, his retentive memory and his reliability in transmission . . ." *Id.* at xxix–xxx. In collecting ahadith, Imam Malik relied on only those "men that he saw had taqwa, scrupulousness, good memory, knowledge and understanding, and who clearly knew that they would be accountable for what they said on the Day of Rising." See Introduction to Malik, supra note 113, at xxix.

132. Introduction to 1 Sahih Al-Bukhari, supra note 3, at xiv–xv (Muhammad Mushin Khan trans.).

133. Six compilations of ahadith are considered genuine and reliable. Named after the compilers, they are (1) Bukhari, (2) Muslim, (3) Abu Dawud, (4) Tirmidhi, (5) Ibn Maja, and (6) al Nasai. The collections of Bukhari and Muslim are held in the most esteem. The ahadith reported in both of these collections are recognized as absolutely authentic. See Introduction to 1 Sahih Muslim, supra note 82, at iv–v. For online complete collections of Sahih Bukhar and Sahih Muslim, see http://www.usc.edu/dept/MSA/reference/searchhadith.html.

134. Quran 39:9.

135. Quran 3:79.

136. Lapidus, supra note 52, at 96.

137. Mishkat Masabih, at hadith 111W; see also Riffat Hussain, Religious Human Rights in the World Today, 10 Emory Int'l L. Rev. 85, 92 (1996).

138. Renard, supra note 51, at 5. The quotation is taken from Ibn-Arabi (d.1240), a Muslim jurist born in Andalusia, Spain. *Id.*

139. Quran 51:47. As the Quran explains "with power did We construct the heaven. Verily, we are able to expand the space thereof." *Id.* The gradual expansion of the universe is an important discovery unavailable to previous generations of Muslims to fully appreciate the meaning of the Quran. Describing human reproduction, the Quran states: "He created you in the wombs of your mothers, creation after creation in three veils of darkness." Quran 39:6. The three veils of darkness have been identified as (1) abdominal wall, (2) uterine wall, and (3) aminochorionic membrane (a sac filled with fluid in which the fetus floats). Maurice Bucaille, The Bible, the Quran and Science 205 (North American Trust 1979).

140. N. J. Coulson, A History of Islamic Law 102 (1964). *Editor note, this Hadith in footnote 140 is weak or fabricated therefore it is unreliable. See Shaikh Naser ul-Dean Al Albani, Silslat Al Ahadith Addaeefa Hadith No. 57.*

141. Coulson, an English scholar of Islam, sums up the metaphors that Muslim authors use to describe the phenomenon of ikhtilaf, or diversity of doctrine: "A tree, whose network of branches and twigs stems from the same trunk and roots; a sea, formed by the merging waters of different rivers; a variety of threads woven into a single garment; even the interlaced holes of a fishing net." *Id.* at 86.

142. In the first four hundred years, Muslim scholars developed an understanding of the protected knowledge of Islam through logic, analysis, mutual dialogue, and consensus. In the next two hundred years, four major schools of jurisprudence, under the scholastic leadership of Abu-Hanifa, Malik, Shafi'i (d.204/820), and Hanbal (d.241/855), were fully developed. "While the Hanafi, Maliki, and Shafi schools agreed that the 'gate of ijtihad' or independent reasoning was closed, . . . the Hanbalis and a minority of Shafi [scholars declined to embrace the doctrine] of taqlid." Lapidus, supra note 52, at 193; see e.g., Burstyn v. Wilson, 343 U.S. 495 (1952) (holding that "it is not the business of government in our nation to suppress real or imagined attacks upon a particular religious doctrine, whether they appear in publications, speeches, or motion pictures").

143. Bid'a is singular, whereas bida is plural. See Gatje, supra note 129, at 21.

144. See *id.*

145. Quran 2:11.

146. Quran 2:12.

147. Yet, in a secular community that extensively allows the freedoms of speech and religion, bid'a or heresy is a protected intellectual and religious viewpoint. Consequently, no church or community may lawfully harm or even silence the heretic. Under the combined effect of free speech and free exercise of religion, the state must allow the heretic to express his views, regardless of how offensive the views are to the church or community. The state may restrict or prohibit public advocacy of heresy only if the heretical speech causes or is most likely to cause a serious law and order situation.

148. The Iranian revolution of 1979, for example, repudiated all innovations and reinstated a more fundamental version of Shi'a Islam. There are movements in almost all Islamic countries, which strive to restore the purity of protected knowledge. Even the Saudi legal system has been greatly influenced by Muhammad ibn Abd Al-Wah-

hab (died 1791) who proposed the elimination of all innovations. Gatje, supra note 129, at 21.

149. Quran 33:40.

150. Mirza Sahib is an abbreviated but respectful name for Mirza Ghulam Ahmed.

151. Quran 61:6.

152. Prophet Muhammad (peace be upon him) said: "I have five names. I am Muhammad and Ahmed. I am Al-Mahl through whom Allah will eliminate Al-Kufr; I am Al-Hashir who will be the first to be resurrected, the people being resurrected thereafter; and I am also Al-Aqib (i.e., there will be no Prophet after me)." 4 Sahih Al-Bukhari, supra note 3, at hadith 732.

153. Quran 33:40. According to the followers of Ahmed, "there will be no Prophet after Muhammad [peace be upon him] who will bring a new law or who will not be completely obedient to [Muhammad (peace be upon him)] . . . [New prophets may] appear, but only through allegiance to Muhammad (peace be upon him)." They also believe that Muhammad (peace be upon him) was the most perfect Prophet, not the last Prophet. See M. Nadeem Ahmad Siddiq, Enforced Apostasy: Zaheeruddin v. State and the Official Persecution of the Ahmadiyya Community in Pakistan, 14 Law & Ineq. 275 n.17 (1995).

154. The Baha'is are similarly situated in Iran. Baha'u'allh claimed to be a Prophet as well. Both Ahmadis and Baha'is innovate Islam in essentially the same way: They both deny that Muhammad (peace be upon him) was God's last Messenger. Note, however, that Muslims seem to have no problems with new prophets within the fold of Christianity, including Joseph Smith of the Mormons.

155. According to the Constitution, "'Muslim' means a person who believes in the unity of oneness of Almighty Allah, in the absolute and unqualified finality of the Prophethood of Muhammad (peace be upon him), the last of the prophets and does not believe in, or recognize as a Prophet or religious reformer, any person who claimed or claims to be a Prophet, in any sense of the word or of any description whatsoever, after Muhammad (peace be upon him)." Pak. Const. art. 260(3)(a).

156. M. Nadeem Ahmad Siddiq, Enforced Apostasy: Zaheeruddin v. State and the Official Persecution of the Ahmadiyya Community in Pakistan, 14 Law & Ineq. 275 n.17 (1995) (citing Zaheeruddin v. State, 26 S.C.M.R. 1718 (Pak. 1993)).

157. For a critique of Pakistani laws and its Supreme Court decisions suppressing the freedom of religion of Ahmadis, see Tayyab Mahmud, Freedom of Religion & Religious Minorities in Pakistan: A Study of Judicial Practice, 19 Fordham Int'l L. J. 40 (1995). Professor Mahmud argues that the creation of Pakistan promised to protect religious minorities, a promise that "regressive and medieval models of Shari'ah" have subverted. *Id.* at 99.

158. See State v. Moran, 784 P.2d 730 (1989).

159. See Werner, Zarof, Slotnick, Stern & Askenazy v. Lewis, 155 Misc.2d 558 (N.Y. City. Civ. Ct. 1992); Alpha Foods Co. v. Valtasaros, 1993 WL 494343, No. B14-92-00626-CV (Dec. 2, 1993).

160. An insider of a software system may improve the source code, but Islam forbids any innovations because the protected knowledge needs no improvements.

161. Ridda is a hadd crime, a crime for which the punishment has been fixed. However, the meaning of ridda is not fixed, except in a very general way, that ridda

is the repudiation of Islam. Professor David Forte, for example, correctly points out that in the early days of Islam, apostasy and treason were synonymous. In Hanafi school of jurisprudence, ridda is most often treated as rebellion. See David F. Forte, Apostasy and Blasphemy in Pakistan, 10 Conn. J. Int'l L. 27, 43–45 (1994).

162. Quran 47:25.

163. Quran 6:68.

164. Quran 49:12.

165. The Prophet prohibited calling a person who has embraced Islamic monotheism a hypocrite. It is irrelevant whether others still think, "he does not love Allah and His Messenger." 9 Sahih Al-Bukhari, supra note 3, at hadith 71. Likewise, the Prophet prohibited Muslims from challenging each other's sincerity of faith.

166. http://www.iio.org/deviant/noi.htm

167. The Quran prohibits anyone from entering a house without permission and commands him to turn away if no one is in the house. Quran 24:27–28. The Sunna also protects the privacy of homes. The Prophet strictly observed the privacy of home. Once a man peeped into the house of the Prophet. The Prophet got up and aimed a sharp-edged arrowhead at him to poke him. 9 Sahih Al-Bukhari, supra note 3, at hadith 26–27.

168. Quran 49:11.

169. Quran 3:77.

170. Historically, ridda was considered a mutiny against Islam. During the Prophet's life, ridda was not simply the repudiation of faith; it amounted to a declaration of war.

171. Murtad is singular; murtaddun is plural.

172. Shari'ah prescribes the death penalty for apostasy, a practice that is "especially troublesome to the concept of democracy." Peter A. Samuelson, Pluralism Betrayed: The Battle Between Secularism and Islam in Algeria's Quest for Democracy, 20 Yale J. Int'l L. 309, 339 (1995). Modern Islamic human rights documents have failed to challenge the death penalty for ridda. *Id.*

173. The Quran does not specify the punishment for apostasy. However, all four schools of jurisprudence prescribe the death penalty. According to Malik and Shafi, the apostate should not be executed for three days during which he may repent and accept Islam. See Shaybani Siyar, The Islamic Law Of Nations 195 (Trans. Majid Khadduri, 1966). Shaybani is an eighth century Muslim jurist. See *Id.* at 27–36.

174. The Satanic Verses of Salman Rushdie, for example, was a contemptuous attack on the integrity of the Quran, the honor of the Prophet, and his pious wives. Because Rushdie was a world-known author, his advocacy of hatred against Islam was taken more seriously. Accordingly, the Iranian Imam issued a death decree against the author.

175. Sahih Muslim, *Supra* note 82, at hadith 413035.

176. Quran 28:56.

177. In the mid twentieth century, the United Nations Charter outlawed the use of force against the territorial integrity of any state. U.N. Charter art. 2, para. 4. Over the centuries, however, nations and empires used war as a lawful means to conduct foreign policy, colonize other nations, and occupy inhabited and uninhabited territories.

178. Quran 23:89–90.

179. The Prophet's father died before he was born. His mother died when he was six. At the age of eight, the Prophet lost his influential grandfather. He was then raised by his loving uncle, Abu Talib. Gatje, supra note 129, at 4.

180. Quran 28:56.

181. Quran 2:256.

182. See Robert N. Shapiro, Of Robots, Persons, and the Protection of Religious Beliefs, 56 S. Cal. L. Rev. 1277 (1983) (examining deception and coercion in conversions); Richard Delgado, When Religious Exercise Is Not Free: Deprogramming and the Constitutional Status of Coercively Induced Belief, 37 Vand. L. Rev. 1071 (1984). Professor Delgado states that "deception, confinement, high pressure proselytization and indoctrination tactics, lack of privacy, threats, pressures to conform and not to criticize, emotional manipulation—constitute coercive persuasion." *Id.* at 1107.

183. Quran 10:108.

184. Quran 4:19 (forbidding inheriting women against their will). 9 Sahih Al-Bukhari, supra note 3, at hadith 78 (Trans. Muhammad Muhsin Khan) (stating that a coerced marriage is invalid). Al-ikrah is a foundational principle of Islamic law. Even in commercial and family matters, coercion and tricks are forbidden. For example, a marriage or a sales contract obtained through coercion is invalid. Likewise, any tricks used in bargains, giving of gifts, or in the contracts of marriages are unlawful, as the Islamic law mandates transparency in inter-human transactions.

185. 9 Sahih Al-Bukhari, supra note 3, at hadith 96.

186. *See* Mohammad Hashim Kamali, Freedom of Religion in Islamic Law, 21 Cap. U.L. Rev. 63 (1992) (explaining that Islam has a well-established tradition of interfaith tolerance).

187. Quran 5:5. The most prominent messengers of God are Moses with the Torah, David with the Zabur (Psalms) and Jesus with the Injil (Gospel). However, the people of the book also include the Sabians and Zoroastrians. The Iranian Constitution recognizes Jews, Christians, and Zoroastrians as protected minorities. In a separate provision, the constitution requires the government and all Muslims to treat non-Muslims in an ethical fashion and respect their human rights. See Ali Khan, Constitutional Kinship Between Iran and the Soviet Union, 9 N.Y.L. Sch. J. Int'l & Comp. L. 293, 318 (1988).

188. It is lawful for Muslims to eat the food of the people of the book and Muslim men may lawfully engage in marriage with Jewish and Christian women.

189. Quran 5:5.

190. In fact, Jesus is mentioned in the Quran far more times than Muhammad (peace be upon him).

191. Quran 16:125.

192. *Id.*

193. The racism that the Nation of Islam advocated against the whites in the United States is unfortunate. Any recruitment of African American men and women into Islam by playing on their racial fears is contrary to everything for which Islam stands. See Ali Khan, Lessons from Malcolm X: Freedom By Any Means Necessary, 38 How. L.J. 79 (1994) (pointing out that Malcolm rejected the racism of the Nation of Islam).

194. "And tell the believing women to lower their gaze (from looking at forbidden things), and protect their private parts (from illegal sexual acts, etc.) and not to show off their adornment . . ." Quran 24:31. The same principle is prescribed for men. Quran 24:30.

195. Educated Muslim women are proud of their faith, they do not like the Western model for the liberation of women. In fact, Western feminist critique of the First Amendment pornography right is in harmony with the Islamic view of treating women as spiritual beings, not as sexual objects. See, e.g., Catherine Mackinnon, Feminism Unbound (1987) (providing feminist critique of pornography protected under the First Amendment); see also Ali Khan, The Hermeneutics of Sexual Order, 31 Santa Clara L. Rev. 47, 93–101 (1990) (explaining despiritualization of women under First Amendment jurisprudence) (upon reflection, however, I have now repudiated the concept of religious neurosis, which was central to my thesis in this article).

196. Quran 72:21.

197. Quran 10:99.

198. Quran 10:100.

199. The Prophet selected suitable time to preach, made sure no one got bored, and advised others to make things easy rather than difficult so that they did not run away from Islam. 1 Sahih Al-Bukhari, supra note 3, at hadith 68–69.

200. Quran 6:68.

201. The Prophet disliked, and even showed anger, when the people asked too many questions. 9 Sahih Al-Bukhari, supra note 3, at hadith 394. He prohibited asking too many questions in disputed religious matters. *Id.* at 392.

202. Quran 33:58.

203. For an aggressive criticism of Islamic practices regarding apostasy, see Donna E. Arzt, Heroes or Heretics: Religious Dissidents Under Islamic Law, 14 Wis. Int'l L.J. 349 (1995). In denying free speech, it is asserted, fundamentalist Muslims "are deceived by their religion." Quran 8:49.

204. "So leave them (alone) to speak nonsense and play until they meet the Day of theirs, which they have been promised." Quran 43:83.

205. Article 19 of the Declaration states: "Everyone has the right to freedom of opinion and expression; this right includes freedom to hold opinions without interference and to seek, receive and impart information and ideas through any media and regardless of frontiers." Universal Declaration of Human Rights, art. 19.

206. "Congress shall make no law respecting an establishment of religion, or prohibiting the free exercise thereof; or abridging the freedom of speech, or of the press; or the right of the people peaceably to assemble, and to petition the Government for a redress of grievances." U.S. Const. amend. I.

207. The American concept of freedom of religion is derived from moral neutrality, presuming that no one religion has monopoly over divine truth:

In the realm of religious faith . . . sharp differences arise. . . . The tenets of one man may seem the rankest error to his neighbor. To persuade others to his own point of view, the pleader . . . resorts to exaggeration . . . and even to false statement. But the people of this nation have ordained that . . . these liberties are . . . essential to enlightened opinion and right conduct on the part of the citizens of a democracy. Cantwell v. Connecticut, 310 U.S. 296, 310 (1940).

208. Several judicial principles articulate the nature and scope of free speech. See, e.g., Police Dep't of Chicago v. Mosley, 408 U.S. 92, 95, 102 (1972) (holding that the government may not regulate speech based on its content unless the regulation can survive strict scrutiny); Perry Educ. Ass'n. v. Perry Local Educators' Ass'n., 460 U.S. 37, 45–49 (1983) (saying that the government cannot lawfully regulate speech when a certain ideology or perspective is the rationale for the restriction); City Council of Los Angeles v. Taxpayers for Vincent, 466 U.S. 789, 804 (1984) (explaining that in the realm of private speech, law may not favor one speaker over another); R.A.V. v. St. Paul, 505 U.S. 377, 381–396 (1992) (stating that viewpoint discrimination is prohibited); Rosenberger v. Rector and Visitors of Univ. of Virginia, 515 U.S. 819, 835–837 (1995) (pointing out that a university may not suppress religious speech under the Establishment Clause of the First Amendment).

209. James Yahya Sadowski, Prospects for Democracy in the Middle East: The Case of Kuwait, 21 SPG Fletcher F. World Aff. 57, 65 (1997) (describing the suppression of political speech in Morocco, Syria, and Algeria).

210. In Kunz v. People of State of New York, 340 U.S. 290 (1951), the Supreme Court struck down the ordinance under which Kunz—who denounced Jews and Catholics "in vicious and unbridled terms" in a congested Manhattan intersection— was convicted. The Free Exercise Clause will protect most religions, including Ahmadis and Baha'is. However, the clause does not secure any religious right to integrity. The clause will protect any sect that innovates or repudiates any existing religion.

211. Due to fear of anti-Semitism, few authors and artists will openly attack Judaism, as they do Christianity. Perhaps due to a possible violent reaction from Muslims, few authors and artists attack Islam.

212. "(T)he swastika . . . is abhorrent to the Jewish citizens of Skokie, and that the survivors of the Nazi persecutions, tormented by their recollections, may have strong feelings regarding its display. Yet it is entirely clear that this factor does not justify enjoining . . . speech." Village of Skokie v. Nat'l Socialist Party, 69 Ill.2d 605, 615 (1978).

213. In fact, it has been suggested that religious speech should be curbed under the establishment clause. See Steven G. Gey, When is Religious Speech Not "Free Speech"? 2000 U. Ill. L. Rev. 379 (2000).

214. I have been teaching Law and Human Rights at Washburn University Law School for the last fifteen years. Over this period, whenever we discuss the competing freedoms of religion and speech, American students are most reluctant to put any restraints on free speech; they are willing to protect even hate speech. Some of these students are devoutly religious individuals.

215. Here the word "art" is used in a broad sense to include literary and artistic works, film, sculpture, songs, and videos.

216. The Rohrabacher Amendment, 136 Cong. Rec. 2865764 (1990).

217. 20 U.S.C. 954(d)(1) (1998).

218. "So, the unpopularity of views, their shocking quality, their obnoxiousness, and even their alarming impact is not enough. Otherwise, the preacher of any strange doctrine could be stopped." Rockwell v. Morris, 12 A.2d 272, 282 (N.Y. App. Div. 1961).

219. Nat'l Endowment for the Arts v. Finley, 524 U.S. 569, 579 (1998).

220. *Id.* at 588.

221. *Id.* at 592 (Scalia, J., concurring).

222. The International Covenant on Civil and Political Rights prohibits hate speech against religion. Article 20(2) states that "(a)ny advocacy of . . . religious hatred that constitutes incitement to discrimination, hostility or violence shall be prohibited by law." The United States has ratified the Covenant with a reservation to Article 20. This reservation is consistent with the Unites States constitutional law that allows hate speech against racial and religious groups. R.A.V. v. City of St. Paul, 505 U.S. 377 (1992) (burning of a cross inside the fenced yard of a black family cannot be punished as prohibited speech).

223. Texas v. Johnson, 491 U.S. 397, 414 (1989).

224. Terminiello v. Chicago, 337 U.S. 1, 4 (1949).

225. "The copyright and trademark laws are such neutral laws of general applicability to which one must adhere for the betterment of the public good, regardless of [one's] religious convictions to the contrary." Urantia Found v. Maaherra, 895 F. Supp. 1329, 1332 (D. Ariz. 1995).

226. In books and musicals, the honor of Jesus has been constantly compromised. In Passover Plot, Jesus has been portrayed "a political machiavel who plotted to fulfill the political prophecies of the Old Testament." Leeds Music Ltd. v. Robin, 358 F. Supp. 650, 653 (S.D. Ohio 1973). In "Jesus Christ Superstar," a musical, he is shown as "a charismatic, rock and roll singer who, through indecision and curiosity, and on a kind of ego-trip, goes to his confused death on the cross." *Id.* at 654.

227. Danielle Caminiti, Brooklyn Institute of Arts and Sciences v. City of New York: The Death of the Subsidy and the Birth of the Entitlement in the Funding of the Arts, 10 Fordham Intell. Prop. Media & Ent. L.J. 875, 876 (2000); see also Brooklyn Institute of Arts and Science v. New York, 64 F. Supp.2d 184, 191 (E.D.N.Y. 1999).

228. "It would be an unwarranted infringement of property rights to require them to yield to the exercise of First Amendment rights where adequate alternative avenues of communications exist. Such an accommodation would diminish property rights without enhancing the asserted right of free speech." Lloyd Corp. v. Tanner, 407 U.S. 551, 567 (1972).

229. "The danger of 'secular fundamentalism,'" says Professor John Esposito, is that secular fundamentalists believe that their worldview is not only best for them but for all the people. See John Esposito, Political Islam and U.S. Foreign Policy, 20 Fletcher F. World Aff. 119, 128 (Fall 1996).

230. For example, the United States will protect The Satanic Verses of Salman Rushdie, ignoring that he intentionally inflicts emotional distress on Muslims. The Islamic world has the opposite reaction. Some Muslims are so distressed that they want to kill the author. In this situation, there is a total breakdown of mutual understanding: The West sees Islamic extremism whereas, the Islamic world sees the spiritual emptiness of secularism.

231. The Islamic distrust of art goes back to the revelations of the Quran, which overturned the pre-Islamic culture rooted in pagan poetry and idolatry. The Quran is opposed to sculpture, but not literature. The Quran warns against poets who

"wander distracted in every valley" but makes an exception for those who believe. Quran 26:224–227; see also Pamela Constable, Ban on Idols Wipes Faces from Afghanistan; Even the Living Feel Taliban Law, Chicago Tribune, April 1, 2001, at 4.

232. Quran 17:53.

233. Quran 31:19. "And lower your voice. Verily, the harshest of all voices is the voice (braying) of the ass." *Id.*

234. The Prophet said that anyone who has in his heart the weight of a muster seed of pride shall not enter Paradise. 1 Sahih Al-Bukhari, *Supra* note 3, at hadith 164.

235. Quran 4:36; 57:23.

236. Malik Al-Muwatta, *Supra* note 112, at 414.

237. Secularists argue that even standards of decency cannot be generalized. Decency means "something very different to a septuagenarian in Tuscaloosa ("a small conservative town") and a teenager in Las Vegas ("the city of gambling")." National Endowment for the Arts v. Finley, 524 U.S. 569, 583 (1998).

238. Quran 23:71.

239. Quran 5:3.

240. Professor Smolin presents an alternative vision even for the United States: "America under God could have liberty without license, democracy without budget deficits, free speech without pornography, familial freedom without sexual revolution. The autonomy-based individualism of the contemporary West can be viewed as rebellion or apostasy from the Christian foundations and discipline that was formative to the West." David M. Smolin, Church, State and International Human Rights: A Theological Perspective, 73 Notre Dame L. Rev. 1515, 1523 (1998).

241. The world-renowned genres of qasida, ghazal, qwalli, and sufi literature are the examples of the freedom of expression. Under the Moghul rule in India, Hindu literature developed along with Muslim literature, enriching the literary tradition of the subcontinent.

242. Under the secular notions of free speech, the standards such as sincere and respectful will be derided as subjective, empty of meaning.

243. And when they (Muslims) hear Al-laghw (dirty, false, evil and vain talk), they withdraw from it and say: "To us our deeds, and to you your deeds. Peace be to you. We seek not (the way of) the ignorant." Quran 28:55. The Prophet also prohibited sinful and useless talk. 9 Sahih Al-Bukhari, *Supra* note 3, at hadith 395.

244. The Prophet prohibited Qil and Qal (sinful and useless talk). *Id.*

245. Quran 33:58.

246. Malik, *Supra* note 112, at 414.

247. According to the protected knowledge of Islam, for example, Jesus is a beloved Prophet of God. Muslims, therefore, dislike when authors and artists ridicule Jesus, God's beloved Prophet and his mother, Mary, a woman "chosen above the women of all nations." Quran 3:42. This respect for Jesus, his mother, and his disciples prompted Muslims to demonstrate on the streets of Manhattan when "Corpus Christi," a musical that depicts Jesus and his disciples as homosexual men, was debuted. Vanessa Thorpe, Review: Arts: What have they done to our Monty?: Broadway Asset-Strippers Have Replaced Sheffield with Buffalo, N.Y. What, No Hot Chocolate?, The Observer, at 6 (Nov. 5, 2000).

248. Islam, however, does not treat all beliefs equally; it will not allow belief systems that corrupt its protected knowledge.

249. Quran 60:8.

250. In the United States, the definition of religion is liberal. Unless the religion is bizarre, clearly nonreligious in motivation, the courts accept the practice as religious. United States v. Kuch, 288 F. Supp. 439 (D.D.C. 1968).

251. Islam is unlikely to protect religions that corrupt the protected knowledge of Islam. Even secular law of intellectual property refuses to protect plagiarized or counterfeit literary and artistic works.

252. "O you who believe! If a rebellious evil person comes to you with a news, verify it, lest you harm people in ignorance, and afterwards you become regretful to what you have done." Quran 49:6.

253. Quran 28:55.

Appendix A

Universal Islamic Declaration of Human Rights

21 Dhul Qaidah 1401—19 September 1981

CONTENTS

> *This is a declaration for mankind, a guidance and instruction to those who fear God.*

> (Al Qur'an, Al-Imran 3:138)

FOREWORD

Islam gave to mankind an ideal code of human rights fourteen centuries ago. These rights aim at conferring honour and dignity on mankind and eliminating exploitation, oppression and injustice.

Human rights in Islam are firmly rooted in the belief that God, and God alone, is the Law Giver and the Source of all human rights. Due to their Divine origin, no ruler, government, assembly or authority can curtail or violate in any way the human rights conferred by God, nor can they be surrendered.

Human rights in Islam are an integral part of the overall Islamic order and it is obligatory on all Muslim governments and organs of society to implement them in letter and in spirit within the framework of that order.

It is unfortunate that human rights are being trampled upon with impunity in many countries of the world, including some Muslim countries. Such violations are a matter of serious concern and are arousing the conscience of more and more people throughout the world.

I sincerely hope that this *Declaration of Human Rights* will give a powerful impetus to the Muslim peoples to stand firm and defend resolutely and courageously the rights conferred on them by God.

This *Declaration of Human Rights* is the second fundamental document proclaimed by the Islamic Council to mark the beginning of the 15th Century of the Islamic era, the first being the *Universal Islamic Declaration* announced at the International Conference on The Prophet Muhammad (peace and blessings be upon him) and his Message, held in London from 12 to 15 April 1980.

The *Universal Islamic Declaration of Human Rights* is based on the Qur'an and the Sunnah and has been compiled by eminent Muslim scholars, jurists and representatives of Islamic movements and thought. May God reward them all for their efforts and guide us along the right path.

Paris 21 Dhul Qaidah 1401 Salem Azzam
19th September 1981 *Secretary General*

> *O men! Behold, We have created you all out of a male and a female, and have made you into nations and tribes, so that you might come to know one another. Verily, the noblest of you in the sight of God is the one who is most deeply conscious of Him. Behold, God is all-knowing, all aware.*

(Al Qur'an, Al-Hujurat 49:13)

PREAMBLE

WHEREAS the age-old human aspiration for a just world order wherein people could live, develop and prosper in an environment free from fear, oppression, exploitation and deprivation, remains largely unfulfilled;

WHEREAS the Divine Mercy unto mankind reflected in its having been endowed with super-abundant economic sustenance is being wasted, or unfairly or unjustly withheld from the inhabitants of the earth;

WHEREAS Allah (God) has given mankind through His revelations in the Holy Qur'an and the Sunnah of His Blessed Prophet Muhammad an abiding legal and moral framework within which to establish and regulate human institutions and relationships;

WHEREAS the human rights decreed by the Divine Law aim at conferring dignity and honour on mankind and are designed to eliminate oppression and injustice;

WHEREAS by virtue of their Divine source and sanction these rights can neither be curtailed, abrogated or disregarded by authorities, assemblies or other institutions, nor can they be surrendered or alienated;

Therefore we, as Muslims, who believe

a) in God, the Beneficent and Merciful, the Creator, the Sustainer, the Sovereign, the sole Guide of mankind and the Source of all Law;

b) in the Vicegerency (Khilafah) of man who has been created to fulfill the Will of God on earth;

c) in the wisdom of Divine guidance brought by the Prophets, whose mission found its culmination in the final Divine message that was conveyed by the Prophet Muhammad (Peace be upon him) to all mankind;

d) that rationality by itself without the light of revelation from God can neither be a sure guide in the affairs of mankind nor provide spiritual nourishment to the human soul, and, knowing that the teachings of Islam represent the quintessence of Divine guidance in its final and perfect form, feel duty-bound to remind man of the high status and dignity bestowed on him by God;

e) in inviting all mankind to the message of Islam;

f) that by the terms of our primeval covenant with God our duties and obligations have priority over our rights, and that each one of us is under a bounden duty to spread the teachings of Islam by word, deed, and indeed in all gentle ways, and to make them effective not only in our individual lives but also in the society around us;

g) in our obligation to establish an Islamic order:

i) wherein all human beings shall be equal and none shall enjoy a privilege or suffer a disadvantage or discrimination by reason of race, colour, sex, origin or language;

ii) wherein all human beings are born free;

iii) wherein slavery and forced labour are abhorred;

iv) wherein conditions shall be established such that the institution of family shall be preserved, protected and honoured as the basis of all social life;

v) wherein the rulers and the ruled alike are subject to, and equal before, the Law;

vi) wherein obedience shall be rendered only to those commands that are in consonance with the Law;

vii) wherein all worldly power shall be considered as a sacred trust, to be exercised within the limits prescribed by the Law and in a manner approved by it, and with due regard for the priorities fixed by it;

viii) wherein all economic resources shall be treated as Divine blessings bestowed upon mankind, to be enjoyed by all in accordance with the rules and the values set out in the Qur'an and the Sunnah;

ix) wherein all public affairs shall be determined and conducted, and the authority to administer them shall be exercised after mutual consultation (*Shura*) between the believers qualified to contribute to a decision which would accord well with the Law and the public good;

x) wherein everyone shall undertake obligations proportionate to his capacity and shall be held responsible pro rata for his deeds;

xi) wherein everyone shall, in case of an infringement of his rights, be assured of appropriate remedial measures in accordance with the Law;

xii) wherein no one shall be deprived of the rights assured to him by the Law except by its authority and to the extent permitted by it;

xiii) wherein every individual shall have the right to bring legal action against anyone who commits a crime against society as a whole or against any of its members;

xiv) wherein every effort shall be made to

(a) secure unto mankind deliverance from every type of exploitation, injustice and oppression,

(b) ensure to everyone security, dignity and liberty in terms set out and by methods approved and within the limits set by the Law;
Do hereby, as servants of Allah and as members of the Universal Brotherhood of Islam, at the beginning of the Fifteenth Century of the Islamic Era, affirm our commitment to uphold the following inviolable and inalienable human rights that we consider are enjoined by Islam.

I. RIGHT TO LIFE

a) Human life is sacred and inviolable and every effort shall be made to protect it. In particular no one shall be exposed to injury or death, except under the authority of the Law.

b) Just as in life, so also after death, the sanctity of a person's body shall be inviolable. It is the obligation of believers to see that a deceased person's body is handled with due solemnity.

II. RIGHT TO FREEDOM

a) Man is born free. No inroads shall be made on his right to liberty except under the authority and in due process of the Law.

b) Every individual and every people has the inalienable right to freedom in all its forms—physical, cultural, economic and political—and shall be entitled to struggle by all available means against any infringement or abrogation of this right; and every oppressed individual or people has a legitimate claim to the support of other individuals and/or peoples in such a struggle.

III. RIGHT TO EQUALITY AND PROHIBITION AGAINST IMPERMISSIBLE DISCRIMINATION

a) All persons are equal before the Law and are entitled to equal opportunities and protection of the Law.

b) All persons shall be entitled to equal wage for equal work.

c) No person shall be denied the opportunity to work or be discriminated against in any manner or exposed to greater physical risk by reason of religious belief, colour, race, origin, sex or language.

IV. RIGHT TO JUSTICE

a) Every person has the right to be treated in accordance with the Law, and only in accordance with the Law.

b) Every person has not only the right but also the obligation to protest against injustice; to recourse to remedies provided by the Law in respect of any unwarranted personal injury or loss; to self-defence against any charges that are preferred against him and to obtain fair adjudication before an independent judicial tribunal in any dispute with public authorities or any other person.

c) It is the right and duty of every person to defend the rights of any other person and the community in general (*Hisbah*).

d) No person shall be discriminated against while seeking to defend private and public rights.

e) It is the right and duty of every Muslim to refuse to obey any command which is contrary to the Law, no matter by whom it may be issued.

V. RIGHT TO FAIR TRIAL

a) No person shall be adjudged guilty of an offence and made liable to punishment except after proof of his guilt before an independent judicial tribunal.

b) No person shall be adjudged guilty except after a fair trial and after reasonable opportunity for defence has been provided to him.

c) Punishment shall be awarded in accordance with the Law, in proportion to the seriousness of the offence and with due consideration of the circumstances under which it was committed.

d) No act shall be considered a crime unless it is stipulated as such in the clear wording of the Law.

e) Every individual is responsible for his actions. Responsibility for a crime cannot be vicariously extended to other members of his family or group, who are not otherwise directly or indirectly involved in the commission of the crime in question.

VI. RIGHT TO PROTECTION AGAINST ABUSE OF POWER

Every person has the right to protection against harassment by official agencies. He is not liable to account for himself except for making a defence to the charges made against him or where he is found in a situation wherein a question regarding suspicion of his involvement in a crime could be *reasonably* raised

VII. RIGHT TO PROTECTION AGAINST TORTURE

No person shall be subjected to torture in mind or body, or degraded, or threatened with injury either to himself or to anyone related to or held dear by him, or forcibly made to confess to the commission of a crime, or forced to consent to an act which is injurious to his interests.

VIII. RIGHT TO PROTECTION OF HONOUR AND REPUTATION

Every person has the right to protect his honour and reputation against calumnies, groundless charges or deliberate attempts at defamation and blackmail.

IX. RIGHT TO ASYLUM

a) Every persecuted or oppressed person has the right to seek refuge and asylum. This right is guaranteed to every human being irrespective of race, religion, colour and sex.

b) Al Masjid Al Haram (the sacred house of Allah) in Mecca is a sanctuary for all Muslims.

X. RIGHTS OF MINORITIES

a) The Qur'anic principle "There is no compulsion in religion" shall govern the religious rights of non-Muslim minorities.

b) In a Muslim country religious minorities shall have the choice to be governed in respect of their civil and personal matters by Islamic Law, or by their own laws.

XI. RIGHT AND OBLIGATION TO PARTICIPATE IN THE CONDUCT AND MANAGEMENT OF PUBLIC AFFAIRS

a) Subject to the Law, every individual in the community (*Ummah*) is entitled to assume public office.

b) Process of free consultation (*Shura*) is the basis of the administrative relationship between the government and the people. People also have the right to choose and remove their rulers in accordance with this principle.

XII. RIGHT TO FREEDOM OF BELIEF, THOUGHT AND SPEECH

a) Every person has the right to express his thoughts and beliefs so long as he remains within the limits prescribed by the Law. No one, however, is entitled to disseminate falsehood or to circulate reports which may outrage public decency, or to indulge in slander, innuendo or to cast defamatory aspersions on other persons.

b) Pursuit of knowledge and search after truth is not only a right but a duty of every Muslim.

c) It is the right and duty of every Muslim to protest and strive (within the limits set out by the Law) against oppression even if it involves challenging the highest authority in the state.

d) There shall be no bar on the dissemination of information provided it does not endanger the security of the society or the state and is confined within the limits imposed by the Law.

e) No one shall hold in contempt or ridicule the religious beliefs of others or incite public hostility against them; respect for the religious feelings of others is obligatory on all Muslims.

XIII. RIGHT TO FREEDOM OF RELIGION

Every person has the right to freedom of conscience and worship in accordance with his religious beliefs.

XIV. RIGHT TO FREE ASSOCIATION

a) Every person is entitled to participate individually and collectively in the religious, social, cultural and political life of his community and to establish institutions and agencies meant to enjoin what is right (*ma'roof*) and to prevent what is wrong (*munkar*).

b) Every person is entitled to strive for the establishment of institutions whereunder an enjoyment of these rights would be made possible. Collectively, the community is obliged to establish conditions so as to allow its members full development of their personalities.

XV. THE ECONOMIC ORDER AND THE RIGHTS EVOLVING THEREFROM

a) In their economic pursuits, all persons are entitled to the full benefits of nature and all its resources. These are blessings bestowed by God for the benefit of mankind as a whole.

b) All human beings are entitled to earn their living according to the Law.

c) Every person is entitled to own property individually or in association with others. State ownership of certain economic resources in the public interest is legitimate.

d) The poor have the right to a prescribed share in the wealth of the rich, as fixed by Zakah, levied and collected in accordance with the Law.

e) All means of production shall be utilised in the interest of the community (*Ummah*) as a whole, and may not be neglected or misused.

f) In order to promote the development of a balanced economy and to protect society from exploitation, Islamic Law forbids monopolies, unreasonable restrictive trade practices, usury, the use of coercion in the making of contracts and the publication of misleading advertisements.

g) All economic activities are permitted provided they are not detrimental to the interests of the community (*Ummah*) and do not violate Islamic laws and values.

XVI. RIGHT TO PROTECTION OF PROPERTY

No property may be expropriated except in the public interest and on payment of fair and adequate compensation.

XVII. STATUS AND DIGNITY OF WORKERS

Islam honours work and the worker and enjoins Muslims not only to treat the worker justly but also generously. He is not only to be paid his earned wages promptly, but is also entitled to adequate rest and leisure.

XVIII. RIGHT TO SOCIAL SECURITY

Every person has the right to food, shelter, clothing, education and medical care consistent with the resources of the community. This obligation of the community extends in particular to all individuals who cannot take care of themselves due to some temporary or permanent disability.

XIX. RIGHT TO FOUND A FAMILY
AND RELATED MATTERS

a) Every person is entitled to marry, to found a family and to bring up children in conformity with his religion, traditions and culture. Every spouse is entitled to such rights and privileges and carries such obligations as are stipulated by the Law.

b) Each of the partners in a marriage is entitled to respect and consideration from the other.

c) Every husband is obligated to maintain his wife and children according to his means.

d) Every child has the right to be maintained and properly brought up by its parents, it being forbidden that children are made to work at an early age or that any burden is put on them which would arrest or harm their natural development.

e) If parents are for some reason unable to discharge their obligations toward a child it becomes the responsibility of the community to fulfill these obligations at public expense.

f) Every person is entitled to material support, as well as care and protection, from his family during his childhood, old age or incapacity. Parents are entitled to material support as well as care and protection from their children.

g) Motherhood is entitled to special respect, care and assistance on the part of the family and the public organs of the community (*Ummah*).

h) Within the family, men and women are to share in their obligations and responsibilities according to their sex, their natural endowments, talents and inclinations, bearing in mind their common responsibilities toward their progeny and their relatives.

i) No person may be married against his or her will, or lose or suffer dimunition of legal personality on account of marriage.

XX. RIGHTS OF MARRIED WOMEN

Every married woman is entitled to:

a) live in the house in which her husband lives;

b) receive the means necessary for maintaining a standard of living which is not inferior to that of her spouse, and, in the event of divorce, receive during the statutory period of waiting (*iddah*) means of maintenance commensurate with her husband's resources, for herself as well as for the children she nurses or keeps, irrespective of her own financial status, earnings, or property that she may hold in her own rights;

c) seek and obtain dissolution of marriage (*Khul'a*) in accordance with the terms of the Law. This right is in addition to her right to seek divorce through the courts.

d) inherit from her husband, her parents, her children and other relatives according to the Law;

e) strict confidentiality from her spouse, or ex-spouse if divorced, with regard to any information that he may have obtained about her, the disclosure of which could prove detrimental to her interests. A similar responsibility rests upon her in respect of her spouse or ex-spouse.

XXI. RIGHT TO EDUCATION

a) Every person is entitled to receive education in accordance with his natural capabilities.

b) Every person is entitled to a free choice of profession and career and to the opportunity for the full development of his natural endowments.

XXII. RIGHT OF PRIVACY

Every person is entitled to the protection of his privacy.

XXIII. RIGHT TO FREEDOM OF MOVEMENT AND RESIDENCE

a) In view of the fact that the World of Islam is veritably *Ummah Islamia,* every Muslim shall have the right to freely move in and out of any Muslim country.

b) No one shall be forced to leave the country of his residence, or be arbitrarily deported therefrom without recourse to due process of Law.

EXPLANATORY NOTES

1. In the above formulation of Human Rights, unless the context provides otherwise:

a) the term 'person' refers to both the male and female sexes.

b) the term 'Law' denotes the *Shari'ah*, i.e., the totality of ordinances derived from the Qur'an and the Sunnah and any other laws that are deduced from these two sources by methods considered valid in Islamic jurisprudence.

2. Each one of the Human Rights enunciated in this declaration carries a corresponding duty.

3. In the exercise and enjoyment of the rights referred to above every person shall be subject only to such limitations as are enjoined by the Law for the purpose of securing the due recognition of, and respect for, the rights and the freedom of others and of meeting the just requirements of morality, public order and the general welfare of the Community (*Ummah*).

The Arabic text of this *Declaration* is the original.

GLOSSARY OF ARABIC TERMS

SUNNAH—The example or way of life of the Prophet (peace be upon him), embracing what he said, did or agreed to.

KHALIFAH—The vicegerency of man on earth or succession to the Prophet, transliterated into English as the Caliphate.

HISBAH—Public vigilance, an institution of the Islamic State enjoined to observe and facilitate the fulfillment of right norms of public behaviour. The "Hisbah" consists in public vigilance as well as an opportunity to private individuals to seek redress through it.

MA'ROOF—Good act.

MUNKAR—Reprehensible deed.

ZAKAH—The 'purifying' tax on wealth, one of the five pillars of Islam obligatory on Muslims.

'IDDAH—The waiting period of a widowed or divorced woman during which she is not to remarry.

KHUL'A—Divorce a woman obtains at her own request.

UMMAH ISLAMIA—World Muslim community.

SHARI'AH—Islamic law.

REFERENCES

Note: The Roman numerals refer to the topics in the text. The Arabic numerals refer to the Chapter and the Verse of the Qur'an, i.e., *5:32* means Chapter 5, Verse 32.

I	1	Qur'an Al-Maidah *5:32*
	2	Hadith narrated by Muslim, Abu Daud,Tirmidhi, Nasai
	3	Hadith narrated by Bukhari
II	4	Hadith narrated by Bukhari, Muslim
	5	Sayings of Caliph Umar
	6	Qur'an As-Shura *42:41*
	7	Qur'an Al-Hajj *22:41*
III	8	From the Prophet's address
	9	Hadith narrated by Bukhari, Muslim, Abu Daud, Tirmidhi, Nasai
	10	From the address of Caliph Abu Bakr
	11	From the Prophet's farewell address
	12	Qur'an Al-Ahqaf *46:19*
	13	Hadith narrated by Ahmad
	14	Qur'an Al-Mulk *67:15*
	15	Qur'an Al-Zalzalah *99:7–8*

IV	16	Qur'an An-Nisa *4:59*
	17	Qur'an Al-Maidah *5:49*
	18	Qur'an An-Nisa *4:148*
	19	Hadith narrated by Bukhari, Muslim, Tirmidhi
	20	Hadith narrated by Bukhari, Muslim
	21	Hadith narrated by Muslim, Abu Daud, Tirmdhi, Nasai
	22	Hadith narrated by Bukhari, Muslim, Abu Daud, Tirmidhi, Nasai
	23	Hadith narrated by Abu Daud, Tirmidhi
	24	Hadith narrated by Bukhari, Muslim, Abu Daud, Tirmidhi, Nasai
	25	Hadith narrated by Bukhari
V	26	Hadith narrated by Bukhari, Muslim
	27	Qur'an Al-Isra *17:15*
	28	Qur'an Al-Ahzab *33:5*
	29	Qur'an Al-Hujurat *49:6*
	30	Qur'an An-Najm *53:28*
	31	Qur'an Al Baqarah *2:229*
	32	Hadith narrated by Al Baihaki, Hakim
	33	Qur'an Al-Isra *17:15*
	34	Qur'an At-Tur *52:21*
	35	Qur'an Yusuf *12:79*
VI	36	Qur'an Al Ahzab *33:58*
VII	37	Hadith narrated by Bukhari, Muslim, Abu Daud, Tirmidhi, Nasai
	38	Hadith narrated by Ibn Majah
VIII	39	From the Prophet's farewell address
	40	Qur'an Al-Hujurat *49:12*
	41	Qur'an Al-Hujurat *49:11*
IX	42	Qur'an At-Tawba *9:6*
	43	Qur'an Al-Imran *3:97*
	44	Qur'an Al-Baqarah *2:125*
	45	Qur'an Al-Hajj *22:25*
X	46	Qur'an Al Baqarah *2:256*
	47	Qur'an Al-Maidah *5:42*
	48	Qur'an Al-Maidah *5:43*
	49	Qur'an Al-Maidah *5:47*
XI	50	Qur'an As-Shura *42:38*
	51	Hadith narated by Ahmad
	52	From the address of Caliph Abu Bakr
XII	53	Qur'an Al-Ahzab *33:60–61*
	54	Qur'an Saba *34:46*
	55	Hadith narrated by Tirmidhi, Nasai

	56	Qur'an An-Nisa *4:83*
	57	Qur'an Al-Anam *6:108*
XIII	58	Qur'an Al Kafirun *109:6*
XIV	59	Qur'an Yusuf *12:108*
	60	Qur'an Al-Imran *3:104*
	61	Qur'an Al-Maidah *5:2*
	62	Hadith narrated by Abu Daud, Tirmidhi, Nasai, Ibn Majah
XV	63	Qur'an Al-Maidah *5:120*
	64	Qur'an Al-Jathiyah *45:13*
	65	Qur'an Ash-Shuara *26:183*
	66	Qur'an Al-Isra *17:20*
	67	Qur'an Hud *11:6*
	68	Qur'an Al-Mulk *67:15*
	69	Qur'an An-Najm *53:48*
	70	Qur'an Al-Hashr *59:9*
	71	Qur'an Al-Maarij *70:24–25*
	72	Sayings of Caliph Abu Bakr
	73	Hadith narrated by Bukhari, Muslim
	74	Hadith narrated by Muslim
	75	Hadith narrated by Muslim, Abu Daud, Tirmidhi, Nasai
	76	Hadith narrated by Bukhari, Muslim, Abu Daud, Tirmidhi, Nasai
	77	Qur'an Al-Mutaffifin *83:1–3*
	78	Hadith narrated by Muslim
	79	Qur'an Al-Baqarah *2:275*
	80	Hadith narrated by Bukhari, Muslim, Abu Daud, Tirmidhi, Nasai
XVI	81	Qur'an Al Baqarah *2:188*
	82	Hadith narrated by Bukhari
	83	Hadith narrated by Muslim
	84	Hadith narrated by Muslim, Tirmidhi
XVII	85	Qur'an At-Tawbah *9:105*
	86	Hadith narrated by Abu Yala—Majma Al Zawaid
	87	Hadith narrated by Ibn Majah
	88	Qur'an Al-Ahqaf *46:19*
	89	Qur'an At-Tawbah *9:105*
	90	Hadith narrated by Tabarani? Majma Al Zawai
	91	Hadith narrated by Bukhari
XVIII	92	Qur'an Al-Ahzab *33:6*
XIX	93	Qur'an An-Nisa *4:1*
	94	Qur'an Al-Baqarah *2:228*
	95	Hadith narrated by Bukhari, Muslim, Abu Daud, Tirmidhi, Nasai

   96 Qur'an Ar-Rum *30:21*
   97 Qur'an At-Talaq *65:7*
   98 Qur'an Al-Isra *17:24*
   99 Hadith narrated by Bukhari, Muslim, Abu Daud, Tirmidhi
  100 Hadith narrated by Abu Daud
  101 Hadith narrated by Bukhari, Muslim
  102 Hadith narrated by Abu Daud, Tirmidhi
  103 Hadith narrated by Ahmad, Abu Daud
XX 104 Qur'an At-Talaq *65:6*
  105 Qur'an An-Nisa *4:34*
  106 Qur'an At-Talaq *65:6*
  107 Qur'an At-Talaq *65:6*
  108 Qur'an Al-Baqarah *2:229*
  109 Qur'an An-Nisa *4:12*
  110 Qur'an Al-Baqarah *2:237*
XXI 111 Qur'an Al-Isra *17:23–24*
  112 Hadith narrated by Ibn Majah
  113 Qur'an Al-Imran *3:187*
  114 From the Prophet's farewell address
  115 Hadith narrated by Bukhari, Muslim
  116 Hadith narrated by Bukhari, Muslim, Abu Daud, Tirmidhi
XXII 117 Hadith narrated by Muslim
  118 Qur'an Al-Hujurat *49:12*
  119 Hadith narrated by Abu Daud, Tirmidhi
XXIII 120 Qur'an Al-Mulk *67:15*
  121 Qur'an Al-Anam *6:11*
  122 Qur'an An-Nisa *4:97*
  123 Qur'an Al-Baqarah *2:217*
  124 Qur'an Al-Hashr *59:9*

Appendix B

The Constitution of Medina
622 C.E.

In the name of God the Compassionate, the Merciful.

This is a document from Muhammad the prophet (governing the relations) between the believers and Muslims of Quraysh and Yathrib, and those who followed them and joined them and labored with them.

They are one community (umma) to the exclusion of all men.

The Quraysh emigrants according to their present custom shall pay the bloodwit within their number and shall redeem their prisoners with the kind-ness and justice common among believers.

The B. 'Auf according to their present custom shall pay the bloodwit they paid in heatheism; every section shall redeem its prisoners with the kindness and justice common among believers. The B. Sa ida, the B. 'l-Harith, the B. Jusham, the B. al-Najjar, the B. 'Amr b. 'Auf, the B. al-Nabit and the B. al-'Aus likewise.

Believers shall not leave anyone destitute among them by not paying his redemption money or bloodwit in kindness.

A believer shall not take as an ally the freedman of another Muslim against him.

The God-fearing believers shall be against the rebellious or him who seeks to spread injustice, or sin or animosity, or corruption between believers; the hand of every man shall be against him even if he be a son of one of them.

A believer shall not slay a believer for the sake of an unbeliever, nor shall he aid an unbeliever against a believer.

God's protection is one, the least of them may give protection to a stranger on their behalf. Believers are friends one to the other to the exclusion of outsiders.

To the Jew who follows us belong help and equality. He shall not be wronged nor shall his enemies be aided.

The peace of the believers is indivisible. No separate peace shall be made when believers are fighting in the way of God. Conditions must be fair and equitable to all.

In every foray a rider must take another behind him.

The believers must avenge the blood of one another shed in the way of God.

The God-fearing believers enjoy the best and most upright guidance.

No polytheist shall take the property of person of Quraysh under his protection nor shall he intervene against a believer.

Whoever is convicted of killing a believer without good reason shall be subject to retaliation unless the next of kin is satisfied (with blood-money), and the believers shall be against him as one man, and they are bound to take action against him.

It shall not be lawful to a believer who holds by what is in this document and believes in God and the last day to help an evil-doer or to shelter him. The curse of God and His anger on the day of resurrection will be upon him if he does, and neither repentance nor ransom will be received from him.

Whenever you differ about a matter it must be referred to God and to Muhammad.

The Jews shall contribute to the cost of war so long as they are fighting alongside the believers.

The Jews of the B. 'Auf are one community with the believers (the Jews have their religion and the Muslims have theirs), their freedmen and their persons except those who behave unjustly and sinfully, for they hurt but themselves and their families.

The same applies to the Jews of the B. al-Najjar, B. al-Harith, B. Sai ida, B. Jusham, B. al-Aus, B. Tha'laba, and the Jafna, a clan of the Tha'laba and the B. al-Shutayba. Loyalty is a protection against treachery. The freedmen of Tha 'laba are as themselves. The close friends of the Jews are as themselves.

None of them shall go out to war save the permission of Muhammad, but he shall not be prevented from taking revenge for a wound. He who slays a man without warning slays himself and his household, unless it be one who has wronged him, for God will accept that.

The Jews must bear their expenses and the Muslims their expenses. Each must help the other against anyone who attacks the people of this document. They must seek mutual advice and consultation, and loyalty is a protection against treachery. A man is not liable for his ally's misdeeds. The wronged must be helped.

The Jews must pay with the believers so long as war lasts.

Yathrib shall be a sanctuary for the people of this document.

A stranger under protection shall be as his host doing no harm and committing no crime.

A woman shall only be given protection with the consent of her family.

If any dispute or controversy likely to cause trouble should arise it must be referred to God and to Muhammad the apostle of God. God accepts what is nearest to piety and goodness in this document.

Quraysh and their helpers shall not be given protection.

The contracting parties are bound to help one another against any attack on Yathrib.

If they are called to make peace and maintain it they must do so; and if they make a similar demand on the Muslims it must be carried out except in the case of a holy war.

Every one shall have his portion from the side to which he belongs.

The Jews of al-Aus, their freedmen and themselves have the same standing with the people of this document in purely loyalty from the people of this document. Loyalty is a protection against treachery. He who acquires ought to acquire it for himself. God approves of this document.

This deed will not protect the unjust and the sinner. The man who goes forth to fight and the man who stays at home in the city is safe unless he has been unjust and sinned. God is the protector of the good and God-fearing man and Muhammad is the apostle of God.

Commentary on the Constitution of Medina

Ali Khan

The first Islamic state was founded not in the shadow of swords, as is commonly believed in some circles, but in the security of a social contract, called the Constitution of Medina. By all counts, the Medina Constitution lit the torch of freedom by establishing a Free State for a pluralistic community composed of Muslims, Jews, and pagans. This unprecedented Free State, the first of its kind in the intellectual and political history of human civilization, was founded by none other than Prophet Muhammad himself in the Gregorian year of 622, that is, more than thirteen hundred years before the Universal Declaration of Human Rights (1948) envisaged a modern pluralistic, religiously tolerant Free State.

In 622, the Prophet and his followers were forced to leave the increasingly oppressive city of Mecca, which had become a place of religious intolerance and persecution. In the hope of peace and freedom, they migrated to Medina. The year 622 which is known as the year of migration or the *hijrah* set in motion two important Islamic events. Chronologically, this is the year that starts the Islamic Calendar. Politically, this is the year when the Medina Constitution was agreed upon and written into law. At the time the Medina Constitution was written, however, the Quran was far from complete as it was still being revealed to the Prophet; and the Muslim community, though gradually increasing in numbers, was still no more than a total of 200 men, women and children.

Most scholars accept the authenticity of the Medina Constitution, though the original document has not been found. Scholars fail to agree, however, whether the Medina Constitution is a single contract or a compilation of multiple agreements reached at different times. A close reading of the document reveals that its provisions are most coherent when read as a compilation of two separate agreements. Muhammad Hamidullah makes a persuasive case that the Medina Constitution, because of its tone and phraseology, was not drafted in a single sitting. He divides the document into two parts. Part 1 (i.e., articles 1–23) addresses mutual relations among Muslims. Part II (i.e., articles 24–47) contains rules to regulate intercommunal affairs between Muslims and Jews.[1] This textual division of the Medina Constitution, though necessary to make the most sense of the document, does not undermine its underlying organic appeal to found Islamic Free State on principles of equality, equity, and religious freedom.

The most organic feature of the Medina Constitution is that it establishes an Islamic Free State on the basis of a social contract. A point of contrast must be noted here: The Western political theory of social contract, derived from the works of Hobbes, Rousseau and Rawls, presupposes a fictional state of nature, and draws various normative and structural inferences. Hobbes installs a mighty sovereign who commands absolute power over the people to "keep them all in awe." Rousseau's theory of social contract lodges sovereignty in the will of the people. This highly abstract notion of the general will lead to all sorts of distortions, including the legitimization of totalitarian democracies. Rawls is no better because, despite some brilliant insights, he anchors his theory in an artificial device of the "veil of ignorance." Contrary to these fictional, artificial, and theoretical accounts of social contract, the Islamic Free State is founded on the reality of an actual agreement among real people of diverse ethnic and religious groups. This reality based social contract is not even a theory or an inspirational constitution to be implemented in the future. The Medina Constitution offered social contract in real time, in real space, to real people through a real agreement, hundreds of years before the theory of fictional social contract gained widespread approval, mostly in the West.

An equally impressive and timeless contribution of the Medina Constitution is the normative establishment of a pluralistic community. The Constitution's opening articles state that Muslims of Quraysh and Yathrib, and those who followed them and joined them and labored with them, are one community to the exclusion of all men. These provisions assert that the immigrant Muslims of Mecca and native Muslims of Medina constitute one community. Conceptually, the Constitution establishes the concept of *the community of believers* (ummat–al mumunin). The community of believers treats all Muslims with equal respect and dignity. It dissolves the distinction between natives and immigrants, offering principles of equality and justice to all Muslims, regardless of their origin of birth, nationality, tribe, or any other ethnic or racial background. It does not allow natives to have superiority over immigrants or vice versa. The Islamic Free State is therefore not exclusively identified with any one tribe or culture but is expanded to include immigrants with diverse dialects, cultures, and social habits. The modern concept of citizenship, practiced in some Muslim states, which excludes immigrant Muslims from the rights of citizenship on a permanent basis, would be incompatible with the letter and spirit of the Medina Constitution.

Part II of the Constitution further expands the scope of community that the Islamic Free State protects. Articles 25–35 mention a legion of Jewish tribes, such as 'Auf, Najjar, Harith, Sai'ida, Jusham, Aus, Tha'laba, and Jafna, granting each tribe the right to be "one community with the believers." This expansive concept of the community is most significant because an Islamic Free State is no longer conceived as an exclusively Muslim nation. In modern terms, an Islamic state can be a religiously pluralistic state. Any attempts to cleanse an Islamic state of the peoples of other religions would be incompatible with the dictates of the Medina Constitution.

Furthermore, the Medina Constitution does not treat all Jews as one monolithic population. It treats them as a religious population but recognizes their diverse ethnic, cultural, or linguistic characteristics, just as it acknowledges similar diversity within the Muslim population. This comprehensive recognition of each distinct Jewish group in a separate Article of the Constitution bestows equal dignity and respect upon all Jewish tribes with whom the social contract was made, rejecting the concept that some Jews are superior to others. Each Jewish tribe in the Constitution is placed on an equal footing with each other as well as with the community of believers, i.e., Muslims.

Article 25 grants the freedom of religion, stating that "the Jews have their religion and the Muslims have theirs." Prophet Muhammad is of course no moral relativist or, for that matter, secular. He is God's Prophet, seeing God in all aspects of life. The model of life he presents is spiritual, a model under which human beings are constantly conscious of God, devoted to God, and live and die for God. And the religion of Islam that the Prophet transmitted to the humanity contained no flaws. Despite this absolute confidence in the truth of Islam, the Medina Constitution, made in the midst of God's revelations to the Prophet, does not establish a self-righteous State, compelling its citizens to adhere to the official religion of Islam. And despite the Prophet's openly expressed belief that the Divine Torah has been altered, the Medina Constitution nonetheless frames a Free State under which Jews are free to practice their religion as they believe it. This normative freedom to practice one's religion as one believes it, and even if it is contrary to Muslim beliefs, demonstrates the highest possible form of religious tolerance. The Medina Constitution refutes theories that insist that only secularism can protect religious freedom.

In addition to protecting religious freedom, the state that the Medina

Constitution establishes is a pluralistic state. The Medina Constitution is not simply an accord among Muslims. It is also a treaty between distinct religious communities, Jews and Muslims. By implication of its underlying principle, the Islamic Free State is not confined to Muslims but is open to the followers of all monotheistic religions and even beyond, for after all Medina was both monotheistic and pagan.

Yet another remarkable feature of the Medina Constitution is its recognition that a lawful agreement is always subject to supra-normative constraints. In modern terms, for example, agreements contrary to state policies and values are unenforceable. In the international legal system, agreements contrary to *jus cogens* or peremptory norms carry no validity. Recognizing supra-normative constraints, Article 47 explicitly states that this Constitution "will not protect the unjust and the sinner." Thus, the Medina Constitution was not an accord reflecting "political realities" or "ugly compromises." It was indeed a morally honest agreement, true to the revealed (and to be revealed) words of the Quran, and made under the Prophet's guidance. As such, the value of the Medina Constitution lies in its moral authenticity and in its virtue that a social contract among diverse peoples can be reached on the basis of freely expressed consent.

Among the Islamic sources of law, the Medina Constitution should not be treated as a distinct source of law and jurisprudence. It is part of the Prophet's Sunna. The Quran remains the supreme source of law, and nothing in the Medina Constitution can be invoked to trump the Quran's text. Since the Sunna is fully compatible with, and always subservient to, the Quran, the Medina Constitution is remarkable in its compatibility with the Quran's principles of inter-human behavior. For example, the Medina Constitution's religious freedom is in accord with the Quran that lays out the principal idea of spiritual freedom to practice one's religion as one believes it. "To you be your Way, and to me mine."[2]

Anver Emon, a student of Professor Khaled Abou El Fadl, has written a well-argued article to demonstrate that modern scholars are reading too much into the Medina Constitution. "The fact that recent Muslim authors often address a presumed constitutional theory implicit in the document may have more to do with twentieth century politics in the Muslim world than with anything inherent in the text."[3] Emon's argument, however, misses the point that the Medina Constitution, as part of the Prophet's Sunna, is an eternal source of guidance and each community of believers in the constant flow of time may tap into this source to derive meaning and guidance for structuring a life consistent with the values of the Quran and the Sunna, the Basic Code of Islam.[4]

NOTES

1. Muhammad Hamidullah, Majmu al-Watha'iq al-Siyasiyya fi al-Ahd al-Banawi wa al-Khaliafa al-Rashida (1941).

2. Quran 109:6.

3. Anver Emon, *Reflections on the Constitution of Medina*, 1 UCLA Journal of Islamic and Near Eastern Law 103, 133 (2001–2002).

4. Ali khan, The Reopening of the Islamic Code: The Second Era of Ijtihad, 1 University of Saint Thomas Law Journal 341 (2003).

Index

Muhammadan, term, 8
Muhammad ibn Abdullah (Prophet), 8,
    143; and hadith, 12–14; and Sunnah,
    4, 12–14
mulkyyah, 137
mulkyyaht al-elm, term, 168n13
Muslim, term, 177n155
Muslim bin al-Hajjaj, Abu al-Hasan,
    12–14
Muslim community: American, 1–2;
    characteristics of, xi; reaction to blas-
    phemy, 136, 160–61, 163, 182n230
Muslim jurisprudence, term, 3
mutilation of corpses, Islamic law on, 81,
    89

al-Nasai, 12
Nasreen, Taslima, 167n9
National Endowment for the Arts
    (NEA), 161
Nation of Islam, 10, 33n81, 179n193
Nessab, 53
nominate contracts, types of, 101–2
non-compulsion, principle of, 157–59
*Nooranita bte Kamaruddin v. Faiez bin
    Yeop Ahmad*, 128–29
Noorbee v. Ahmed Sanusi, 125
Nubian Islamic Hebrews, 10

obligatory acts, 23
oil-based prosperity, and contract law,
    97

Pakistan, family law in, 128
PBUH, definition of, 33n58
people of the book, 82, 158, 179n187
perfect society, as punishment rationale,
    56–57
permitted acts, 23
Pictet, Jean, 67–68
pilgrimage. *See* hajj
pluralism, Islam and, 165, 205–7
polygamy, 113
polytheists, war on, 71–90
positive law, versus Islamic law, x, 43
Powers, David, 131–32
prayer, 9; as protected, 146

prenuptial agreements, 119, 124
prisoners of war: escape of, 90; treatment
    of, Islamic law on, 84–90
privacy: of belief, 155; Islamic law on, 45;
    UIDHR on, 196
prohibitory norm, common violation of,
    impact of, 52–53
property: divorce and, 124–26; inheri-
    tance of, Islamic law on, 115; UIDHR
    on, 194; in wartime, Islamic law on,
    38–84
Prophet. *See* Muhammad ibn Abdullah
proportionality doctrine, 48–50
protected knowledge, 135–84; dissemi-
    nation of, 156–60; innovating,
    153–54; versus intellectual property,
    137–38; nature of, 137–46; of Qur'an,
    138–42; repudiating, 155–56; of Sun-
    nah, 142–45; trust of, 146–48; under-
    standing, 151–53
public interest: and law, 18–19; wars of,
    68–71
public participation, UIDHR on, 192
punishment, 43–64; characteristics of,
    46–53; gradation of, 53; rationales
    for, 53–57; for ridda, 155–56; social
    benefit of, 45

qanun al Islamia. *See* Islamic law
Qazaf, 56
qist, term, 119
qiyas, 6, 18
Qur'an, 11, 169n46; on gender equality,
    118; protected knowledge of, 138–42;
    and Shari'ah, 4; and Sunnah, 143. *See
    also* interpretation
Qusas crimes, 51–53; definition of,
    59n14

Rahim, Abdur, 18
Ramadan, 9; as protected, 146
Ramadan, Hisham M., ix–xi, 43–64
Ramadan, Said, 3
ransom, 85–86
Rawls, John, 206
rebels, war on, 68–70
reciprocation, rule of, 80–81

About the Editor and Contributors

Irshad Abdal-Haqq, Esq. practices economic development law in Washington, D.C, and has served as legal counsel to numerous Washington-area Islamic organizations since 1981. His degrees include J.D., Georgetown University Law Center, 1981, and M.A.T. (Legal Education) Antioch University, 1984. In addition to having served as an adjunct professor of law at various universities, Abdal-Haqq is the former executive director of the Council on Legal Education Opportunity.

Hafiz Nazeem Goolam senior lecturer in the Department of Jurisprudence, Faculty of Law, at the University of South Africa.

Mahmoud Hoballah served as director of Islamic Center, Washington D.C. and was professor of ethics and psychology, Al-Azhar University, Cairo, Egypt.

Ali Khan is professor of law at Washburn University's School of Law.

Noor Mohammed is professor of law emeritus at University of Baltimore School of Law, Baltimore, Maryland. LL.M., 1961, Minnesota; LL.M., 1962; J.S.D., 1968, Yale; et al.

Hisham M. Ramadan is a visiting professor at Michigan State University College of Law. His degrees include: LL.B., Ain Shams University, Cairo, Egypt; LL.M., Auckland University, New Zealand; LL.M. (Criminal Law), State University of New York at Buffalo; and S.J.D., The University of Wisconsin.

Ahmed Zaki Yamanai is Former Minister of Petroleum and Mineral Resources of the Kingdom of Saudi Arabia. LL.B, Cairo University, 1951; LL.M, New York University School of Law, 1954; and LL.M, Harvard School.